BEYOND SCEPTICISM AND REALISM

BEYOND SCEPTICISM AND REALISM

*A Constructive Exploration of Husserlian
and Whiteheadian Methods of Inquiry*

by

ERVIN LASZLO

THE HAGUE

MARTINUS NIJHOFF

1966

PREFACE

I have written this work to make a point. To make it, I was compelled to put forward views regardless of whether they corresponded to my personal convictions or not. I am neither as sceptical as my 'argument from consciousness' suggests, nor as realist as my 'argument from being' would lead one to believe. These are *prototypes* for the arguments that would be advanced by an uncompromising methodical sceptic and a consistent and systematic realist; their purpose is not to affirm the principles of scepticism and realism, but to demonstrate them by exemplification. However, I can say with Wittgenstein that, once the significance of these models has been grasped, they can be discarded as ladders one has already scaled, for they show that truly consistent scepticism and realism are not contradictory, and therefore they negate their own basic assumptions.

Since I mantain that a proposition which satisfies the sceptic as well as the realist may be construed as an instance of meaningful metaphysics, I hope that, with these constructive analyses of the sceptical method of Husserl and the realist method of Whitehead, I may have contributed towards the rehabilitation of metaphysics in contemporary philosophy.

Fribourg, Switzerland, October 1964.   E. L.

CONTENTS

PART I

SCEPTICISM AND REALISM:
THE PROBLEM AND THE METHOD

BASIC ASSUMPTIONS AND
PREDETERMINED ARGUMENTS

I

Of the many modes of thought which underlie the history of philosophy there are two which are fundamental to all meaningful discourse concerning the nature of reality. Of these two ways of seeing the world one is based on the importance of acquiring insight into the facts fundamental to our explanation of the remarkable fact of there being a world, and the other on the importance of the unique possibilities of proof offered by re-examining our beliefs concerning the world from the viewpoint of our consciousness. The former position is basically realistic and places trust in the development of a scientific, controlled mode of grasping the world that surrounds the individual. The latter is fundamentally sceptical and searches for sound premises among the multitude of sensations which furnish our most immediate contact with reality. The realistic conception (which could also be called 'naturalism' or 'objectivism') places the individual and his consciousness within a world, promising to explain his own nature in the course of its primary business of explaining the order of the world. The sceptical position (which can also be denoted 'sensationalism', 'phenomenalism' or 'subjectivism') considers the world as it is presented in immediate experiences, and promises to clarify the nature of the world in the course of explaining the constitutive activity of consciousness.[1] Consciousness is one aspect of the natural world for the realist; the natural world is one aspect of consciousness for the sceptic. Notwithstanding mutual accusations of untenable premises and fallacious reasoning between proponents of these conflicting world-views, both positions have proven to be equally tenable and capable of providing

---

[1] While "scepticism" is used in a variety of senses, I shall use it exclusively in the above, primarily methodological one.

the ground for consistent as well as significant conclusions. The question of their truth and value is anterior to the adoption of the basic assumptions which underlie each of these positions; no analysis of conclusions can decide the question of the ultimate validity of sceptical and realist modes of thought.

The situation is rendered difficult in view of the fact that both the sceptic and the realist may claim (quite correctly, in fact) a pure form of empiricism. It is said, for example, that physics (and natural science in general) is rigorously empirical, being based on observation for its protocol statements and again for their verification. Nothing, it is held, is postulated in physics which would contradict, or not be implied by, observational evidence. Contrarily to this contention, the sceptic claims that physics, and natural science in general, is based on implicit realist premises which have to be acknowledged before the validity of the conclusions could be established. Much misunderstanding is usually involved in such arguments, and, since the subject of this inquiry is precisely the contrast between sceptical and realist modes of reasoning, the basic issue at stake, namely the meaning of 'empiricism' in the two contrasting and apparently contradictory uses, should be defined before going any further.

There is a kind of dichotomy in empirical philosophical construction from the earliest Hellenic philosophers to our day which, in my opinion, stems from the effective presence of seldom analyzed, axiomatically adopted basic assumptions. They can be one of two kinds: either they are to the effect that the experiencing agent is in the world; or to the effect that the world is in the experiencing agent. This is surely a crude statement of the issue, but it does connote the reason why 'empiricism' can be claimed in equal measure by sceptics and realists. Both sides assert – quite justifiably in the light of their basic assumptions – the principle of 'empiricism', claiming a strict adherence to empirical evidence. But the difference between them, though reducible to fine shadings in the formulation of the problem, is by no means negligible. Empiricism, in the sense of an inquiry based on the assumption that the subject is in the world, can infer the world from experience independently of the subject, and, when the subject is also inferred, it is inferred as part of the world through an already determined conception of it. On the other hand, an investigation of experience under the assumption that the world is given in the experience of the subject, must decide about the nature of the subject before it could legitimately determine the nature of the world. The subject is determined for the realist by the nature of the world of which he is a component or particular aspect – for the sceptic the world is determined by the subject of whose consciousness it is a component and a particular aspect. Empiricism is shared by both, in the sense that the contention of proceeding on the basis of an analysis of experience is justified in both cases. But under what intrinsic presuppositions the experiential data is evaluated is not specified in the claim, and this implicit differentiation can be responsible for much of the misunderstandings between sceptically and realistically oriented thinkers. The natural scientist tends to reject rigid ontological categories and concepts and believes to hold himself strictly to empirical evidence. He might claim, for example, that he is presuppositionless in his procedure and that although the sceptic can be as sceptical as he likes concerning the existence of the world, he would come to the same results as scientists do, if he would comprehend modern scientific procedure. But the sceptic can counter by pointing to the 'naïve acceptance' of the 'naturalistic standpoint' and to the 'physicalist realism' of the natural scientist who is not concerned to prove the existence of the events he is talking about, but presumes to go right on to determine their functions and regulative principles. The sceptic's objection is even stronger to the endeavour of the ontologist and metaphysician who also postulate 'substance' and 'reality' and sometimes have even had the audacity to claim that their notions are derived from an analysis of experience.

In an impartial assessment of the issue I believe that we shall come to the conclusion that both scepticism and realism are justified in the light of their own basic presuppositions. If we assume that the experient exists, and that whatever exists besides must be inferred from his experiences, the world is taken, methodologically at least, as being given *in* experiences. This sceptical manner of reasoning is something like this, "I think (i.e. I experience), therefore I exist; therefore, if I am to find out what else exists, I must explore my experiences. In so doing I can note what events I experience and in which sequence I experience them. Thus I can come to conclusions concerning the things I experience through the regularities which these things manifest."

The realist manner of reasoning, in contradistinction to the above, may be something like the following, "I am born into a world which has existed before me and which will exist when I am gone. I experience this world, and my experiences are the occasions which render knowledge of the world possible. If I am to come to reliable conclusions concerning this world, I must explore my experiences. In so doing

I can note what events I experience and in which sequence I experience them. Thus I can come to conclusions concerning the things I experience through the regularities which these things manifest."

Now, it is evident that if my exemplification of the two modes of reasoning is basically correct, they start from different premisses but reach the same conclusion as to how knowledge can be acquired. It would seem, then, that the choice of the premisses, determined by the sceptical and the realist basic assumptions, is immaterial. This, unfortunately, is not the case. For, while both basic assumptions lead to the exploration of experience and both mean by 'experience' the experience of the world, the sceptic assumes that the world is given in his experience, while the realist assumes that his experience is given in the world.

But, you may object, is this not a mere play on words? I think that it is much more than that. When we follow the reasoning of the sceptic we must think of 'experience' in terms of experience given to the subject, i.e. of direct sense-experience. On the other hand, notwithstanding the fact that the experience of the realist is also communicated through the senses, i.e. is also *sense*-experience, the sensory quality of the realist's experience is of a transitory character significative merely of the communication of events from the external world to the mind of the observer. This cannot be affirmed without circularity of the sense-experiences of the sceptic in the light of his basic assumption. The sceptic is trying to see if he can infer that the events he experiences exist independently of the fact of his experiencing them, and assuming that the events of his experiences are independent of the act of experiencing means admitting as premiss the conclusion to be proven. Hence for the sceptic sense-experience is significative of sensory events and of 'worldly' events only if verified statements can be advanced concerning the worldliness of his experiences. The realist can dispose of the need for such proof: for him experiences are worldly, and proof needs to be advanced only concerning the contrary event: that experiences may also be illusory, and thus non-worldly (e.g. hallucinations, dreams, and so forth).

The sceptic as well as the realist can make empirical observations and note regularities. If the sceptic comes to the conclusion that his experiences include the experience of objects and of events involving objects (here 'object' is used in the widest sense, to include all relatively constant and identifiable phenomena) his objects are cognitive constructs from his sense-experiences, i.e. they are *sense*-objects. If the realist comes to the conclusion that his experiences include objects and objective events, however, his sense-experience represents for him evidence of the existence of objects 'in the world': his objects are not entirely reducible to sense-objects, but represent the sensory perception of *physical* objects.

At this point again, the argument may be accused of making a mountain of a molehill, enlarging terminological differences into basic, but in fact specious, differences in meaning. To counter this objection, let us pursue the consequences of this reasoning. We have sense-objects on the one hand and physical objects on the other. Both have been inferred from experiences and we may admit without contradiction that the same, or at least fundamentally analogous, experiences have led to the postulation of both. A sense-object is established by noting the events and sequences of experience just as a physical object is. But the former signifies the objective content of experience under the assumption that the world is given in experience; therefore, the world given in experience has (some) objective content. The latter signifies the objective content of experience under the assumption that experience is given in the world; therefore, the experience given in the world has (some) objective content. So far there is no irremediable contradiction: it is agreed that experience has objective contents. With that, the things actually experienced, i.e. the contents of reflexive human experience, are similarly explained regardless of whether the terminology of the explanatory theories is sensationalist or physicalist.

But, the similarity of explanation extends merely to the fleeting occasions of actual experience. When experience is that *in* which the world is given, and not merely *how* the world is given, the objects constructed from experience are sense-objects; when experience is *how* the world is given, the sense-objects have either physical counterparts, or are the perceptions of physical objects (depending on whether an immanentist or a transcendentalist epistemological position is adopted). Now, the determinant feature of sense-objects is that they are objects constructed of sense-experiences. If so, sense-objects are meaningfully existent when the sense-experiences of which they are constructed are given. It is contradictory to speak of the existence of a sense-object in the absence of the components of which it is constituted. The world is given in experience under this assumption, and if the world consists (partly at least) of objects, these objects are given when the corresponding experiences are given. If we assert that they are given in the absence of the experience of their sensory components we entertain an inconsistent notion, for it is contradictory to speak of the actuality of a sense-object while denying the actuality of the sense-experiences constituting it. If this simple statement is contested, the basic assumption which justifies it is challenged, and as a consequence the statement no longer follows from it as legitimate conclusion. But what form can such a challenge take? The contested assumption is that the world is given in experience. Its challenge would be that the world is given not *only* in experience, but also in itself, i.e. independently of being experienced. Such a challenge, however, is a direct affirmation of the realist basic assumption, for if the world exists in any measure beyond experience, the limits of experience are transcended, and whatever is experienced, is contained in a wider realm *of* which the experiential events signify the experiences. (If there is no such signification, the transcendent portion of the world is "noumenal".) Hence any challenge of the statement that sense-objects are given if, and only if, the corresponding sense-experiences are given, immediately and directly implies the realist basic assumption.

Under the realist assumption the experienced object is significative of a physical object and it may be held without contradiction that the physical object exists in the absence of its experiential counterpart (its sensory 'evidence'). As long as the inquiry is restricted to actual experience, the differences between the conclusions entailed by the sceptical and the realist basic assumptions do not amount to more than differences in sensationalist and physicalist terminology. But when inferences are being drawn from actual experience, the paths of the two modes of reasoning diverge. Knowledge is sought in experience by the sceptic as well as by the realist, and both have a rightful claim to the title of empiricist. But, if only the reality of the data of sensory experience is affirmed as premiss, only the reality of "sense-data" (even if explicated into the objective content of 'the world') is tenable as conclusion; if the reality of the world is affirmed and the facticity of sense-data is held evidence of it, then the reality of the world is a legitimate conclusion. Both conclusions are affirmed in the respective premisses. Both beg the question therefore, but *petitio principii* is a fallacious procedure only if the assumed premisses are illegitimate for some other reason than their relation to the conclusion. In view of the fact that one of the two basic assumptions must be made, for a third possibility is excluded (except the one of conjoining them, which, however, is confused and inconsistent), the question remains, which one is the more indicated? This raises the necessity of deciding between modes of thought which have been dominant in western philosophy since the earliest times, being represented already by Gorgias on the one hand, and by Anaximander on the other. The decision is ultimately whether we should consider that advantage should be taken of the possibilities offered to man by his unique position in the scheme of things, or of the unique capacity of the human mind to transcend his position and view the world as a vast architecture of specifiable facts. Plato inclined to the former view, Aristotle to the latter. And there is a significant germ of truth in saying with Coleridge, "every man is born an Aristotelian or a Platonist".[1] While it would be surely an exaggeration to attempt to subsume each thinker in the history of ideas under one or the other category without careful specifications and allowing for elements in his thought which may be common to both, I believe it is not exaggerated to claim that most systematic thinkers could be analyzed to a predominantly realist-objectivist, or sceptical-subjectivist mode of approaching their problems. Clear-cut decisions are possible in some cases – such as those of Berkeley and Marx (who probably represent the extreme forms of sceptical subjectivism and realist objectivism) – but already Hegel appears to argue from a realist basic assumption (the "Absolute Idea" is the "whole" functioning as 'the world') but with strongly subjectivist concepts, while Locke argues conversely, from a sceptical basic assumption ("all knowledge is through sense-experience") but tinged with prominently objectivist features (i.e. the 'primary qualities').

The arguments for scepticism, as those for realism, are too many-sided and too weighty to permit a unilateral decision. The history of thought amply testifies to the fact that neither scepticism nor realism can be disproven any more than conclusively proven. Both have values and disvalues: scepticism provides us with insight into the foundations of our knowledge, and realism permits large-scale concept and theory formation. But scepticism, if presuppositionless, is inadequate to supply us with the rational justification of the ideas we normally entertain of reality; and realism, although adequate in this respect, is based on the premiss that our experiences refer to a physical world without being in a position to substantiate it.

In relation to their basic premises, the most sceptical conclusion is as valid as the most encompassing realist principle. Even solipsism and cosmological metaphysics can be of equal validity if they follow from their respective basic assumptions without involving contra-

---

[1] 'Table Talk' in *Coleridge: Select Poetry and Prose*, p. 491

dictions and redundant notions. And neither their values nor their disvalues are sufficiently disparate to justify disregarding one in favour of the other in an objective inquiry into the nature of reality. Rather than accepting one or the other basic assumption without question, the task of the philosopher should be to clarify and define them, and to attempt to determine how the experiential descriptions of the sceptic could be meaningfully related to the adequate theories of the realist.

II

I have implied that scepticism and realism present the basic issues in constructive thought and that some sort of a division between philosophers according to whether they are sceptics or realists should be possible. This division is more evident in the thought of the so-called 'speculative' philosophers (even though a sceptic is anything but speculative) than in the case of any 'analytic' thinker, the latter refraining from taking his proper position with respect to speculative issues unless there are solid reasons for doing so. As solid reasons may be advanced either both for scepticism and for realism or for neither, but not for one only and not for the other, analytic thinkers are usually loath to commit themselves on this point. They tend to 'favour', or 'incline to', one or the other, but would usually refuse to be called either a sceptic or a realist. These titles are customarily reserved for the more speculative idealists, ontologists, materialists, phenomenologists, phenomenalists, and their kin.

But it is sometimes thought (e.g. by Ingarden in his thoughtful book on the existence of the world[1]) that the basic element of conflict is the issue of idealism *vs.* realism, rather than scepticism and realism. Marxist-Leninists on the other hand, define the basic issue as the antithesis between idealism and materialism. For Whitehead the fundamental division of philosophy is into objectivism and subjectivism, and in Husserl's view the decisive conflict is between immanentism and transcendentalism. It would be forced to subsume all these antithetical pairs under one common heading, but it is feasible, I believe, to establish priority between them.

When "scepticism" is defined as a methodological limitation of knowledge, restricting 'knowledge' to statements made in immediate and verifiable reference to incontrovertible empirical fact, and when "realism" is defined as the proposition that facts are not dependent

[1] Roman Ingarden, *Der Streit um die Existenz der Welt*, Band 1, Tübingen, 1964.

on their knowledge, then the sceptic holds that fact to be existent which he experiences, and the realist holds facts existent regardless of whether he knows them or not. Since no fact may exist for the sceptic for which he has no experiential evidence, and no fact is dependent for its existence upon experiential evidence for the realist, all facts exist to the measure to which they are experienced (or are inferred from experiences) for the sceptic, and no facts cease to exist when not experienced for the realist. Hence the sceptic begins from 'inside', and seeks facts which could be said to be 'outside' his consciousness, while the realist begins from 'outside' (of his own experience) and validates his assumptions as true knowledge when he finds corresponding facts 'inside'. Scepticism is concordant with idealism and subjectivism, realism implies objectivism and materialism; but scepticism may also be objectified in systems of objective idealism, and realism subjectified as psychologism or panpsychism. A great variety of constructive philosophical positions is possible, but they are reducible to a previous choice between the sceptical and the realist basic assumptions.

I have suggested that the basic assumption of scepticism is 'world-in-experience', and the basic assumption of realism is 'experience-in-world', and that the choice of these basic assumptions is prior to any argument advanced concerning the nature of reality. The argument based on the sceptical assumption (that the world is given in experience) affirms the experient, and the contrary assumption (the experient being in the world) affirms the world. When the over-all pattern of these arguments is considered, it will be evident that the sceptical mode of reasoning is to argue *from* the subject's consciousness, and, using internally consistent concepts and inferences, to come up with an explanation of the world as given to consciousness. Such an argument may be said to adopt "consciousness" as its root-axiom. In contradistinction to this sceptical mode, the pattern of realistic argumentation is to assume the existence of the world, and, in clarifying *how* the world is, and *what* there is in the world, also to provide an explanation of the facts of experience. These facts will be 'world-facts', deduced from an analysis of experience as referring to the world. Experience pertains to the realm of consciousness for the sceptic, and it refers to the existent world for the realist. The sceptic emphasizes *consciousness*; the realist accentuates *being*. In schematizing and simplifying the sceptical and the realist patterns of argumentation, we may henceforth refer to the former as presenting an 'argument from consciousness' and to the latter as evolving an 'argument from being'. These terms are introduced to function merely as signposts helping the thinker to familiarize himself with the topography of basic assumptions and make him see the effect they have on philosophical (and even on scientific) reasoning; I do not presume to suggest that all inquiries into reality may be directly and unequivocally reduced to either "consciousness" or to "being" as root-axiom. I do believe, however, that the universe of meanings attached to these terms has connotations which significantly predominate in most systematic investigations into nature and experience.

In systematic philosophy the role of these concepts should be thoroughly investigated. In arguing from consciousness we should inquire whether there is any reason to posit 'the world', and, if we argue from being, we must see whether there are grounds to assume that any aspect of experience is entirely mine, and mine alone. I have come to the conclusion[1] that no *fully* convincing reasons can be found for either of these statements: in the consistent 'argument from consciousness' there are no sufficient reasons to assume the existence of others, and in consequence experience remains private; and in the consistent 'argument from being' there are no convincing grounds to isolate particular aspects and events of experience fully from the rest, and thus to obtain some experiences which are private, and entirely divorced from the public ones. (For if there is the least link between what we call the 'private' and the 'public' aspects and events of experience, by that token the privacy of the 'private' experience disappears, for that link determines the experience to be at least in some regards 'public' and thus different from what it were if all experiences were private.)

But if both the argument from being and the argument from consciousness can be criticized to analyticity and covert circularity, we may well ask whether factual empirical statements are altogether possible?

My proposition is that the consistent arguments of the sceptic and the realist may contain sound and significant empirical statements and that *jointly* they may permit the resolution of the difficulty. The indicated method will be to disregard all forms of cross-inferences (which I shall term 'reductionism') and concentrate on the consistent arguments 'from consciousness' and 'from being'. The kind of propositions entailed by scepticism and realism must be independently determined, without permitting inferences from any concept or principle of one argument to affect the formulation of concepts and

---

[1] *cf.* below, pp. 65 *ff.*

principles in the other. I suggest that it is entirely possible, and even probable, that the consistent arguments of the sceptic and of the realist deal with actual matters of fact correctly, and that the denial of the incompatibility of meaning would lead to the resolution of the conflict without raising up the difficulties contained in reductionism. As Ramsey said,[1] when a dispute between two parties is chronic, there must be some false assumption common to the arguments of both, the denial of which will lead to the resolution of the dispute. If I deny that the meanings inherent in the theories of the sceptic and the realist are mutually exclusive, I do so in the attempt to resolve their dispute without committing inconsistencies. Demonstration of this denial is by showing that the root-axioms 'being' and 'consciousness' determine the respective arguments, and that all terms determined by these root-axioms function analogously within the context of their respective propositions. And if 'consciousness' functions in the sceptical argument analogously to 'being' in the argument of the realist, the incompatibility of meaning carried by these terms is fused and resolved by virtue of the compatibility of their propositional function.

That "consciousness" and "being" have radically different meanings when used as labels cannot be denied, for such denial leads to the grave difficulties encountered in reductionism. But we may deny that these terms function differently with respect to the framework of reference in which they serve as premiss and thus that the contradiction is valid. This simple denial may lead to the resolution of the chronic dispute of the sceptic and the realist by demonstrating that the disputed issues are non-contradictory in the light of the structure of the arguments by which they are disputed. There is no contradiction in affirming that this may be the case. But neither would there be a contradiction in affirming the opposite. However, hypotheses must be advanced in order to be verified or falsified. Purely as a working hypothesis, this assumption deserves to be investigated. After all, it is not entirely unlikely that "consciousness" and "being" are equivalent terms in arguments which look at the world 'from inside' and 'from outside' and that, since the two perspectives afford inverse views of the same facts, the sceptic and the realist, even if they argue from different basic assumptions and thus make use of divergently predetermined arguments, should advance empirical statements which are severally true and jointly also factual.

[1] F. P. Ramsey, *Foundations of Mathemathics*, pp. 115–116.

FALLACIES OF REDUCTIONISM

The point of view here advanced is to the effect that inquiries into the nature of things are based either on evidence in the form of events directly given to consciousness in immediate experience, or on evidence evaluated as referring to, or being caused by, an objective realm of being existing independently of its perception. The hypothesis asserts that evidence as given to consciousness determines a set of propositions which deal with the world within the context of conscious experience, while evidence evaluated as referring to, or being caused by, the physical world determines a set of propositions which concerns consciousness merely as one part or aspect of the physical world.

My assertion is that no cross-inferences are possible between arguments 'from consciousness' and 'from being', and, if proposed, are necessarily ampliative. There are few thinkers who would wish to maintain this assertion in such a strict form. Those who acknowledge it as a real problem, but deny that it is insurmountable, advance the type of arguments which, for convenience's sake, may be collectively denoted as 'reductionism'. By "reductionism" I mean then, the effort to demonstrate that the physical world of the realist contains in some sense the world of immediate experience, communicated to consciousness in the form of primary evidence, and that, conversely, the primary evidence communicated to consciousness in immediate experience signifies in some definite manner the existence of the physical world. Hence two major varieties of reductionism are possible: one would argue from the data of consciousness to the physical world, and the other from the physical world to the data of consciousness. I shall term the former 'epistemic reductionism' and the latter 'physical reductionism' and note that epistemic reductionism is based on arguments 'from consciousness', and physical reductionism on arguments 'from being'.

My purpose at present is to show the difficulties inherent in being committed to reductionism in either form. I shall introduce the terms "epistemic fact" and "physical fact" to stand, respectively, for evidence taken as immediate data of consciousness, and evidence evaluated as referring to, or being caused by, some part or aspect of the physical world. Thus both kinds of 'facts' are experiential facts, but they are differently assessed. Using these concepts, the proposition is that the 'epistemic reductionist' argues *from* consciousness *to* being, and the 'physical reductionist' argues *from* being *to* consciousness, with the former inferring physical facts from his epistemic facts, and the latter assessing some of his physical facts as epistemic facts. If reductionism in either form is feasible, epistemic and physical facts are mutually implicative, representing on the one hand, the inference of the physical world from consciousness, and on the other, the deduction of consciousness from the physical world. The reductionist affirms not only that there are epistemic as well as physical facts, but asserts that (some) epistemic events signify the presence of physical objects, and (some) physical objects give rise to epistemic events. I shall argue against this thesis and show that while it is impossible to maintain, another solution to the problem may be at hand.

I

I shall distinguish three major degrees of reductionism to which the epistemic and physical reductionist may wish to commit himself. The first of these is the demonstration of the *identity* of epistemic and physical facts. This is the most ambitious of the three, and I shall consider it first.

The demonstration of identity involves generalization from consciousness for the epistemic reductionist, and deduction from being for the physical reductionist. Now the difficulty encountered by the former concerns the problem of induction jointly with the problem of the 'privacy' of immediate experience. Induction, for which closed system, mutual relevance, determinism and simplicity are held to be preconditions [1] is particularly problematic in view of the fact that the premises are the items of experience presented to consciousness. Consciousness, as Hume has already shown, cannot be consistently affirmed to provide the ground for postulating a principle of causality (or

[1] *cf.* J. M. Bochenski, *Zeitgenössische Denkmethoden*, V.20. p. 123

even of functional concomitance) without indulging in non-evidential assumptions, and thus at least partially assuming the conclusion to be proven. Logically, the difficulty is that no general truths may be derived from the particular events presented to consciousness, and epistemologically, that it is most difficult to maintain that the data of immediate experience are 'public', and thus permit of generalization. Hence the major weak points in the argument for the identity of epistemic and physical facts of the epistemic reductionist are that (i) he admits the validity of general truths concerning experiential events; (ii) he applies his assumed general principles to infer physical objects from epistemic events and assumes that he has shown thereby that epistemic events have lost their 'private' character. His procedure is thus basically non-demonstrative and fallible.

The case for the demonstration of the identity of the two types of facts by the physical reductionist is not any more encouraging. It rests on the assumptions that whatever is given in experience refers in some evident and meaningful manner to an objective realm of being which is not dependent upon being known, and that the exploration of experience as referring to objective being clarifies and explains the immediate data of experience. The physical reductionist is committed to maintaining that the world is given independently of his apprehensions and that his task lies in showing that he can deduce the facts of his own experience from his knowledge of the assumed existence of the physical world, and thus demonstrate the identity of physical and epistemic facts. But at best he can prove the conclusion he is concerned to advance by assuming it in his premiss: the physical world is prejected to his investigations, while it functions as the verifier of his conclusions. Hence the procedure of the physical reductionist is open to objections on grounds of circularity; his conclusions remain hypothetical.

There are weighty considerations against the feasibility of demonstrating full identity between epistemic and physical facts regardless of whether we argue from consciousness and its epistemic facts, or from being and its physical facts. However, it may be said that the aim of the reductionist is valid, but his programme is too ambitious. He should be content with demonstrating that epistemic and physical facts are *equivalent*. Instead of full identity, a kind of descriptive equivalence should suffice to make his point. This is the second degree of reductionism, and it applies equally to the epistemic and to the physical reductionist. The task is to show that epistemic and physical facts may be described without contradictions. The demonstration of this point, however, must face the argument traditionally advanced against epistemological realism. It may be resumed as the claim that epistemic facts necessarily take place *when, where,* and *as* apprehended, while physical facts do not.

Take for example, the 'epistemic' and the 'physicalist' explanation of the event identified as the musical note *A*. The 'epistemic' explanation considers it as a sound, a sound let us say, ascribed to hitting the middle *A*-key of a piano, and having diverse relations to other sounds perceived at that time and, with sounds perceived at previous times and associated with that particular sound, with other experiences of the subject then and previously, etc. In fact, the note *A* may be analyzed to very fine nuances, and it will still remain a sound of a particular quality. Now take the 'physicalist' explanation. It involves the mechanistic principles inherent in the production of 440 vibrations per second, the transmission of vibration to the air, the wave of corresponding frequency travelling from the string to the surrounding area and, as this area includes the observer, also to his ear. There it is held to produce vibrations of the ear-drum, which are transmitted by the nervous system to the brain, and are perceived in complex cognitive processes as the sound 'middle *A* of the piano'. What the epistemic explanation involves is the quality of the sound. That which the physicalist explanation describes is a series of events explainable by laws of causality or concomitance, of which the end-result is a cognitive sensation of sound, but which itself consists of the transmission of motion from string to air, to ear-drum, to brain. In other words, the physical explanation deals with the motion of micro-physical particles which are neither perceivable in themselves, nor as motion, but which produce as a final resultant, a perceivable quality. It is fairly obvious that the analysis of the sound itself will never lead us to infer these motions. There is no element of the sound which could give us a clue that it is something radically different from what it seems to be, namely that it consists of a series of mechanistic, wave, and physiological events, terminating in electric impulses in the brain. In order to arrive at the knowledge of these events, we must pre-suppose others which transcend the data of experience, but are such that they result in experiences. Thus, by the procedure of the physical reductionist the 'subjectivity' of the given person is subordinated to the 'objectivity' of events – a procedure which is contrary to that of the epistemic reductionist for whom the knowledge of objects is to be inferred from the experience of the subject, with the result that he is committed to consider the subject's own subjectivity as the measure of all objectivity.

The example of the epistemic and physicalist explanation of a sound was to show that a given event cannot be described without contradictions under the assumptions of an argument 'from consciousness' and 'from being'. This conclusion applies not only to sounds, but to almost all percepts. The perception of colour finds an entirely different set of explanations when taken as a physical fact, and when taken as an epistemic one. The epistemic reductionist attempts to find the physical fact in each item of perception by an analysis of the given features of the percept, and the physical reductionist tries to show that the percept as physical fact results in the percept as epistemic fact. However, the former can speak merely of qualities inherent in the presentation of the given event to consciousness, while the latter is bound to have recourse to principles which are not presented to consciousness, but produce an effect which is claimed to be the perceived datum. The physical reductionist moves in the realm of physical facts which is entirely closed to the epistemic reductionist. The former comes up with events in function of explanations which are inaccessible to arguments based on the analysis of epistemic facts.

I contended that epistemic facts take place *then*, *there*, and *as* perceived, while physical facts are bound to none of these conditions. I have tried to show that physical facts *cannot* be consistently explained as taking place in 'reality' in the form wherein they are perceived. The divergence between the two types of facts extends also to the *time* at which they are held to occur, and this is what I shall consider next. The epistemic reductionist is committed to maintain that the events he analyses are simultaneous with his apprehension of them. The physical reductionist cannot agree to this, primarily in view of the 'time-lag' argument he is obliged to consider. When given events are treated as physical facts, they refer to a series of interlocked events all of which involve the transmission of energy in time and space. The argument is relevant in that an event which is spatially removed from its experience is also temporally removed, so that the postulation of the physical world brings with it the claim that all particulars of that world are not only removed from the subject in space, but are also removed from him in time. Thus whatever facts are experienced are done so with an intervening amount of space and time. Time elapses between the occurence of each event 'out there', and its experience 'in here'. Even if the elapsed time is infinitesimal, it cannot be ignored. In the physicalist explanation the object is *not* simultaneous with its experience, and it *cannot* be simultaneous with it. Hence if an item of experience refers to something real *of* which it is an experience, then that to which it refers precedes its occurrence. Perception is necessarily subsequent to the thing perceived. Consequently the physical reductionist cannot assume that the object exists then, when it is perceived. This is a further point to the disadvantage of a demonstration of the equivalence of physical and epistemic facts.

Spatial divergence between these modes of explanation may be exemplified by the argument of illusion. A mirror image already displaces the 'real' locus of the experienced event, and all refraction of sound, light, as well as the simulation of any sensory event represents divergences between the object as epistemic and as physical fact. But it is impossible to account for spatial displacement on the basis of events evaluated as epistemic facts, for such facts have no existence aside from their apprehension. (It is noteworthy in this context that both Moore and Russell abandoned the distinction between 'sense-data' and 'sensation' which they had originally suggested to define sense-data and their apprehension.) In the consistent Humean view, epistemic facts do not point or refer to anything beyond themselves, while physical facts gain their significance precisely by virtue of their reference to, and implication of, a causal or functional network of relations.

If the above, rather overworked objections to epistemological realism hold true, then the demonstration of the equivalence of epistemic and physical facts encounters insurmountable difficulties. In that event, however, we may resort to the third degree of reductionism – a still more modest one than the second. It concerns the claim that epistemic and physical facts may be given complementary explanations. If neither identity nor descriptive equivalence may be demonstrated with respect to any of these facts, perhaps their over-all *complementarity* can. This requires that we develop a scheme for accounting for physical facts, and another for accounting for epistemic facts and then show that the two classes of facts are complementary.

The conditions for demonstrating the complementarity of the classes of epistemic and physical facts, as I see it, are two in number: (i) the natural universe must be fully known and it must be an organically interrelated series of physical facts, each part implying, by virtue of its nexus to all others, the nature or structure of the whole; (ii) human experience must be completely known, down to its most minute events, and all predicates must be true judgments. Now the first condition stipulates a system of physical facts, and the second a system of epistemic facts. If we allow that both are feasible and grant that they have been established, we could have two systems which are mutually complementary: *if* physical facts are so organized that each fact is interconnected with the whole, and *if* epistemic facts take place and are known, *then* the epistemic facts of 'one' equal the physical facts of 'one of the many' constituting the natural universe. Hence if the organistic hypothesis dealing with physical facts is true, and if the epistemological hypothesis explicating epistemic facts is true, then the latter is contained in the former with the result that the true knowledge of epistemic facts is the true knowledge of physical facts from the viewpoint of one; and the true knowledge of physical facts is the true knowledge of epistemic facts from the viewpoint of the many. Then, and only then, could we be assured that the species of epistemic and physical facts are truly complementary. Their complementarity does not signify proof of either identity or equivalence, however, since all that has been accomplished was the demonstration that epistemic and physical facts may be given mutually complementary explanations.

But the feasibility of demonstrating the complementarity of epistemic and physical facts through the formulation of complementary physicalist and epistemological systems is overshadowed by the consideration that, if not logical, then serious practical obstacles stand in the way of accomplishing this task. Finding evidence of the organic interconnection of physical facts is one thing, and building the relatively scant knowledge we have of these interconnections into a consistent cosmology is another. Knowledge of some of our experience is undoubtedly possible, but knowledge of *all* our experience is dubitable. The reductionist could thus hold that complementarity is a theoretical possibility and that he has evidence in its favour in the form of both epistemic and physical facts, but he cannot maintain that the demonstration of complementarity is possible with the conceptual tools at our disposal, and in the light of our actual knowledge of the universe and of ourselves.

II

The above, rather pessimistic conclusions have a wide range of implications, for science as well as for philosophy. If epistemic facts and physical facts remain disjunctive as far as our actual knowledge goes, and if we have no more than a suspicion that they may be the same facts after all, the empiricism of natural science is put into question.

If we cannot show that the data of our immediate experience are necessarily identical with what we take to be facts relevant to the physical world, in what can the empiricism of the natural scientist consist? For, as Ayer remarked, there would be no contradiction in denying that any given set of statements about atoms and electrons was true, or even meaningful, while at the same time maintaining the truth of statements which affirm the existence of the physical objects which we claim to percieve. And from this it follows, continues Ayer, that whatever may be said in defence of the causal theory, it cannot be regarded as furnishing an analysis of our perceptual judgments.[1] If I correctly interpret his remarks, Ayer's assertion corresponds to mine in that he denies the necessary equivalence of the facts discovered through the 'causal theory' (which are physical facts) and those which would furnish an analysis of our 'perceptual judgements' (which would be epistemic facts). Thus it is questionable that science can be said to deal with experiential events, since it usually operates on the basis of *some* hypothesis involving "cause" in the widest sense of the term.

I suggest that the difficulty does not entail doubting of the empiricism of natural science, for 'empiricism' in the context of scientific realism has a radically different meaning from that which it has in the context of a sceptical epistemology. Both concern experienced events, but one treats these events as physical, and the other as epistemic facts.

The empiricism of the natural scientist consists of an evaluation of the events serving as his grounds of verification as a specified set of physical facts presented to his perceptive faculties. These facts are judged to be such that their presence or absence either verifies or falsifies the hypothesis. The hypothesis can deal with facts other than those directly apprehended by the observer by virtue of an analogy (sometimes – misleadingly in the present context – referred to as 'epistemic correlation') existing between the data of observation denoted by concepts through inspection, and the unobservable scientific objects denoted by concepts through postulation. When the correlation of the two types of data is one-one, a precise analogy

[1] *cf.* A. J. Ayer, *The Problem of Knowledge*, 'Perception'.

obtains, and the theory embracing unobserved facts is verified by the data available to direct inspection. But this misleadingly designated 'epistemic correlation' does not mean that scientific empiricism is a successful form of physical reductionism: it is not the mere presence of the observed data, but the significance attributed to their presence (or absence) in regard to the hypothesis which prescribes their verificatory or falsificatory function. It is a precondition of verification that the inspected events be evaluated as physical facts, and not as epistemic ones; as public 'space-time point-events', and not as 'private sense-data'. Since the hypothesis prescribes that the apprehended data be treated as physical events, related to, and hence implying, other physical events, the ground of verification of physical theories are apprehended physical facts, and not presented epistemic facts. Consequently the scientist's 'empiricism' (in his own realist framework of assumptions) remains intact. That he deals with facts which are only partially perceptual, is due to the scope of inquiry specified by his realist basic assumption according to which not all facts are data of apprehension; our perceptive faculties are limited to a given genus of facts, and it is not the sum of facts that is limited to our range of perception. Perception is limited to certain wave-lengths of light, sound, certain velocities, quanta and qualia; beyond this range physical events remain meaningful and factual, but not perceptual. Hence, the function of the scientific hypothesis is to reduce the meaningful and factual, but not perceptual facts to the range of apprehended events. It magnifies the smaller-than-perceptual, shrinks the larger-than-perceptual, and in between refers one perceptual event to another by noting their interconnection. But the 'perceptual' event of science is treated as a *physical* fact, by virtue of attributing to it precisely those implications which define its function within the hypothesis. Hence sounds, shapes, textures, tastes, odours, etc. are treated as physical facts: they are given realist explanations. My contention is that, as explained by the scientist, events (though they are in fact 'experienced'), are neither identical nor equivalent to the immediate data of consciousness, for if they were, they would lose the relational properties which specify their function within the hypothesis. Despite the 'epistemic correlation', the empiricism of science is not reducible to the sense-world of the sceptic and, as a consequence, science is internally consistent, remaining entirely within the realm of realism.

Science deals with physical facts exclusively; but philosophy deals with physical as well as with epistemic facts. Doing so, however, should mean undertaking two distinct inquiries in an effort to demonstrate at least their complementarity as inclusive classes of facts. To do this, two philosophers would be required: one to profess realism, the other scepticism. If each remains consistent throughout the argument, each will deal either with physical or with epistemic facts, but not with both. Owing to the limitations of our stock of knowledge, such an effort has negligible chances of bringing about convincing results. Furthermore, the temptation of interpreting one type of fact as containing, referring to, or signifying the other type, appears to be too great to resist. This statement can be substantiated by an analysis of the work of most investigators of the nature of reality, and I shall refer here to some by way of example.

On the side of realism, Marx and Engels have been among the most radical ones in modern philosophy. Nevertheless, they were not content to postulate a cosmology (dialectical materialism) and a sociology (historical materialism), but went on to formulate a theory of knowledge, borrowing its categories (i.e. 'matter', 'reflection', 'dialectical relation', etc.) from their physicalist realism (termed 'scientific materialism'). But not even Whitehead could refrain from interpreting his metaphysical results as furnishing an analysis of of epistemic facts. He thus affirmed that the justification of his metaphysical principles is to be sought "(i) in our direct knowledge of the actual occasions which compose our immediate experience, and (ii) in their success as forming a basis of harmonising our systematised accounts of various types of experience, and (iii) in their success as providing the concepts in terms of which an epistemology can be framed." [1] Even more striking is his assertion that "if you start from the immediate facts of our psychological experience, as surely an empiricist should begin, you are at once led to the organic conception of nature . ." [2], while maintaining that "mental activity is one of the modes of feeling belonging to all actual entities to some degree, but only amounting to conscious intellectuality in some actual entities." [3]

Conversely, Husserl, the champion of systematic doubt in contemporary philosophy, felt obliged to sustain the validity of his 'transcendental reduction' (by which the 'natural standpoint' of science is to be radically grounded) by holding that there are aspects of the immediate

[1] *Science and the Modern World*, Ch. 10.
[2] *Idem*, Ch. 4.
[3] *Process and Reality* , Part I, Ch. I, Sect. VI.

facts of experience which lead to knowledge of the world and hence have 'metaphysical results'. "A priori, my ego, given to me apo-dictically – the only thing I can posit in absolute apodicticity as existing – can be a world-experiencing ego only by being in communion with others like himself: a member of a community of monads, which is given orientedly, starting from himself." [1]

While few realist philosophers content themselves with science's brand of empiricism but search for the justification of their systems in the immediate facts of experience, few sceptics resist the temptation to proceed beyond the evidence at hand and delve into the realm of metaphysics (Hume was one of the few capable of this feat). Thereby realists tend to become physical reductionists, reinterpreting their physical facts as epistemic ones, and sceptics emerge as epistemic reductionists, assessing their epistemic events as physical facts.

III

If my conclusions are valid, they forbid the proposition of statements which could satisfy the sceptic as well as the realist. Consequently unless we allow that one of them is entirely in the wrong, we cannot obtain statements which 'mirror' (to use a fashionable term) the structure of the world. Yet, this is required of propositions by many logical and linguistic analysts. Russell, for example, concludes his *An Inquiry Into Meaning and Truth* with the affirmation that, "com-plete metaphysical agnosticism is not compatible with the main-tainance of linguistic propositions ... For my part, I believe that, partly by means of the study of syntax, we can arrive at considerable knowledge concerning the structure of the world". [2] But how, we may ask, could a language mirror the structure of the world if it tolerates two internally consistent sets of meaning? Russell himself is far from disregarding this problem, although he assesses it differently than I do. "We think that grass is green, that stones are hard, and that snow is cold. But physics assures us that the greeness of grass, the hardness of stones, and the coldness of snow, are not the greeness, hardness, and coldness that we know in our own experience, but something very different". [3] However, Russell maintains that the 'naïve realism' which prompts us to believe that grass is green, stones

---

[1] Husserl, *Cartesian Meditations*, § 60.
[2] B. Russell, *An Inquiry Into Meaning and Truth*, 'Language and Metaphysics'.
[3] *Idem*, 'Introduction'.

are hard, and snow is cold, leads to physics. "Naïve realism leads to physics, and physics, if true, shows that naïve realism is false. Therefore naïve realism, if true, is false; therefore it is false."[1] Contrarily to this assumption, I have been concerned to show that the 'naïve realism' which Russell defines as 'the doctrine that things are what they seem', does not lead to physics, but conduces rather to scepticism. For if we seriously wish to maintain that things are what they seem, we cannot allow that they should be different from what we experience them to be. Physics does just that, however. On the other hand, the subjectivist doctrine of *esse est percipi* is a logical (though perhaps ordinarily unlikely) conclusion to be derived from Russell's brand of 'naïve realism', for here things not only are, but cannot be anything other, than what they seem. Modern physics *presupposes* that things may be other than what we experience them to be; it incorporates a most sophisticated brand of realism. If my argument is correct, we are back at the disjunction of the epistemic facts of the sceptic and the physical facts of the realist, for the former does not lead to the latter, and hence cannot be falsified by it. It would seem then that no proposition could claim to correctly refer to non-linguistic events, since every proposition can always be contradicted by reference to an entirely different set of propositions.

The pessimistic assessment of the problem is based on the theory of meaning according to which words are labels for things and events. As labels for physical and epistemic facts the terms used by the sceptic and the realist are mutually exclusive: their basic assumptions preclude the legitimacy of reductionist cross-inferences between the referents of their terms. But the pessimistic evaluation of the problem does not take into account the theory of 'meaning-as-use' of terms within given propositions. I suggest that this theory of meaning may furnish a solution to the problem posed by the disjunction of epistemic and physical facts. I am led to this consideration in view of the fact that even if their root-axioms determine that sceptical and realist arguments should consist of different principles and different terms, they do not determine that the final conclusions should have a categorically different syntactical structure. If we allow that the sceptic as well as the realist has a right to his own valid language (or 'language-game'), and if we also assume that they reach analogous conclusions, each in his own language, then the function of terms in their final propositions will be identical, and, insofar as the meaning of terms is

[1] *Ibid.*

determined by their use within their language, the identical function of terms would signify identical meanings. When the sceptic says "consciousness", the realist says "being"; when the sceptic speaks of "epistemic facts", the realist considers "physical facts". These are disjunctive terms when used as labels for the things to which the sceptic and the realist assumes that they correspond. But they may nevertheless turn out to be identical in virtue of the isomorphism of the systems of assumptions wherein they are stated. If they do, "scepticism" and "realism" become invalid. On the other hand the conclusions they state remain valid and non-contradictory. Meaning-as-use within the total system of assumptions of scepticism and realism may transform the semantic orientation of both. It may remove the sceptical predisposition of the one, and the realist assumptions of the other, and enable one to consider them as propositions about matters of facts. "Scepticism" and "realism" become meaningless; the statements expressed in sceptical and in realist terminology remain meaningful.

This assertion is proposed as a working hypothesis to be tested in the following investigations. It can be considered a verifiable hypothesis if we construct valid 'prototype' arguments for scepticism and for realism, and collate the structure of the resulting conclusions. If the decisive propositions of the two arguments turn out to be isomorphic, the disjunction of epistemic and physical facts may be considered spurious, since it depends upon the interpretation of their terms as labels for the events to which they are held to correspond. Insofar as this theory of meaning is held to be inferior to the theory according to which meaning is determined by the function of terms in the given arguments and the sceptical and realist arguments have isomorphic structure, epistemic and physical facts possess identical meanings. Re-interpretation, and not reduction by means of cross-inferences, would hold the key, then, to the correct approach to the problem.

Hence, crudely but simply put, what I am suggesting is that what we need to do is first, to treat all facts as epistemic, second, to treat all facts as physical, and third, to compare our two accounts. If they check structurally, we do not need to reduce one account to the other, for the distinction between them is spurious. I believe that we would then have as good an account of reality on our hands as we are likely to obtain in philosophical inquiry.

THE PHENOMENOLOGICAL, ONTOLOGICAL AND LINGUISTIC METHODS

I shall next examine the relevance of the phenomenological, ontological and linguistic methods to the problem of scepticism and realism. The criticism I shall advance of these methods will be in function of the assessment of the main issues of this problem as I have stated it above.

The methods I shall discuss are not the only ones currently held and evolved by philosophers, nor are they the only relevant ones. The reason for choosing the above methods is that they are most influential in contemporary thought as well as highly relevant to the problem at hand. I shall restrict my study of these methods to the ideas of the thinkers whose work could be considered the most competent in and representative of their particular field; consequently I shall consider the phenomenological method in the light of Husserl's later works, the ontological method through Whitehead's philosophy of organism, and the linguistic method through the work of the Oxford and Cambridge analysts.

I. TRANSCENDENTAL PHENOMENOLOGY AND PHILOSOPHY OF ORGANISM: A CONFRONTATION

To give a preliminary characterization of the type of thought incorporated by these philosophies, I shall point to the following facts. (i) For Husserlian transcendental phenomenology: the task of philosophy is to re-examine all previous thought and all established beliefs by suspending judgments predicating reality and treating the world as an 'acceptance-phenomenon' given to consciousness. We, as philosophers, are to "make a new beginning, each for himself and in himself".[1] (ii) For Whitehead's philosophy of organism: "the true method of philosophical construction is to frame a scheme of ideas, the best that one can, and unflinchingly to explore the interpretation of experience in terms of that scheme".[2] Whitehead's own scheme is a cosmological metaphysics assuming the primacy of being over consciousness. "The principle I am adopting is that consciousness presupposes experience, and not experience consciousness. It is a special element in the subjective forms of some feelings. Thus an actual entity may, or may not, be conscious of some part of its experience".[3] Hence experience becomes the "self-enjoyment of being one among many, and of being one arising out of the composition of many",[4] and "the primary situation disclosed in cognitive experience is 'ego-object amid objects' ".[5]

The striking result of the adoption of 'consciousness' as root-axiom by Husserl and of 'being' as basic premiss by Whitehead is the fact that for Husserl experience *must* be that of the thinker, for he alone can effect the transcendental reduction to the contents of his consciousness and thus fulfill the philosophical task of the phenomenologist, while for Whitehead experience *must* be that of an entity among others and arising from the constitution of others, for only then can the scheme of philosophy of organism be upheld.

But Husserl does not wish to stay on the level of pure consciousness all along his investigations any more than Whitehead restricts himself to an analysis of the conditions of being. Both thinkers tend to transgress into the domain of the other: Husserl in attempting to derive proof for 'other minds' and 'physical things' (*Physikalische Dinge*) from the 'primordial', 'apodictic', 'first' or 'evidential' facts of consciousness emerging in the course of the descriptive delineation of its contents, and Whitehead in trying to analyse perceptual judgments to the apprehension of metaphysical facts. The way toward ontology lies in a critical re-examination of the givenness of things to consciousness for Husserl, while for Whitehead the way toward theory of knowledge is through the re-examination of the data of experience with the conceptual tools developed in his cosmological scheme.

Both these approaches preclude reductionism, if my postulate is true according to which a consistent inquiry arguing from conscious-

---

[1] *Cartesian Meditations (CM)*, §3.
[2] *Process and Reality (PR)*, 'Preface'.
[3] *PR*, Part II, Ch. I, Sect. VI.
[4] *PR*, Part II, Ch. VI, Sect. II.
[5] *Science and the Modern World (SMW)*, Ch. 9.

ness ends by affirming consciousness, and that a similar statement can be made with respect to arguments from being. Thus, if I am right, Husserl should conclude that only consciousness exists and the 'world' exists as an element in consciousness, deriving its 'being' from its mode of givenness; and Whitehead should conclude that the natural universe is an objective fact independently of whether or not it is perceived and known by any conscious cognitive agent. Both of these assumptions are substantiated by a study of the above thinkers' work; but, there also are aspects of their work which are contrary to this assumption. I would like to point here to both aspects in turn.

It is often said that Husserl's phenomenology has solved the problem of idealism and realism. When this claim is made, 'idealism' is used in a connotation which is fundamentally analogous to the one I lend to 'scepticism', i.e. it signifies the thesis that the world exists *in* consciousness. (It is immaterial in this respect whether we allow for the existence of only 'my' consciousness, or hold that there may also be 'other minds': in either event the world is given in *a* consciousness.) To uphold the above claim, it is necessary to show that Husserl gives equal emphasis to "the world" and to "pure consciousness". An affirmation of the former at the expense of the latter would signify a tendency toward realism, the inverse case points to a leaning toward scepticism (='idealism'). By this yardstick a complete affirmation of 'the world' is unconditional realism, and the full affirmation of 'pure consciousness' connotes total (i.e. in my eyes consistent) scepticism. Phenomenology cannot assume either one of these clear-cut positions without sacrificing the phenomenological reduction of the 'real world' to 'pure consciousness' – the fundamental postulate of the phenomenological method. It is evident, then, that the method already presupposes a judicious distribution of emphasis on these contrary poles: on the subjective (consciousness) and the objective (the world). The question is, however, whether or not this balanced emphasis can be maintained in the light of the conclusions derived from the investigations themselves. On the one hand phenomenology, in order to effectively 'ground' our knowledge of the world in evidential data, must presuppose that the world exists; on the other hand it is obliged to proceed by assuming the *cogito* as the sole indubitable fact. If the former assumption is justified by the results of the application of the latter, phenomenology would indeed resolve the dichotomy of realist and idealist patterns of thought. But it may also be that the adoption of 'consciousness' as root-axiom does not permit the postulation of the existence of the world with a certainty equal to that with which it affirms the existence of the *cogito*. If my postulate is correct, this should, in fact, be the case. Husserl would be unjustly reproached then with idealism; his idealist conclusions would be those of a consistent thinker arguing according to the basic assumption of scepticism. To decide this issue I shall refer here to those passages from Husserl's voluminous work which, it seems to me, throw the clearest light on the relevant issues.

In Chapter III of Volume I of the *Ideen* (*'Die Region des reinen Bewusstseins'*) Husserl considers the problem of determining the status of consciousness in the phenomenological inquiry. He considers that our actual ways of reasoning force us to posit the underlying 'physical reality' of the things communicated to us as experiences, even though their reality could also be of another kind.[1] It is possible that our sensory world is the last world, that, in other words, there is no physical world 'behind' it.[2] There is nothing in all this, insists Husserl, which would entail that a world, or a thing of any kind *must* be given. The existence of the world is the correlate of manifold experiences signified by certain essential constitutions. But it does not follow that actual experience could only take place in connections which let us infer the world's existence. Such a conclusion is not justified either by the very essence of apprehension (*Wahrnehmung*) or by any other form of experiential apprehension.[3] It is quite possible to think that experience refuses to provide evidence of the existence of things, with the result that no unequivocally postulable, existent world would be given.[4] These are the meditations of a consistent

---

[1] "Der tatsächliche Gang unserer menschlichen Erfahrungen ist ein solcher, dass er unsere Vernunft zwingt, über die anschaulich gegebenen Dinge (die der Cartesianischen imaginatio) hinauszugehen und ihnen eine "physikalische Wahrheit" unterzulegen. Er könnte aber auch ein anderer sein."
Edmund Husserl, *Ideen zu einer reinen Phänomenologie und phänomenologischen Philosophie*, Vol. I, p. 110, The Hague, 1950.

[2] (es) ist auch denkbar, dass unsere anschauliche Welt die letzte wäre, 'hinter' der es eine physikalische überhaupt nicht gäbe . . .", *ibid.*, p. 110.

[3] Anderseits ist mit alledem nicht gesagt, dass es überhaupt eine Welt, irgendein Ding geben *muss*. Existenz einer Welt ist das Korrelat gewisser, durch gewisse Wesensgestaltungen ausgezeichneter Erfahrungsmannigfaltigkeiten. Es ist aber *nicht* einzusehen, dass aktuelle Erfahrungen *nur* in solchen Zusammenhangsformen verlaufen können; rein aus dem Wesen von Wahrnehmung überhaupt und der anderen mitbeteiligten Arten erfahrender Anschauungen ist dergleichem nicht zu entnehmen." *Ibid.*, p. 114.

[4] ". . es ist denkbar, dass es im Erfahren von unausgleichbaren und nicht nur für uns, sondern an sich unausgleichbaren Widerstreiten wimmelt, dass die Erfahrung mit einem Male konsequent sich gegen die Zumutung, ihre Dingsetzungen jemals einstimmig durchzuhalten, widerspenstig zeigt, dass ihr Zusammenhang die festen Regelordnungen der Abschattungen, Auffassungen, Erscheinungen einbüsst, und dass das wirklich in infinitum so bleibt – dass es keine einstimmig setzbare, also seiende Welt mehr gibt." *Ibid.*, p. 115.

sceptic, and the answer Husserl gives is worthy of his formulation of the problem.

No real Being (says Husserl) is necessary for the being of consciousness itself. The immanent being is therefore without doubt an absolute Being in the sense that in principle it *nulla "re" indiget ad existendum.* On the other hand the world of the transcendental *"res"* is entirely dependent upon consciousness.[1] There is a veritable abyss between the meaning of consciousness and reality. Here a horizon which is only presumptive, with a never absolutely given, merely accidental kind of Being relative to consciousness; there a necessary and absolute Being, never given in the presumptive manner which leaves open the possibility of the non-being of the apprehended.[2] Thus it is clear that when we consider consciousness in 'purity', it has to have validity as a for-itself-closed context of Being, into which nothing can penetrate and from which nothing can escape, which has no spatio-temporal 'outside' . . .[3] ; on the other hand the entire spatio-temporal world has, in its own sense, merely an intentional Being, one which consciousness posits in its experiences and which can be viewed and determined only as being identical with unequivocally motivated experience-manifoldnesses (*Erfahrungsmannigfaltigkeiten*) – beyond that it is a Nothing . . .[4]. Reality, the reality of the particular thing and also the reality of the whole world, is essentially lacking in independence. In its absolute sense it is nothing at all, it has no 'absolute essence'

[1] "*. . kein reales Sein,* kein solches, das sich bewusstseinmässig durch Erscheinungen darstellt und ausweist, *ist für das Sein des Bewusstseins selbst* (im weitesten Sinne des Erlebnisstromes) *notwendig.*"
Das immanente Sein ist also zweifellos in dem Sinne absolutes Sein, dass es prinzipiell nulla 're' indiget ad existendum.
Anderseits ist die Welt der transzendenten 'res' durchaus auf Bewusstsein, und zwar nicht auf ein logisch erdachtes, sondern aktuelles angewiesen" Ibid., pp. 115–116.
[2] "Zwischen Bewusstsein und Realität gähnt ein wahrer Abgrund des Sinnes. Hier ein sich abschattendes, prinzipiell nur mit präsumptiven Horizonten und nie absolut zu gebendes, bloss zufälliges und bewusstseinrelatives Sein; dort ein notwendiges und absolutes Sein, prinzipiell nicht durch Abschattung und Erscheinung (in präsumptiver Weise, die immerfort das Nichtsein des Selbst-Wahrgenommenen offen lässt) zu geben." Ibid., p. 117.
[3] "Also wird es klar . . . . . , dass trotz alledem Bewusstsein, in '*Reinheit*' betrachtet, als ein für *sich geschlossener Seinszusammenhang* zu gelten hat, als ein Zusammenhang *absoluten Seins,* in den nichts hineindringen und aus dem nichts entschlüpfen kann; der kein räumlich-zeitliches Draussen hat . . ." Ibid., p. 117.
[4] "Andererseits ist die ganze *räumlich-zeitliche Welt,* der sich Mensch und menschliches Ich als untergeordnete Einzelrealitäten zurechnen, *ihrem Sinne nach blosses intentionales Sein,* also ein solches, das den blossen sekundären, relativen Sinn eines Seins *für* ein Bewusstsein hat als in Bewusstseinssubjekten durch Erscheinungen erfahrbares und sich als Bewährungseinheit von Erscheinungen möglicherweise in infinitum bewährendes. Es ist ein Sein, das das Bewusstsein in seinen Erfahrungen setzt, das prinzipiell nur als Identisches von einstimmig motivierten Erfahrungsmannigfaltigkeiten anschaubar und bestimmbar – *darüber hinaus* aber ein Nichts ist, . . ." Ibid., p. 117.

(*absolutes Wesen*), it has the essence from something which is only intentional, only conscious, respectively imaginable, realizable in possible manifestations.[1]

It would seem that Husserl finds no proof in consciousness to justify the assertion of the physical reality of its contents. Is it conceivable, then, that the real, physical world does not exist in the first place? If there is no proof to assert that it does exist, there could be no contradiction in asserting this as a possibility. But Husserl would disagree to this, and here the roots of epistemic reductionism are discernible. He remarks, "the Being of consciousness, though modified by an annihilation of the object-world (*Dingwelt*), would not be touched as regards its own existence" [2], and reflectively adds, "*Also modifiziert allerdings*" ('Hence modified at any rate'). The annihilation of the world, according to him, would simply mean that those contexts of experience which permit the connections (*Zusammenhänge*) of theoretical reason would be excluded.[3] Implicit in this statement is the belief that experience, as it actually takes place, does furnish those contexts which permit theoretical reason to postulate the real, physical world by some direct inference. Were there no such direct implications of some experiential contents for the existence of the physical world, the corresponding contents of consciousness would not need to be modified if the real world did not exist. But the indications given by Husserl are scarce as to what correlates the physical world has in conscious experience which directly imply the former's existence. He only tells us that if the physical world did not exist, the connections of experiences would be typically other than they in fact are, insofar as the motivations of experience, fundamental for the development of physical concepts and theories, would fall away. But the 'things' (*Dinge*) would still afford the continuous manifoldness of appearance as intentional unities which they would afford if the

---

[1] "Realität, sowohl Realität des einzeln genommenen Dinges als auch Realität der ganzen Welt, entbehrt wesensmässig (in unserem strengen Sinne) der Selbständigkeit. Es ist nicht in sich etwas Absolutes und bindet sich sekundär an anderes, sondern es ist in absolutem Sinne gar nichts, es hat gar kein 'absolutes Wesen', es hat die Wesenheit von etwas, das prinzipiell *nur* Intentionales, *nur* Bewusstes, bwz. Vorstellbares, in möglichen Erscheinungen zu Verwirklichendes ist." *Ibid.*, p. 118.

[2] ". . . *das Sein des Bewusstseins*, jedes Erlebnisstromes überhaupt, *durch eine Vernichtung der Dingwelt zwar notwendig modifiziert, aber in seiner eigenen Existenz nicht berührt würde.*" *Ibid.*, p. 115.

[3] "Denn Vernichtung der Welt besagt korrelativ nichts anders, als dass in jedem Erlebnisstrom (dem voll, also beiderseitig endlos genommenen Gesamtstrom der Erlebnisse eines Ich) gewisse geordnete Erfahrungszusammenhänge und demgemäss auch nach ihnen sich orientierende Zusammenhänge theoretisierender Vernunft ausgeschlossen wären." *Ibid.*, p. 115.

physical world *did* exist.[1] Thus Husserl appears to argue that not the factual content of experience, but merely the motivations which permit us to evolve physical concepts and judgments, would be affected by the annihilation of the world. It is difficult to see how this proposition can be maintained together with the one that the motivations, directed *at* the content of experience, are also *determined by* the things given in experience. Certainly, motivation for building physical concepts and making physical judgments should be provided by the actual givenness of the thing we designate 'physical', and if these things remain unaffected by the annihilation of the world (i.e. if they are identical regardless of whether or not the physical world exists), our motivations for constructing ideas and theories concerning the physical world should be unaffected by, and independent from, any answer pertaining to the question concerning the existence of the world.

However, let us for the sake of argument assume that these motivations (or any other component of conscious experience you wish) would be modified if and when the world did not exist. If such were the case, the physical world would determine these particular experience-correlates, and thus assume primacy with respect to them. This assumption, however, contradicts Husserl's thesis concerning the absolute primacy of pure consciousness. It is immediately evident that such primacy could only be consistently maintained if no aspect of the real world is held to be capable of determining any aspect of the world of consciousness. And this is in fact affirmed by Husserl in that he says that there are no causal relations (in the sense of mutual dependence) between the reality of consciousness and of the world.[2] If we take him at his word, however, we shall admit no reasons for the modification of the realities of consciousness if and when the real world ceases to exist. On the other hand, Husserl evidently overstates the case in denying relations of dependence between pure consciousness and the physical world, for, even if such denial hypostatizes the absolute primacy of consciousness, it renders the inference of an apo-

---

[1] "Die Erfahrungszusammenhänge wären dann eben entsprechend andere und typisch andere, als sie faktisch sind, sofern die Erfahrungsmotivationen fortfielen, welche für die physikalische Begriffs- und Urteilsbildung gründende sind. Aber im grossen und ganzen könnten sich uns im Rahmen der gebenden *Anschauungen*, die wir unter dem Titel 'schlichte Erfahrung' befassen (Wahrnehmung, Wiedererinnerung usw.), 'Dinge' darbieten ähnlich wie jetzt, sich in Erscheinungsmannigfaltigkeiten kontinuierlich durchhaltend als intentionale Einheiten." *Ibid.*, pp. 110–111.

[2] "[Bewusstsein, in 'Reinheit' betrachtet] ... von keinem Dinge Kausalität erfahren und auf kein Ding Kausalität üben kann – vorausgesetzt, dass Kausalität den normalen Sinn natürlicher Kausalität hat, als einer Abhängigkeitsbeziehung zwischen Realitäten." *Ibid.*, p. 117.

dictically existent external reality logically impossible. If Husserl
would be content with a purely hypothetical external reality, his
position would be consistent. But he formulates the doctrine of constitution (*Konstitutionslehre*) and in so doing he assumes causal
relations between experiences presented to consciousness and the
physical body (*Leib*) through which they are perceived.[1] While Husserl
does consider the possibility of constituting an 'objective nature'
on the level of solipsism [2], his arguments are inconsistent with his
definition of 'pure consciousness'. He wishes namely to understand
the 'true' or 'objective' thing as 1) that which is presented under
'normal' as opposed to 'anomalous' conditions, and as 2) the identical
stock of qualities which obtain when all relativity is rigorously disposed
of and fixed. Given these conditions, Husserl affirms, and given an
objective knowledge of the psycho-physical constitution of the experient subject and of the existing conditionality between subject and
object in addition, we can determine how the thing in question must
be constituted for the particular – normal or anomalous – subjectivity.[3]
This makes sense – but only if we define 'normalcy' in reference to the
physical conditions of perception. If we agree to this, as Husserl does,
we assume that the actual presentation of the given thing is dependent
upon the physical conditions of perception. But then we presuppose
causal determination between the conditions of perception and the
presentation of the object to consciousness, i.e. we assume the causal
dependence of the contents of consciousness upon events in the physical
world. This, however, is in contradiction with the posited nature of
'pure consciousness'.

But let us concede the point and ask, instead, what the criteria are
for deciding which perceptions are normal and which are not. The
criteria for normalcy, according to Husserl, rest on the possibility of
correcting impressions received through one sense-organ by recourse

---

[1] *cf. Ideen*, Vol. II, paragraph 18, 'Die Aistheta in Bezug auf den aisthetischen Leib'.
[2] *cf. Ideen*, Vol. II., pp. 77–78.
[3] ". . . unter dem Titel 'wahres' oder 'objektives' Ding [ist] noch ein Doppeltes zu ver-
stehen:
    1) *das Ding*, wie es sich mir unter *'normalen' Bedingungen* darstellt, demgegenüber alle
anderen dingartigen Einheiten – die unter 'anomalen' Bedingungen konstituierten – zum
'blossen Schein' herabsinken;
    2) der identische Bestand an Qualitäten, der sich unter *Absehung von aller Relativität*
herausarbeiten und logisch-mathematisch fixieren lässt: das physikalische Ding. Kennt
man dieses und besitzt man ausserdem objektive Erkenntnis der psychophysischen Beschaf-
fenheit der erfahrenden Subjekte sowie der bestehenden Konditionalitäten zwischen Ding
und Subjekt, so lässt sich daraus objektiv bestimmen, wie das betreffende Ding für die
jeweilige Subjektivität – normale oder anomale – anschaulich beschaffen sein muss." *Ibid.*,
pp. 77–78.

to impressions received by others. If one organ provides evidence for changes in the outer world which, in the light of the evidence of the other organs, turns out to be anomalous, we are dealing with 'appearances' (*Schein*) and not with reality. But what if some sense-organs are incapacitated, and thus cannot provide the necessary corrections? The danger is present then, Husserl says, that under these conditions objective nature could not be constituted. Yet this danger is eliminated when we abolish the abstraction which we have maintained up to now, and take into account the conditions of the factual constitution: that in reality the experient subject is not a solipsistic one, but one among many.[1] Now if we agree to *this* proposition, we are committed to regard the entire method of phenomenological investigation as a heuristic instrument without intrinsic truth-value, to be used as long as it is useful, and discarded when it no longer is, since here the realist premiss (the subject as 'one among many') is simply assumed, in view of the fact that the sceptical premiss entails a solipsistic and hence displeasing conclusion.

When normalcy is defined by the correction of the impressions received through one sense-organ by the impressions received through another, the absolute Being of consciousness is subordinated to the Being of the body which determines the contents of consciousness. But when the incorrigibility of possibly fallacious impressions received through the organs of one's own body is postulated, the primacy of consciousness collapses not only with respect to the Being of one's own body, but also with respect to the Being of the world: the only way a fallacious constitution of objective reality could be corrected in such a case is by recourse to the perceptual judgments of other people. Hence there are cases when the constituting consciousness is corrigible by what should properly be its constituted contents, namely 'other

---

[1] "Solange wir Fälle nehmen, in denen die Veränderungen der Aussenwelt, die uns ein anomales Wahrnehmungsorgan vortäuscht, durch das Zeugnis der anderen Organe als 'scheinbare' erwiesen werden, ist die Scheidung von 'Schein' und Wirklichkeit immer gegeben, wenn auch im Einzelfalle unentschieden bleiben mag, *was* Schein und *was* Wirklichkeit ist. Nehmen wir aber einmal an, dass ein Subjekt stets nur normale Wahrnehmungen hätte, und niemals eine Abwandlung irgend eines seiner Organe erführe, oder aber, dass es eine Abwandlung erführe, bei der nicht die Möglichkeit der Korrektur bestände (Verlust des gesamten Tastfeldes, psychische Erkrankungen, die den gesamten Wahrnehmungstypus verändern), dann entfielen die bisher angenommenen Motive für die Scheidung von 'Schein' und 'Wirklichkeit', und die Stufe der 'objektiven Natur' könnte von einem solchen Subjekt nicht erreicht werden. Die Gefahr, dass es unter den angenommenen Bedingungen gar nicht zur Konstitution der objektiven Natur kommen könnte, wird aber beseitigt, sobald wir die Abstraktion aufheben, die wir bis jetzt aufrecht erhalten haben, und die Bedingungen in Rechnung ziehen, unter denen die *faktische* Konstitution steht: dass nähmlich das erfahrende Subjekt in Wahrheit *kein solipsistisches* ist, sondern eines unter vielen." *Ibid.*, p. 78.

minds', 'analogously apperceived' in their respective bodies. Then, however, the 'grounding' of evidence in the apodictic Being of consciousness falls away, and we are obliged to accept the judgment of others as superior to the evidence of our own experience. For, in the final analysis, how else could any one individual determine whether or not any or all of his sense-organs convey a correct or a deceptive picture of the external world to him?

These and analogous internal contradictions traverse the main body of Husserlian thought. They have not only permitted, but have been very likely the main cause of the splitting of the phenomenological movement into 'transcendental phenomenology', 'ontological phenomenology' and 'existentialism'. Husserl may be interpreted as a consistent sceptic (and accused of being an 'idealist') as well as a methodical ontologist grounding common belief in the natural world with the phenomenological *epoché*. It is evident, however, that much to the consternation of the ontologists and existentialist among his disciples, Husserl's scepticism came progressively to the fore in his later works (e.g. in the *Cartesian Meditations*). Nevertheless, there are no indications that Husserl would have renounced belief in the existence of the world beyond consciousness. As a result the internal contradictions, due to the contrary assumptions inherent in the sceptical root-axiom and the reductionist doctrine of constitution, became more acute in the later works.

But for the present inquiry Husserl is important in his capacity of a sceptic systematically applying the Cartesian method of universal doubt and not in the capacity of a presumptive reductionist. Hence the reductionist aspects of Husserlian phenomenology are not the ones which interest us here, and they need not be considered in detail. It is merely to be pointed out that the ontological ('München-Göttinger') School, as well as the existentialist branch of second and third generation phenomenologists have experienced serious difficulties in using the premisses of transcendental phenomenology for epistemic reductionism, and have introduced changes whereby the investigation loses much of its strict adherence to the cogito as criterion of evidence.[1]

---

[1] Existentialists, such as Sartre, criticise the transcendence-concept of consciousness, holding it to be circular and replacing it with an immanentist concept. Among the more orthodox ontological-phenomenologists, Ingarden and Konrad-Martius have criticised the 'transcendental reduction' which, according to the latter, makes the world into a 'world-phenomenon' while through the use of the simpler *epoché* it remains exactly as it is, in its universal mode of givenness. (cf. H. Konrad-Martius, 'Zwei phänomenologische Richtungen', *Phaenomenologica* IV. The Hague p. 180.)

Relevant to this argument is the fact that in striking contrast to the problems encountered by phenomenologists, thinkers such as Whitehead experience remarkably little difficulty in getting past subjectivism and positing the existence of the world. Husserl is obliged by his method of systematic doubt to derive physical entities from the cogito; Whitehead, however, takes them as given. This is not an accidental, but an entirely basic divergence between the type of thlnking represented by Husserl and Whitehead. It shows that, while Husserl admittedly argues from consciousness, Whitehead argues directly from being. This is not to say, however, that Whitehead admits the axiomatic nature of his notion of being. He substantiates it by a view of experience wherein his notion of being is indicated. But it is evident that his view of experience is derived from his views on the nature of the world, i.e. from his concepts of 'being'. In discussing Philosophic Method [1] Whitehead explicitly states that all final actualities have the metaphysical character of occasions of experience.[2] He condemns the type of epistemological construction in which Husserl engages as an "attitude of strained attention". While he does not explicitly refer to Husserl, the assertion that in such attitude "the data are the patterns of sensa provided by the sense organs (which) is the sensationalist doctrine of Locke and Hume" and the subsequent inclusion of Kant into this category with the reservation that for him the "data are somewhat narrower than for Hume: they are the sensa devoid of their patterns" [3] leaves no doubt that the kind of transcendental philosophy which has arisen in Germany in the 19th century, and which has influenced Husserl through Brentano, would also come under the heading of the attitude of 'strained attention'.

But Whitehead is never dogmatic; he is among the first to realize that his own way of philosophising represents one specific method. In discussing method he explicitly states, "So far as concerns methodology, the general issue of the discussion will be that theory dictates method, and that any particular method is only applicable to theories of one correlate species." [4] He goes even further in reducing theories and the methods they determine to 'working hypotheses': "This close relation of theory to method partly arises from the fact that the relevance of evidence depends on the theory which is dominating the

---

[1] *Adventures of Ideas (AI)*, Ch. 15.
[2] *Ibid.*
[3] *Ibid.*
[4] *Ibid.*

discussion. This fact is the reason why dominant theories are also termed 'working hypotheses'." [1]

Thus, when Whitehead proposes a definition of 'Speculative Philosophy' he asks us to take it as a working hypothesis.[2] It is evident, however, that he holds his own working hypothesis adequate for accounting for the subjective world of consciousness concordantly with the objective world of being. "The world within experience is identical with the world beyond experience, the occasion of experience is within the world and the world within the occasion. The categories have to elucidate this paradox of the connectedness of things: – the many things, the one world without and within." [3] Now by 'categories' Whitehead means the categories of his philosophy of organism: that scheme is to provide for a comprehension of reality in harmony with the data of immediate experience. "Speculative Philosophy can be defined as the endeavour to frame a coherent, logical, necessary system of general ideas in terms of which every element of our experience can be interpreted. Here 'interpretation' means that each element shall have the character of a particular instance of the general scheme." [4] The problems dealt with by epistemology are envisaged by Whitehead as problems of metaphysics, to be solved by the construction of a 'coherent, logical, necessary system of general ideas'. Epistemological inquiry thus appears to be integrated into metaphysical schematization. Nevertheless, Whitehead deals with epistemology on its own ground. For example, notwithstanding his assertion that "on the philosophical side any consideration of epistemology has been entirely excluded. It would have been impossible to discuss that topic without upsetting the whole balance of the work" [5], Whitehead does discuss epistemology in the work he refers to (*Science and the Modern World*) and clarifies many of his views on these issues. Since these views have been at the foundation of the scheme of philosophy of organism later expounded in *Process and Reality*, it is illuminating to consider what Whitehead has to say on epistemology in the earlier work.

Whitehead's deeply rooted belief that experience is the experience of the totality presented in a limited form, is evident when he talks of "faith in the order of nature". He seems to be talking also of his own faith in saying that it "springs from direct inspiration of the nature

[1] *Ibid.*
[2] *Ibid.*
[3] *Ibid.*
[4] *Ibid.*
[5] *SMW*, 'Preface'.

of things as disclosed in our own immediate present experience . . . to experience this faith is . . . to know that our experience, dim and fragmentary as it is, yet sounds the utmost depths of reality . ." [1]. For later he firmly asserts that "if you start from the immediate facts of our psychological experience, as surely an empiricist should begin, you are at once led to the organic conception of nature . ." [2]. Now the 'empiricism' Whitehead speaks of comes to light in his 'objectivism' which, counterposed to 'subjectivism' is the central issue of his theory of knowledge. He gives three reasons for his objectivism, and these reasons shed light on the orientation of Whitehead's thought in regard to the problem of scepticism and realism. "Apart from the detailed criticism of the difficulties raised by subjectivism in any form, my reasons for distrusting it are three in number. One reason arises from the direct interrogation of our perceptive experience. It appears from this interrogation that we are *within* a world of colours, sounds, and other sense-objects, related in space and time to enduring objects such as stones, trees, and human bodies. We seem to be ourselves elements of this world in the same sense as are the other things which we perceive . . . My second reason for distrusting subjectivism is based on the particular content of experience. Our historical knowledge tells us of ages in the past when, so far as we can see, no living being existed on earth. Again it tells us of countless star-systems, whose detailed history remains beyond our ken . . . But all these things which it appears certainly happened, are either unknown in detail, or else are reconstructed by inferential evidence. In the face of this content of our personal experience, it is difficult to believe that the experienced world is an attribute of our own personality . . . My third reason is based upon the instinct for action. Just as sense-perception seems to give knowledge of what lies beyond individuality, so action seems to issue in an instinct for self-transcendence. The activity passes beyond self into the known transcendent world. It is here that final ends are of importance . . . It follows therefore that the world, as known, transcends the subject which is cognisant of it." [3]

This is not the place to give a detailed critique of these premisses, which, in the above quoted 'three reasons for distrusting subjectivism', attempt to substantiate Whitehead's ontological, and epistemologically realist method of philosophical construction. It should be merely

---

[1] *SMW*, Ch. 1.
[2] *SMW*, Ch. 4. A similar assertion is found in *Symbolism, Its Meaning and Effect*, (S) I. 13.
[3] *SMW*, Ch. 5.

pointed out that the direct interrogation of experience is assumed to prove that we are *within* an external world, and that the latter consists of objects and qualities. This is held to be evidence that we are *in* the world, just as are the other things we perceive. We may deny or accept this premiss and the inference. If we categorically deny it, we are dogmatic sceptics and further ontological discussion is reduced to pure conjecture. If we accept it, we may either hold that the perceived objects and qualities are such as given (or essentially such) or that there may be a wide margin of error. Husserl held the latter view when he said "Not only can a particular experienced thing suffer devaluation as an illusion of the senses; the whole unitarily surveyable nexus, experienced throughout a period of time, can prove to be an illusion, a coherent dream." [1] According to this view further discussion of known entities must be based on some apodictic evidence that they are factually such as perceived. If we accept this, then historical knowledge must be grounded in a critical re-examination of *my* experience. Hence the historical knowledge which Whitehead gives as his second reason for distrusting subjectivism is subject to the outcome of the critical examination. Knowledge based on the assumption that things *are* and that they are *such* (or basically such) as we experience them, becomes doubtful. Whitehead, however, does not indulge in these doubts: hence historical knowledge (which is essentially public), is considered by him as valid evidence.

Whitehead's third reason, that action implies a transcendent world into which it passes from the self, represents an acceptance of the first reason (that we are *within* an external world) and not a fresh argument. This basic statement is merely repeated, and action, in addition to sense-perception, evaluated in reference to it. But, as I shall try to show, neither perception nor action necessarily and strictly imply an external world.[2]

In writing his own cosmology, Whitehead built it on these somewhat naïve and intuitionistic epistemological premisses. In *Process and Reality* itself there is no systematic descent below the level of the 'actual entities'. The epistemological argument of that work must be pieced together from diverse statements such as "if experience be not based upon an objective content, there can be no escape from a solipsist subjectivism" [3] and "the experience enjoyed by an actual

[1] Husserl, *CM*, § 7 (in the translation of Dorion Cairns).
[2] *cf.* Part II, below.
[3] *PR*, Part II, Ch. VI, Sect. IV.

entity is that entity *formaliter*".[1] The concept of actual entity is an accepted root-axiom which gains its specific content by the elaboration of a relational scheme wherein actual entities interact. Thus 'being' *qua* the 'actual entity' (or 'occasion') is axiomatic to the scheme itself. This basic axiom is mitigated by the introduction of universals in the form of 'eternal objects', but universals are no less rationalistic than concepts of existence are. When universals are introduced they make up the substance of actuality in conjunction with existents. Yet neither universals nor existents are direct elements of experience as given to consciousness. They are already representative of inferences, explaining rather than describing that which is experientially given. Such ontological explanations are rejected *qua* axioms in the type of 'argument from consciousness' which Husserl proposed, but they are admitted in the form of conclusions concerning the constitution of physical objects (*Physikalische Dinge*). Hence the accent and the direction of arguments in Husserl and Whitehead are contrary, but they share a common concern: the substantiation of their theories by reductionism.

As I have suggested earlier, the reductionism of Husserl is of the 'epistemic' variety, and that of Whitehead of the 'physical' kind. Now it is significant that both thinkers came close to attempting to meet the conditions I outlined for demonstrating the complementarity of epistemic and physical facts: they both posited the organic interconnection of physical facts, and tried to demonstrate that the knowledge of experience furnishes the evidence for it. Whitehead constructed the metaphysical scheme of philosophy of organism and explained experience consistently with its categories; Husserl, on the other hand, analysed the data of experience and believed to have found evidence therein of the unitary interconnection of metaphysical realities. Discussing the 'Metaphysical results of our explication of experiencing someone else' [2] Husserl asserts "Actually . . . *there can exist only a single community of monads*, the community of *all* co-existing monads. Hence there can exist *only one Objective world*, only one objective time, only one Objective space, only one Objective Nature. Moreover this one nature *must* exist, if there are any structures in me that involve the co-existence of other monads." The imperative 'must' is evidence that the sole chance of a methodical sceptic to penetrate the barriers of ego-centricism erected by his own scepticism

---

[1] *PR*, Part II, Ch. I, Sect. VI.
[2] *CM*, § 60.

is to find facts 'in me' (i.e. in the thinker's primary experience) which testify to the organic interconnection of my Ego with other Egos and other objects in general. The condition of reductionism is seen by Husserl, no less than by Whitehead, to lie in the assumption that the analysis of perceptual judgments must furnish evidence of the existence of physical reality through the interconnection of the experience of the particular with the existence of the whole. The goal is the same; the approach is from opposite ends. The result is mutually exclusive universes of meaning.

I have emphasized that the root-axiom of Husserl is 'consciousness' while that of Whitehead is 'being'. I have also presented evidence to the effect that each thinker considers his own root-axiom sufficient to delve into the realm of the other, and thus to reduce notions of being and notions entailed by notions of being ('physical facts') to notions of consciousness and notions entailed by notions of consciousness ('epistemic facts'). Thus, Husserl and Whitehead have figured in this brief confrontation in double roles: Husserl as methodological sceptic and as epistemic reductionist, and Whitehead as systematic realist and as physical reductionist. For purposes of distilling the pure, uncompromising form of scepticism and realism, it will be necessary to eliminate the epistemic reductionism of Husserl and the physical reductionism of Whitehead. This process of pruning will be undertaken in formulating the prototype arguments 'from consciousness' and 'from being'. It is sufficient to remark at present that it is the methodological scepticism of Husserl, and the adequate and systematic realism of Whitehead that represent the ideas and principles vital to the cogent analysis of the problem of scepticism and realism. The reductionist aspects of transcendental phenomenology and of philosophy of organism have to be bracketed, and their essential features – the universal doubt of one, and the constructive realism of the other – elevated to prominence. It is perhaps questionable whether such a purified phenomenology and philosophy of organism may still be called 'phenomenology' and 'philosophy of organism'; it is certain, however, that they will richly deserve being denoted by 'scepticism' and 'realism', philosophical positions which are illustriously exemplified by the work of Husserl and Whitehead.

II. SCEPTICISM, REALISM, AND LINGUISTIC ANALYSIS

The linguistic method is closely associated with the philosophy of common sense in analytic Anglo-Saxon philosophy. The work of thinkers of the school of which G. E. Moore was the first great figure (sometimes referred to as the 'Oxford' and the 'Cambridge' analysts) is characterized by an interest in approaching philosophical problems from the point of view of the language in which they are formulated. They consider their task to lie in the analysis of the formulation of philosophical problems and in the statement of the conclusions. It is usually held by these thinkers that there are good reasons for taking the language of common sense seriously, and that when the language of certain traditional philosophical problems is analysed, a discovery of misunderstandings in the use of words entails the disappearance of the problems themselves.

There is also a more explicit thesis of linguistic analysis which is of interest to this inquiry. It is the thesis which asserts that the meanings of words is their use in ordinary language, and this meaning gives us a clue to the *existence* of the things to which the words are normally used to refer. This doctrine is a logical consequence of the linguistic method introduced by Moore and developed by Wittgenstein and Russell, although not all linguistic philosophers subscribe to it explicitly and without reservations. It has been stated as the Paradigm Case Argument (PCA) and more recently as the Argument from the Standard Examples. In formulating the latter, Urmson claims that philosophical doubt whether something is really an X, as well as doubt whether anything is X, is dispelled "by showing that certain things are standard cases of what the term in question is designed to describe".[1] Philosophical doubt concerning the identification of things such as they are may be overcome by a study of how we refer to them when we use ordinary language in a typical way. Thus, Urmson restates the Paradigm-Case Argument which, in its important expositions, has often been held to disclose knowledge of not only words and the meaning of words, but of the structure and existence of the *world*. The argument holds ordinary language to be a trivial, but reliable guide to knowing (i) *that* things exist; (ii) *how* things exist. Hence the interesting proposition concerning this doctrine is that the PCA is neither a mere game with words, nor only a means

---

[1] J. O. Urmson, 'Some Questions Concerning Validity' in *Essays in Conceptual Analysis*, p. 120.

of detecting their correct and incorrect meanings by reference to the standard cases wherein they are used, but is an instrument for solving philosophical problems. The paradigm use of a word (wherein that word refers to a 'thing' i.e. to a sensory object) is taken as proof of that thing's *existence,* and *manner* of existence. As Austin said, "When we examine what we should say when, what words we should use in what situations, we are looking again not *merely* at words (or 'meanings', whatever they may be) but also at the realities we use the words to talk about." [1] Thus there is an assertion concerning the basic validity for philosophical discourse of words used in ordinary language. This validity is the foundation of the philosophical edifice constructed by Moore and his followers. I am not disputing the assumption of this validity, but merely wish to point out the fact that if it is true, the problem of scepticism and realism is a pseudo-problem, made by philosophers, and capable of being resolved by linguistic analysis. For, when the meaning of a word is taken to be its use, then the meaning reflects the kind of objects, states of affairs, and situations in general, wherein the word is used. Under the assumption of 'meaning-as-use',[2] meaning is a linguistic fact, and linguistic facts do more than serve communication – they also serve to denote our thinking about reality. So far, so good. My objection is not to this assertion, but to the refusal of its proponents to admit that ordinary language does not necessarily give us that picture of the world which a thoroughgoing analysis of any part or aspect of the world may give us, even if at the cost of a different use (or 'misuse') of the words occurring in ordinary language. Ordinary language, it is assumed, discloses the ultimate truth about the nature of things. If this is true, then linguistic analysis using the PCA is the indicated method for philosophic inquiry. But, if there is any doubt concerning this basic issue (upon which the ontological value of the PCA rests) then other methods must be employed to test the philosopher's faith in ordinary language. Now, since an analysis of ordinary language, assuming meaning-as-use, no matter how pregnant and clear, cannot bring us proof without circularity, the only way the proposition of meaning-as-use can be tested is by assuming that it is not applicable to certain test cases. In that way the meaning of a word can be considered independently of its use, and a new meaning of a word would

[1] J. L. Austin, 'A Plea for Excuses' in *Proc. of the Arist. Soc.*, N.S., LVII, p. 8. In fact, Austin examined most of the problems I raise here and believed to have succeeded in solving them by means of linguistic analyses. *cf.* especially his *Sense and Sensibilia*, Oxford, 1962.

[2] This term has been well defined by P. Butchvarov in 'Meaning-as-Use and Meaning-as-Correspondence', in *Philosophy*, 1960, 3.

not necessarily connote its misuse, but could, eventually, represent a deeper apprehension of some fact or aspect of that thing.

In a sense traditional philosophy has operated on this premiss, and it has come in for much criticism from linguistic analysts on this account. But – more importantly – controlled empirical inquiries into the nature of reality also propose uses of words which are different from the uses they find in ordinary language, for not even the empirical natural sciences, the most rigorously controlled of empirical inquiries, can operate purely by means of an ideal language, but must use words borrowed from ordinary language in a novel way. Terms suggestive of solidity, extension, colour, sound, taste, smell, and of a combination of sensory qualities often find novel and specific uses in science (and in philosophy based on scientific methods or on scientific findings), and, while it is difficult to consider the scientific use of the words a 'misuse', it is contradictory to so consider their ordinary use. In the former event a serious check (if not in practice, then in philosophic theory) to scientific hypotheses would be provided by the demand that science keep to the ordinary use of words or use signs or custom-made language exclusively; in the latter case the basic element of truth, necessary for rendering normal linguistic communication credible, would be removed. But the adequate exemplification of scientific use (or misuse) of ordinary words would require a study in itself, and since my purpose is merely to introduce this contention, and not to conclusively prove it, I shall only remark that terms of ordinary language are often used in scientific discourse in a quite novel sense.

Not only natural science, but most disciplines undertaking a systematic study of any one part or aspect of the world come up, in the course of the investigations, with uses of ordinary terms which violate their standard usage. The investigators are not primarily concerned with the correspondence of their use of the words with their use in linguistic paradigm cases, for their task is not general social communication by means of language but specialized research. Thus, after a preliminary definition of the sense in which a word will be used (insofar as its use significantly differs from its ordinary use) investigators tend to employ it without further apologies as designated, notwithstanding the fact that a person who has not been acquainted with the definition proposed for that word would be likely to misunderstand it.

If the meaning of a word is its use, and if its use is correct, then the meaning of the word in the paradigm case is equivalent to knowledge of the thing it refers to: this conclusion is tenable only if we hold the premisses upon which the given language operates *sound*. This again, depends on the criteria we set. Ordinary language is based on practice, and practice is how we seem to get along in the world. Whatever comes up against our practice (as criterion) is changed so that it accords better with our exigencies. But how we best get along with each other and with our natural environment does not necessarily furnish us with true statements concerning either each other or our natural environment. Practice as criterion is valid for daily intercourse and survival. But whether these presuppose acquaintance with ultimate truths is another matter. It must be granted that there may be other criteria for proving statements than the one applied in ordinary language – the medium of communication in a socially interdetermined civilized community. I suggest that there are two mutually independent criteria each of which requires and justifies a specifically philosophical language: one such criterion being *experientiality*, the other *adequacy*.[1]

The criterion 'experientiality' requires a discourse based on the basic premiss "consciousness", wherein words are labels for things given to consciousness. Provided we accept experientiality as supreme criterion, we will have full justification for engaging in discourse in the sceptic's language. Now if experientiality is not acknowledged as supreme criterion, and practice is also rejected, then we may come to the conclusion that *adequacy* is the criterion we are looking for. Adequacy corresponds to the exigencies of full explanation, and inasmuch as neither arguments measured against the criterion of experientiality, nor arguments based on utility in practice can provide us with sufficient grounds of explanation, realism may appear fully indicated. In that event we shall argue from "being", and create a language (or 'language-game') which is other than the language of experience and ordinary language, since its rule is determined by reference to the adequacy of realist explanations. Now if we change these criteria, we can engage in discourse in three different languages: ordinary language, the language of scepticism and the language of realism. Each of these can be evolved to have a name for each object, and one object for each name. But when we compare the names we use as labels for things in each language, we will find that the same symbol stands for three different meanings. Thus "object" means in ordinary language a thing which we have traffic with either actually or potentially, while in the sceptic's language it means an epistemic entity constituted of private-

---

[1] *Cf.* 'The Criteria of Proof' below.

sense-data, and in the realist's language an ontic entity existing independently of being known, and affording sense-data to whoever equipped with sense-organs happens to be in its immediate presence. The decision as to which of these languages is valid and preferable is the decision as to which criterion we choose to adopt. It is my conviction that the criterion justifying the use of ordinary language is insufficient, since it combines the *assumptions* that must be made if the criterion of a realist language is to be satisfied with the *restrictions* entailed by the application of the criterion of the sceptic's language. Hence I share Butchvarov's conclusion, that "it is not this kind [i.e. the kind attainable through an inquiry into the uses of words in ordinary language] of knowledge that we try to attain in science and philosophy and it is not this kind of knowledge that one usually means when he talks about our knowledge of the world".[1] This statement is fully justified in the light of the disjunction of all discourse into references to private and to public events. But the everyday use of a word does not immediately exhibit this dichotomy. A word such as "stone" seems to refer to a thing (either as a universal concept, or as the name of a particular) which is ostensibly clearly known by all people using that word in its meaning wherein it may be considered a standard case. But, is that meaning of the word really identifiable with the stone as it 'really' is? According to the PCA its usage contains vital information as to its nature and existence. But the vital information to be discovered in the paradigm case is different from some uses of the word considered by qualified people to represent superior insight into the nature and existence of the stone. Thus, a geologist would be likely to qualify the standard use (hence meaning) of the stone; and a physicist would probably reject it. To a specialist in the study of the genus of facts to which a 'stone' belongs, that stone turns out to be a somewhat, and under some points of view (taken as a molecular or atomic complex, for example) a radically different thing or fact from the standard referent of the word "stone". This, however, is usually considered with approval as a necessary scientific abstraction. But when a philosopher proposes a similar abstraction, rejecting the ordinary meaning-as-use of the stone in the light of the criterion he is using, he is immediately criticized for making pseudo-problems of things which are evident in ordinary reference.[2] The scientist, on the

---

[1] P. Butchvarov, 'Knowledge of Meanings and Knowledge of the World' in *Philosophy*, 1964. 2,

[2] More recently S. Morris Engel defended the philosopher against such criticism in his brilliant study, 'Isomorphism and Linguistic Waste', in *Mind*, 1965.1.

other hand (it is held) is justified, for his use of the word will in some
way qualify every man's knowledge of "stone". If in fact a philosopher
who rejects the common use of stone as its true meaning is so far
removed from the spirit of his place and time that his thought has no
appreciable effect upon the use of that word and hence upon general
thinking concerning the referent of the word, then his language
(whether sceptical or realist) represents a form of intellectual exercise,
which may be most satisfactory in itself, but is generally irrelevant.
Yet, the language of few philosophers whose works have survived the
passage of centuries, or even of decades, could be said to be quite as
irrelevant. Their use of words, even if it was at first a plain 'misuse' of
contemporaneous ordinary language, has had some share in shaping
that language, either directly, or by influencing some thinkers (even in
quite practical fields) who have had a discernible share in making our
life what it is, and thus moulding our needs of communication
according to the things to which we refer in daily existence. In a very
fundamental sense, the common use of words tomorrow is the misuse
of those words today. Language is flexible, and it can be altered
by changing the meaning of words. This means, however, that the
meaning of words is not identified – at least, by that person who
thus alters language – with its (then current) use. Even if for all people
meaning is use, at least for one person meaning must be correspondence
to his insight into the nature of its referent – or else language would
ossify once and for all. The fact that it does not, constitutes evidence
that in some key points meaning is not ordinary, but novel use. And
what key points could be more important to the cause of knowledge,
than the novel insights of science and philosophy?

Contrarily to this assumption, the PCA applied to ordinary language
implies that each word is a label of its standard, every-day referent.
It is further argued that the referent when thus discovered, is true
(or as true as the limitations of human knowledge can permit us to
approach truth). Implicit in the argument is that, in the everyday
traffic with things, we think of things basically correctly and unambiguously. That is, the elements of a thing we encounter in everyday
existence are all of a kind, and add up to the true knowledge of that
thing. The claim is made here that it is not so. Every thing (here 'thing'
is used in the sense of an experienced object) contains elements of two
entirely different meanings, both of which are included in its use;
hence in the word as standard case. Each thing to which we refer in
ordinary language is given – directly or indirectly – to consciousness

and is assumed to exist. Hence, by the thesis of meaning-as-use, the meaning of each word is experiential *and* existential. When we engage in the sceptic's 'language-game', words in ordinary language will be seen to treat of experienced things uncritically, presupposing their existence, while if we would use the realist's language-game, words in ordinary language will seem to refer to restricted phenomena, representative of a shallow and delimited aspect of the realm of existence. When we compare the two viewpoints, we shall come up with the conclusion that ordinary language couples the naïveness of realist with the limitations of sceptical discourse. If this conclusion is correct, taking ordinary language as criterion of knowledge of things is doubly handicapped, first by the uncritical assumption of the existence of the things we talk of as objects, and secondly by the limitation of discourse to things which can be actually or potentially experienced and commonsensically represented. Contrarily to these handicaps, systematic scepticism and realism are privileged. The former considers the problems of existence without undue presuppositions, arguing from consciousness and attempting to derive, with some measure of certainty, the character of the events from their givenness to the cogito, while the latter is freed from the limitations of common sense, and can envisage things and events beyond the ken of ordinary experience. The common sense of ordinary language makes the worst of the two positions: it joins the limitations of scepticism with the uncritical attitude of naïve realism.

What then, is to be done? The task, in the light of the above argument, would be to treat ordinary language as an object-language, and propose two mutually independent syntax-languages for its criticism. The purpose of the syntax-languages would be to jointly explain the meaning of words as referents of a unitary and consistent thing. The meaning of words residing in their use as standard cases does not give us such a unitary and consistent thing but merely a superficially united, though fundamentally split entity, consisting (in some variable proportion) of experiential and existential elements. The syntax-languages would analyze each word for one of the two genera of meanings. Thus, one-syntax language would treat all terms as referents of elements of experience, and the other as referents of objective existents. Terms such as 'is' and 'felt' together with all words explicitly connoting 'consciousness' or 'being' would be removed from the object-language and placed into the syntax-languages: terms entailed by consciousness into one, by being into the other.

Such hypothetical syntax-languages correspond to the language of systematic inquiries which adopt either the *cogito* or objective being as root-axiom. Sceptical epistemology and realist metaphysics in their systematic formulation may be considered syntax-languages treating of ordinary language as object-language. Their failure has been to consider their treatment adequate, when in fact it has been partial. If ordinary language consists of an intermixture of experiential and existential meanings, the explanation of either meaning of the words and their ordering in an internally consistent system treats only one of the meanings (albeit systematically) with which we, as normal human beings, traffic in our daily existence. Insistence on the adequacy, or sole feasibility or justification, of one of these inquiries, as opposed to the other, has made for distortions which consisted largely of the explanation of problems dealt with as primary by one inquiry, within the context of the other. Thus systems of sceptical epistemology assigned independent ontic status to some of their concepts, and ontological concepts were thought to derive from, or be directly demonstrated by the facts of immediate experience. That neither concepts of being reached by inference from the cogito, nor concepts of direct experience derived from ontological notions are entirely satisfactory, lies already with the manner by which these concepts were postulated.

One of the resultants of the dissatisfaction with epistemological and ontological discussion was the drive back to some points of agreement and one such point of agreement appears to be provided by ordinary language: hence the attempt to resolve philosophical problems by means of an appeal to the common sense of ordinary language by Moore, Russell, and Wittgenstein. In a sense, their work and that of their followers' represents the development of a purely logical syntax-language in order to eliminate the philosophical misunderstandings which, whether acknowledged or not, have been largely created by the disjunction of discourse between the world of the sceptic and of the realist. But if the meanings of scepticism and realism are legitimately empirical, and if they are contradictory nevertheless, such procedures are ineffective. Before the single value which empirical premises should have could be determined, the argument of the sceptic as well as that of the realist have to be given full consideration.

As Wittgenstein himself admits, operations do not assert anything; only the proposition which is the result of an operation asserts something, and that assertion is determined by the elementary proposition of fact upon which it is based .But the basic facts are unlikely to be discovered with the existing analytic methods. The formulation of these basic propositions must be turned over to the sceptic and to the realist, for only if their statements are meaningful and non-contradictory can the facts be stated. Linguistic analysis has important applications, but first it must be integrated into an encompassing philosophy of philosophy which takes due account of the possibility that each word, each proposition may have two mutually exclusive meanings, and only the structure of the propositions in common. Thus each word, each proposition must be transvalued from the experience of consciousness to the existence of the objective universe. That linguistic analysis developed the tools for conceiving of propositions as structures, and of words as functions within the structures, makes the verification of the transvaluation possible. But the propositions must be made first on the basis of inquiries which take, respectively, *consciousness* and *being,* as the sole basic fact, and derive all further propositions by means of the most indicated inference from this simple assumption. Provided the meaning of the conclusions does not exceed the legitimate scope of meaning of the root-axiom, neither inquiry will transgress into the field of competence of the other, but will render the propositions derived from the root-axiom as explicit and legitimate as logical reasoning permits. Thus sceptical epistemology will deal with propositions referring to private experience, and objectivist realism with propositions concerning public experience. Both will use a philosophical syntax-language designed to clarify one of the two meanings of every word of which the referent is a *thing,* one of these meanings being the thing *qua* epistemic entity, and the other of the thing *qua* ontic entity.

The method I propose involves the following linguistically relevant postulates: (i) ordinary language is an object-language to be explained by two mutually independent syntax-languages. The syntax-languages are those of the consistent sceptic on the one hand, and of the consistent realist on the other. (ii) Validity of these syntax-languages *qua* distinct and mutually exclusive languages rests on the assumption that terms correspond to epistemic facts in the former, and to physical facts in the latter. Meaning is first assumed to be correspondence within each syntax-language. (iii) The languages of the sceptic and of the realist conserve their validity as total systems of assumptions irrespectively of the meaning-as-correspondence of their terms: the third postulate requires the reinterpretation of each syntax-language as a system of assumptions which is determinant of the meaning of its terms. Hence the language of the sceptic and the language of the realist remain valid, but their terms acquire meaning corresponding to their function within the given system.

The PCA finds its use in this method, but it is not an orthodox use: the determination of just what the 'paradigm' or 'standard' case for a given term is, is not through reference to how that word is used in ordinary language, but by noting how it is used in each of the two syntax-languages. Since the PCA argues for meaning-as-use, and 'use' is the logically consistent function of given terms in arguments *from* 'consciousness' and *from* 'being', meaning within the syntax-languages is disjunctive only if the function of terms is dissimilar. But whether or not the function of terms is truly dissimilar, is a matter for non-linguistic inquiry. Linguistic analysis is to be used only as the tool for determining whether propositions referring to non-linguistic events are true or false. The propositions are not determined by how language is used *qua* language, but by how language is used to define epistemic and physical facts. Hence the PCA is used, but in a forbidden sense: as applied to two philosophical 'language-games', rather than to ordinary language itself.

THE CRITERIA OF PROOF

Knowledge, we have seen, may concern events immediately given to consciousness and it may also concern things which are perhaps never data of immediate experience. Which of these forms of knowledge can be considered capable of proof, then? The question of proof is particularly difficult when we admit the equal validity and exclusive insufficiency of two diametrically opposing premisses which never entail propositions concerning each other. The 'knowledge' of the sceptic in many cases is not even a part of the knowledge of the realist (for if they explain the very same things, they explain them differently) and the 'knowledge' of the realist is exposed to grave doubts from the viewpoint of the sceptic. If order is to be made in this extremely difficult situation, we have to introduce criteria for the definition of proof, which are to determine just what we can hold to be veridical knowledge. These criteria have to be extraneous to the investigations themselves, and be clearly established before investigations are being undertaken. As Ayer resumes his conclusions in this respect, "the necessary and sufficient conditions for knowing that something is the case are first that what one is said to know be true, secondly that one be sure of it, and thirdly that one should have the right to be sure. This right may be earned in various ways; but even if one could give a complete description of them it would be a mistake to try to build it into the definition of knowledge, just as it would be a mistake to try to incorporate our actual standards of goodness into a definition of good." [1] Now it is evident that both the sceptic and the realist know that what they say is the case, and that they may even be sure of it. But it is equally evident that unless we espouse their particular root-axiom, we shall not admit that they have the *right* to be sure. It follows that the adoption of the root-axiom is not determined by the arguments

[1] Ayer, *op. cit.*, 'Philosophy and Knowledge'.

proposed on their basis, but must be decided previously. Hence, we need criteria of proof which will let us decide in which context to opt for 'consciousness' and in which for 'being' as basic premiss. But, since neither 'consciousness' nor 'being' are sufficient in themselves for an impartial investigation of the nature of reality, we require criteria for choosing *both* consciousness and being as root-axiom, and a method for testing the validity of the contradictions that would normally result in arguments from them. In addition we must have a criterion to prevent the accumulation of redundant principles. Some of the criteria must function for choosing the premisses, others for checking the inferences.

I suggest that we need two basic 'premiss-criteria', and two 'theory-criteria'. The premiss criteria are *adequacy* and *experientiality* and the theory-criteria are *consistency* and *economy*. The premiss-criteria are alternately applicable: the more we insist on one, the less we shall be able to make use of the other. *Adequacy* requires the postulation of the realm of objective being with the cosmology that is entailed by the assumption of the existence of the natural universe. *Experientiality* demands that each event of experience be examined as given to consciousness and that no inferences unsupported by conclusive evidence be made.

Consistency defines the principle of non-contradiction with respect to the arguments from consciousness and from being, but is restricted to the inferences. Thus, even if consistency in any given context demands the qualification of either root-axiom, that qualification need not be undertaken, for the root-axioms have their own criteria which do not include consistency. Finally, *economy* is the criterion of inference designed to prevent the accumulation of redundant principles which could lead to an unnecessary multitude of consistent, but yet distinct postulates.

Reviewing these criteria, the first point I wish to emphasize is that the concept of "proof" has to be considerably extended; it must extend beyond the deductive arguments of logic and mathematics.

It is a trivial statement that philosophy does not reduce to logic and mathematics, much less to those of their operations which permit deductive inferences. It is equally trivial to assert that most of logic and some of mathematics is based on axiomatic premisses, while philosophy needs empirical ones. Yet, the correct assessment of these basic distinctions can cause much trouble, which is aggravated by confusion in terminology.

A case in point is Waismann's paper, 'How I See Philosophy' [1] wherein he denies proof for philosophic arguments. "Philosophic arguments (says Waismann) are not deductive; therefore they are not rigorous; and therefore they don't prove anything." While Waismann admits that they may 'yet have force' he denies that the term "proof' may be applied to them. It appears then, that the term, according to this interpretation, should be reserved for arguments derived by the deductive formulas of logic and mathematics. This is a possible definition. But, it is unsatisfactory to the extent that in philosophy we would be compelled to hold arguments forceful and compelling, but not proven. This is no doubt prudent if we would otherwise incline toward dogmatism. But the term "proof" is used in an overnarrow sense in *undogmatic* philosophic discourse. We may well consider a philosophic conclusion 'proven' without affirming that it represents the absolute, final, and necessary conclusion. The question can be reduced to a terminological problem, but it is imbued with wide implications, since philosophy, if it not only does not, but *ipso facto cannot* prove anything, will appear to be a kind of intellectual exercise which can do no more than make someone "see things he has not noticed before: *e.g.* to dispel wrong analogies, to stress similarities with other cases and in this way to bring about something like a shift of perspective . . . . [for] there is no way of proving him wrong or bullying him into mental acceptance of the proposal . ." [2]

There is a wide scale of possibilities between bringing about a shift of perspective by stressing certain aspects of the way we see things and bullying someone into the acceptance of a proposal. In between lies the entire range which Waismann tends to call the 'compelling' or 'forceful' arguments. Restricting the use of 'proof' to deductive reasoning, these arguments merge into relatively indistinct and weak suggestions without clear demarcation, since they lack the certainty of proof. Is it not better, then, to extend the use of proof and attempt to define what arguments may be considered as proven, even if they lack the absolute certainty of deductive reasoning?

The ground for extending the use of proof to non-deductive propositions is the fact that there are no empirical propositions which can be justified by an ultimate set of propositions which are themselves deductive. Every deductive proposition must ultimately lead

<hr>

[1] Fr. Waismann, 'How I see Philosophy' in *Contemporary British Philosophy*, 3rd series, London, 1956.
[2] *Ibid.*

to some statement which is not deductive, and which is the reason or justification of the deductive proposition. This is not necessarily a fatal objection to the validity of the given deductive proposition in *all* fields of inquiry (in formal logic it certainly is not), but in metaphysics – as in epistemology – the objection is entirely fatal, unless non-deductive propositions are admitted as capable of proof. "Metaphysics or pure philosophy is the study of the nature of knowledge, of the nature and inter-relations of the ultimate modes of justification of propositions of all types, and is therefore necessarily not a deductive enquiry" affirmed Bambrough in his paper 'Principia Metaphysica' [1] and to his statement I may add that of Russell, according to which "it appears from our analysis of knowledge that, unless it is much more restricted than we suppose, we shall have to admit principles of non-demonstrative inference which may be difficult to reconcile with pure empiricism".[2] Since in metaphysics every conclusion is ultimately based on the non-deductive assumption of the existence of the world, unless we extend the definition of proof to include non-deductive propositions, metaphysical conclusions become distinguishable from pure conjecture only by reference to vague notions of 'power of conviction'. Recourse to descriptive propositions is of no help here, since the sceptic's argument, if it goes beyond consciousness, leads ultimately to some non-deductive statement as well. The type of inquiry into the nature of things which comes properly under the heading of 'philosophy', is rightly considered necessarily charged with non-deductive propositions, but is unnecessarily denied proof for that reason. For philosophy, unlike formal logic, requires not only valid but also sound premises, and sound premises cannot be ultimately deductive: they must be synthetic, yet necessary. We can say that there have been no propositions known of which this could be asserted, but, without committing the error of dogmatic scepticism, we cannot say that there cannot be any synthetic necessary propositions, for this itself, if so affirmed, is a synthetic and necessary statement. It is evident, however, that basic propositions available to philosophical inquiry are either synthetic and not necessary, or necessary, but analytic. If we admit non-deductive propositions as reasons or justifications of propositions derived from them, these primary propositions must be taken as sound premises, and we need criteria to determine which statements should be so considered. These criteria are what I

---

[1] Renford Bambrough, 'Principia Metaphysica', in *Philosophy*, 1964, 2, p. 101.
[2] Russell, *op. cit.*, Introduction.

term 'premiss-criteria'. They function to define the basic propositions which are themselves non-deductive and synthetic, as being also *necessary*. Propositions could be considered valid if the inference conforms to the 'theory-criteria' and sound as well as valid if they are derived from statements satisfying the premiss-criteria. Propositions which are sound as well as valid are neither false nor inconsistent, and may thus be considered 'proven'. The concept of proof is extended by means of introducing specific criteria, and it is the criteria then which deserve further clarification.

A. PREMISS-CRITERIA

(*i*) *Adequacy* is one of the two premiss-criteria. Specifically, it is the criterion of the generality of the statement to be admitted as premiss. It is counterposed to relatively delimited, more or less *ad hoc* propositions. A statement is held to be true as regards its correspondence to the criterion of adequacy if it permits the inference of conclusions which apply to empirical knowledge in general. Adequate statements are at the base of such metaphysical schemes as that of Whitehead's philosophy of organism, and Whitehead himself gave a competent definition of "adequacy". "The adequacy of the scheme over every item does not mean the adequacy over such items as happen to have been considered. It means that the texture of observed experience, as illustrating the philosophic scheme, is such that all related experience must exhibit the same texture. Thus the philosophic scheme should be 'necessary', in the sense of bearing in itself its own warrant of universality throughout all experience . ." [1] It is evident that Whitehead's 'necessary' scheme can be inferred only from synthetic propositions. By the criterion of adequacy, such propositions can be considered *sound* in the event that they provide the foundation for a 'necessary scheme'.

(*ii*) *Experientiality* is the second premiss criterion, specifically the criterion of the immediacy of the facts with which the statement (proposed as premiss) deals. In the optimum event the statement is purely descriptive of the most immediate data of experience. Optimum experientiality involves the suspension of all preconceived judgments about the nature of the thing or state of affairs of which the statement treats. The method for obtaining experiential statements has been worked out by Husserl, who (to choose one of his definitions, among

[1] *PR*, Part I, Ch. I, Sect. I.

many others) characterized and justified it by saying, "the evidence of world-experience would, at all events, need to be criticised with regard to its validity and range, before it could be used for the purposes of a radical grounding of science, and that therefore we must not take that evidence to be, without question, immediately apodictic. It follows that denying acceptance to all the sciences given us beforehand, treating them as, for us, inadmissible prejudices, is not enough. Their universal basis, the experienced world, must also be deprived of its naïve acceptance. The being of the world, by reason of the evidence of natural experience, must no longer be for us an obvious matter of fact; it too must be for us, henceforth, only an acceptance-phenomenon." [1] The total and fully consistent suspension of philosophic judgments concerning the nature of reality reduces 'the world' to 'consciousness'. Under the criterion of experientiality, we can validate sentences describing the contents of consciousness as *sound* premisses.

B. THEORY-CRITERIA

(*i*) *Consistency* is one of the two criteria applicable to conclusions inferred from established premisses. Consistency applies to inferences made from propositions which are accepted as 'sound' on ground of their adequacy or experientiality. When we abstract from the truth of the premisses and consider only the *validity* of the conclusions, we can best exemplify what I mean by the criterion 'consistency' with the method of the natural sciences. These use protocol sentences for premisses and the conclusions which follow from them are as rigorously consistent as the applicable logical and mathematical formulas permit. A scientific theory is true, if its premisses are true. I am not concerned at the moment to discuss whether the empirical premisses of the natural sciences are true, or need to be re-examined, but I only wish to propose that whatever their status may be, a scientific theory is considered proven (even if not using exclusively deductive means of procedure) if it is inferred from the premisses without involving contradictions. The conclusions are then tested by experiments if feasible, and if they pass all tests, they are consolidated into 'theories' by means of further hypotheses. Since science often uses hypothetico-deductive (and reductive) methods, the conclusions are established hypothetically, and are confirmed by the various tests at the scientist's disposal. Hypotheses can be of two kinds: 'descriptive' (in the terminology of

---

[1] Husserl, *CM*, § 7 (tr. by Cairns).

scientific method) forecasting the external circumstances of the event; or 'explanatory', offering causal grounds for it. The explanatory hypotheses can again be of two kinds: either 'hypotheses of law', determining the manner in which the causes or conditions of the event operate, or 'hypotheses of cause' (also called 'genetic hypotheses') determining the causes or conditions responsible for the event. All hypotheses are based on empirical induction, including observation and analytical classification of the premises constituting the protocol data, and selection of similarities which may be generalized. Once the hypothesis is established, it is tested by experimental verification, deduction and reduction, demonstration and explanation, to result finally in the construction of the relevant theory through the systematic organization of the laws and principles included in the verified hypotheses.

A scientific theory is held 'proven' if it consistently colligates the items of its protocolled data. These items are restricted, however, to certain kinds of events, in a preselected sphere of experience. Natural science neither examines the immediacy of its data critically (with the exception of experimental psychology), nor does it examine all data available to empirical observation. Its hypothetico-deductive, inductive-reductive method is free from contradictions, and excels in consistency. When this method is applied to hypotheses based on statements validated by considered criteria, we can obtain a set of principles which are both *valid* and *sound*.

(*ii*) *Economy* is the criterion of the necessity of the postulates. In its general form, *"entia non sunt multilicanda praeter necessitatem"* ('Occam's Razor') it has been accepted in most systematic inquiries. Since the criterion of economy means that of two or more principles of equal value the one involving the fewest and internally most unified elements is preferable, economy as criterion is relative to the given system. It requires that all redundant propositions, concepts, and principles be eliminated. In view of the criteria 'adequacy', 'experientiality' and 'consistency' *economy* as criterion means arguing to valid and uneliminable principles from premises validated by the above criteria. The two premiss- and two theory-criteria jointly prove given propositions, and proven propositions are, to all intents and purposes, 'true' propositions: they are as true as any empirical proposition satisfying the sceptic as well as the realist can be.

However, if the two premiss-criteria are applicable in inverse ratio, we cannot obtain any proposition which would fully satisfy both of them, although each one may be thus satisfied together with the theory-criteria. We may obtain propositions which are either fully *adequate*, consistent and economical, or sufficiently *experiential*, consistent and economical, but none that are jointly adequate, experiential, consistent and economical. In the first of the two possibilities we are dealing with epistemic facts derived from the root-axiom "consciousness", and in the second we are dealing with physical facts argued from the root-axiom "being". Since consciousness and being are mutually exclusive, no internally consistent proposition can refer to epistemic as well as to physical facts.

To resolve the difficulty, we must revalue the meaning of terms in accordance with their function in the total system of assumption in which they figure. The *correspondence theory of truth* is applicable to either of the two possible propositions, but not to both (for each fact can be in itself, either epistemic, *or* physical); the *coherence theory of truth*, however, is applicable to both *provided* we admit two internally consistent, coherent systems, determining the meaning of all terms advanced in their context. In the event that the total system of assumptions in which a given statement is an element determines the meaning of the statement, and if attempts to fix the meaning of isolated statements is fallacious (as Quine suggests) any two internally consistent coherent systems contain different meanings if their structure is divergent, and identical meanings if their structure is isomorphic. Under this theory of truth, which includes as *first* step the correspondence theory, and as *second* step the coherence theory applied to two distinct systems of assumptions, it should be logically possible to satisfy all four criteria conjointly, since *a priori*, it is not determinable whether or not arguments 'from consciousness' have a different structure than arguments 'from being'.

Hence if we assume the semantic theory of meaning-as-correspondence together with the correspondence theory of truth, the meaning of propositions derived from consciousness and from being will be mutually exclusive. When we re-value meaning-as-correspondence as meaning-as-use, and re-assess the correspondence theory of truth in the light of the coherence theory of truth, we may or may not, obtain propositions having different meanings. Whether or not meanings in arguments advanced on the premiss of consciousness will differ from those advanced on the premiss of being, depends on the structural correspondence of the functions of terms within each system of assumptions. Hence, truth is not relativized. If consciousness is a fact, epistemic facts represent the truth. If being is a fact, physical facts represent the truth. If we can determine epistemic facts with the use of the same functional structure with which we determine physical facts, then epistemic facts *mean* physical facts, and physical facts *mean* epistemic facts, notwithstanding the different root-axioms and the different meanings of all terms in the argument when taken as labels.

Truth can only reside in elements common to the arguments from consciousness and being. If we find these common elements, we can advance 'proven' statements, and thus attain 'truth' as far as truth is attainable in philosophical investigations.

PART II

SCEPTICISM:
THE ARGUMENT FROM CONSCIOUSNESS

"CONSCIOUSNESS"

I

The 'argument from consciousness' is to meet the criteria of *experientiality, consistency* and *economy*. This is the argument which is to exemplify consistently sceptical reasoning and serve as the prototype of scepticism for the purposes of this inquiry. If it is to do so, it must proceed from some apodictic, indubitable facts or events, which are not exposed to doubt, either when they occur, or at any time before or after their occurrence. This is a large order, and requires careful consideration.

I have suggested that the concept 'consciousness' is the root-axiom of the sceptic who sets the criterion of experientiality above all other criteria. I assume that he uses "consciousness" in the sense wherein it means the totality of events experienced by the given subject, rather than only those events which are apperceived through introspection. In this sense "consciousness" has been often divided into *content* and *act*. I shall introduce this division later, but will specify it by the use of two terms, one of which is the name of the content, and the other the name of the act. I wish to keep the term "consciousness" purely for the *content*, and I shall use the term "intentionality" to designate the *act*. Thus by 'intentional consciousness' I shall designate the full scope of consciousness, complete with content and act. The reason why I restrict the reference of the term "consciousness" to the content alone, lies therein, that whatever 'act' is present in consciousness is the act whereby the content is examined, and is by that token not available to introspective definition. Perhaps Hamilton meant intrinsically the act rather than the content of consciousness when he said, "Consciousness cannot be defined: we may be ourselves fully aware what consciousness is, but we cannot without confusion convey to others a definition of what we ourselves clearly apprehend. The reason is plain:

consciousness lies at the root of all knowledge." [1] Aside from the problems of communication and of the existence of other minds, the *content* of consciousness may be affirmed to be conveyable, since it is something which is presented to us, and which we apprehend. The unconveyable factor is the *act*, whereby we apprehend that which is presented, because its communication presupposes an infinite regress: every statement of the act of apprehension of an event presupposes a further statement which conveys the apprehension of the apprehension of the event, and so forth. The way out of the difficulty is to define consciousness as the content, i.e. as the sum of events which I apprehend; and to define the act of apprehension by a heuristic hypothetical concept generalising the act into a principle which applies to my apprehensions whether I am aware of my being aware of them or not.

Let us deal at present purely with the content of consciousness, i.e. with "consciousness". This notion includes merely apprehended events, but not their means of apprehension. But just what *are* the events apprehended? The preliminary answer is that, if they are definable, they must be such that they can be named: definitions must follow from the analysis of how we name events. This requirement eliminates such events as 'mystical experiences' and occasions which defy all description. The events we exclude are those which are not really 'events' at all, but complex psychological states which make us say that they are events, at the same time preventing us from acknowledging that they can be named. Whatever takes place can be named in some way or other; it can be named even if it involves tortuous linguistic usage and statements which everyone else except he who proposes them (if he does so in good faith) would be inclined to doubt.

Hence, analysing the pure contents of consciousness involves the problem of determining the 'primary-language', since naming the things given to consciousness without judgments of our utterances means discourse in a truly *primary*-language. Now, it is usually assumed that the primary-language is an object-language (Russell, for example says "I shall define one such language ... I shall call this sometimes the 'object-language' sometimes the 'primary-language' " [2]). The equation of 'objects' with 'primary-data of consciousness' is implicit in the equation of the primary-language with an object-language. It is clear, on the other hand, that the primary-language can only be an object-

---

[1] Sir William Hamilton, *Lectures on Metaphysics*, I, 191.
[2] Bertrand Russell, *An Inquiry Into Meaning and Truth*, Ch. 4.

language if the perception of objects does not presuppose any *act* of cognitive judgment, for whatever judgment is uttered of the named events belongs to a language of a higher-order. Hence the problem of the pure content of consciousness involves at the same time the re-examination of a seldom questioned linguistic thesis.

Before entering upon the detailed consideration of these problems, we must decide upon some points of basic importance. First, we should define the term by which we shall refer to the class of events to be named. I suggest that the term 'sense-datum' is best suited to this purpose: it is basically neutral, and as a neutral term it is well adapted to denote the events of our consciousness in the primary-language. Second, we should determine the correlation of linguistic utterances and non-linguistic events. I suggest a strict one-one correlation between words and non-linguistic events throughout, so that when a is a word or utterance, and A is a non-linguistic event, a if, and only if, A. Thus there will be a *different* sound or utterance for each different event $(a, b, c, \ldots$ correlated to A, B, C, $\ldots)$ and not similarities in events associated by similarities in sound. Hence a is not the name of the class of events A, on the basis of similarities obtaining between $a_1, a_2, a_3, \ldots$ and $A_1, A_2, A_3, \ldots$ as Russell suggests.[1] It is evident that such a primary-language is neither a practicable actual language, nor the analysis of ordinary language to primary components. It is a purely epistemological language, designed to permit (in theory) the description of the contents of consciousness. Hence I shall assume that in this language (i) no judgments of the perceived events are made; (ii) each different event is denoted by a different linguistic utterance; and (iii) the repeated use of an utterance signifies the recurrence of the corresponding non-linguistic event.

The question is, what type of words will such a description contain? Will they be the names of 'things' or only the names of sense-data? It will contain 'object-words' only if sense-data are presented as sense-objects without presupposing acts of cognitive judgment. Now, the traditional view of perception, and the one which is still influential in theory of knowledge, holds that no matter how closely the facts of experience are analysed, they will yield the familiar furnishings of everyday perceptual experience, such as tables, chairs, houses, and other people. A description of these things would be in a primary-language which is also an object-language. Before such a common-sensical view could be accepted, however, it should be subjected to a

[1] *Ibid.*

critical re-examination. In the following I shall undertake such a critical inquiry from the viewpoint of the sceptic, i.e. using the criterion 'experientiality' and arguing 'from consciousness'.

II

To test the verity of the equation of ordinary sense-perception with the immediate data of experience (and hence of primary-language with object-language), we can profit the from the findings of experimental psychology on perception.[1] In making use of these findings, we shall have to take some methodological precautions. Experimental psychology is concerned to give suitable explanations of the workings of mind in regard to the data with which it deals in its protocol sentences; I, on the other hand, am concerned to investigate whether or not objects are given in direct perception. Hence, in this inquiry terms suggestive of physical realism have to be bracketed or reinterpreted. For example, experimental psychologists tend to refer to the ultimate facts of experience as "objective sensations" resulting from "sense-stimuli". It is in place of these terms, suggestive of the physical environment, that I shall use the neutral term "sense-datum" or simply "sensation". Experimental psychologists, whether belonging to the school of Behaviourism, Gestalt-Psychology, Introspectionism or to any other, tend also to directly cloth the reported findings with the explanatory notions they hold to be most indicated. All these notions have to be entirely excluded from this inquiry. Our purpose must be to determine the facts of perception by pure description, without indulging in any explanation of the description. If and when such explanations are introduced, they must be clearly labelled as such.

One of the better known phenomena in experimental psychology is the curious fact that an object ten yards away, which, according to a simple calculation in geometrical optics should have half the height and one-fourth the width it had when it was five yards away, appears, nevertheless, to keep its size. Though the retinal projection of the visual datum of the object shrinks in exact proportion to the distance of the object to the eye, normal perception preserves the dimension of receding (as well as of approaching) objects. Under laboratory conditions, however, the perception of the object *can* be made to correspond to the sense-data which it should have, on the basis of a calcu-

---

[1] Reference will be made to the work of Ehrenfels, Helmholtz, Koffka, Köhler, Wertheimer and their followers.

lation in geometrical optics. (For example, the subject of the experiment may be asked to look through a hole in a screen which blocks out all but the given object, and in addition he may get merely brief flashes of light during which to compare its size at various distances.) This coincidence of sense-data and ordinary sense-perception does not obtain in daily life, however. Under average conditions, objects keep their size notwithstanding the modification of the visual data reaching the eye. Experimental psychologists term this the *constancy of size*, and give various hypotheses to explain it.

The constancy of size is not the only constancy apprehended without having objective foundation in the form of corresponding sense-data; there is also the *constancy of shape*. A circle looks circular when we look at it from a position in line with its centre, so that all points of the circle are equidistant from the eye. The same circle viewed from any other position (but from the side) should look elliptical. Yet, under ordinary conditions, the circle will be perceived as a circle from almost all viewpoints. It can be apprehended as an ellipse, however, under laboratory conditions. In that case ordinary sense-perception coincides with sense-data. Otherwise this coincidence will hold true only when viewed from a position directly facing its centre, and will be cancelled when the relative position of object and subject changes. The circle keeps its circularity even when presented as an ellipse.

The *constancy of brightness* has been much discussed in psychology since Helmholtz published his *Physiologische Optik*. To mention the most relevant aspects of his findings: it is found that the observer sees brightnesses as more constant than would correspond to the varying intensities of light in retinal projection. When a black surface is highly illuminated and a white surface is given less light, the variations in brightness can balance the reflecting capacities of the surfaces and we can have the black surface reflect as much light as the white surface. Therefore, as far as the brightness reaching the eye is concerned, both surfaces should be perceived as identical shades of grey. Yet, this is not the case. The black surface is normally perceived as black, and the white as white. While under laboratory conditions the perception of brightnesses can be made to correspond to the brightness of the surfaces, such correspondence obtains only under special conditions.

Constancies of localization are equally remarkable. When the subject fixates on a point before him, the distribution of visual data on the periphery of his field of vision is constant if no change has been introduced into the field as a whole. But if he moves his eyes and fixates on another point, the distribution of visual data should change in his entire field of vision, since the retinal projection of all the things he is viewing will be modified. But the 'objects' in his field of vision do not appear to move in such cases: thier spatial position seems to be independent of their retinal position.

Another known divergence between sense-data and ordinary perception obtains when in stroboscopic experiments (such as those of Wertheimer) the successive presentation of two lights at points not too distant from one another results in the perception of movement between the lights ('stroboscopic movement'). Nevertheless, in this event also, laboratory conditions or special training can dispel such perceptions, and not movement, but only a 'grey flash' will be seen.

Then there are phenomena known as the *constancies of speed*. While the same physical movement may be seen from different distances and for each distance there will be a corresponding retinal speed, the variation of the latter does not seem to influence the former: the apprehension of the movement preserves the speed as constant.

Constancies are not the only area of variance between the factually given sense-data and the phenomena of ordinary perception, however. Another area of variance has been discovered by Ehrenfels, and has since been responsible for much interest in problems such as the above. Contrarily to the theory that local stimuli determine the resulting perceptions, Ehrenfels found that not isolated stimuli (i.e. 'sense-data') but *sets* of stimuli determine what we perceive. When soap is dissolved in water, for instance, the appearance of the liquid is unclear, or 'turbid'. But if we isolate a small area of the visual object (by looking through a hole in a screen, for example) we shall find that we see a distinct shade of grey: the 'turbid' quality of the percept will have disappeared. Similarly, in tactile experience roughness is dependent upon the experience of an extended area, for no character of roughness is present in a local tactile datum. Ehrenfels discovered a number of qualities which appear only upon the presentation of extensive sets of data, and gave them the name "Gestaltqualitäten". The school of psychology later known as 'Gestalt Psychology' has originated from this discovery, but has greatly extended its import by evolving its own full-sized theory of mind. This, however, lies outside the scope of the present investigation. But the relevant and factual conclusion of one of its founders, Wolfgang Köhler, is highly illuminating, and, in the cited passage, does not propose explanatory concepts. ". . . many would say that the shape of a pencil or of a circle is projected upon the retina.

Clearly, when spoken without caution, these words contain the experience error. In the mosaic of all retinal stimuli, the particular areas which correspond to the pencil or the circle are not in any way singled out and unified. Consequently, the shapes in question are also not functionally realized. Our thinking may select and combine any retinal spots we wish; in this fashion, all possible shapes, including those of the pencil and of the circle, may imaginatively be imposed upon the retina. But, so far as retinal stimulation is concerned, such procedures are entirely arbitrary. Functionally, the shapes of the pencil and the circle are just as little given in retinal projection as those of angels or sphinxes." [1]

In the sceptic's analysis, Köhler's words mean that sense-data ('stimuli') do not give us the shapes of those familiar objects which we take to be present in our ordinary perception of the world. These shapes are the products of our selective 'thinking', (i.e. of some cognitive act) and are, as far as the factual presence of visual data are concerned, *entirely arbitrary*. With that, we have encountered the limits of an experimental and physiological study of perceptive processes. As Köhler himself concludes, "For some time to come it will be impossible to investigate the dynamics of visual processes in direct physiological observation. At present we can do no more than draw conclusions from a comparison of retinal patterns with visual facts." [2]

Shape, size, brightness, position, speed, and thus the constant spatial and temporal characteristics of 'objects' are not directly perceived, but must be held to be the product of some cognitive or perceptive act. Their objective source need not be doubted, nor need innate ideas be called into play. But, the mere presence of sense-data as given to consciousness is apparently not a sufficient ground to account for our ordinary perception of objects. While schools of psychology contend as to the explanation of our nevertheless reliable knowledge of objective events, they all agree in bringing in hypotheses to explain *that* which is given to us in experience *as* we experience it. The facts of experience need to be supplemented by such systems of explanation as the 'empirical hypothesis', the 'machine theory', the 'Gestalt theory' and behaviourism. These are theories which explain, each in its own way and with satisfactory self-consistency, the facts with which they deal. They deal, however, with a relatively restricted

[1] Wolfgang Köhler, *Gestalt Psychology*, ch. VI.
[2] *Ibid.*

genus of facts. The task of the philosopher should be to analyze and
explore the wider implications of these findings.

The implications I wish to examine at present concern the contents
of consciousness as defined by the character of the language which
describes 'objective sensations'. That language will be a truly primary-
language; but will it be an object-language? When object-language is
defined as consisting of objects-words, and otherwise being the same
as primary-language, it will be an object-language only if the non-
linguistic events which it describes can be designated by object-words
without presupposing acts of cognitive judgments.

Now, the condition for describing any datum of perception as an
'object' is that it should exhibit the characteristics of things which we
can denote with object-words. Which kind of things we can denote
with object-words depends very largely on how we define "object".

Thus we have to ask, just what kind of a thing *is* an object? In the
widest sense, an 'object' is anything towards which consciousness is
directed. In that sense *every* primary-language is an object-language,
and the entire discussion is superfluous. This wide meaning of 'object'
has its drawbacks, however. It does not differentiate between events
which we could denote with object-words, and those which we could
not. Such experiential events as moods, dreams, hallucinations,
attitudes, and the like, must be differentiated in some definite manner
from events such as stones, trees and houses, notwithstanding the fact
that consciousness may be directed toward all of them. Hence I shall
restrict the meaning of 'object' to events in experience which have the
most general character shared by stones, trees and houses. The
definition of this general character is most difficult, however, in that in
most definitions we are compelled to use words charged with presuppositions. If we say, 'an object is a complex of sense-data endowed with
spatial extension and temporal endurance', we presuppose concepts of
space and time; if we say, 'an object is the event which has solidity', we
presume that the tactual datum testifying to resistence to pressure
is the criterion of 'objectness'; while if we assume that object is
whatever recurs in a recognisable form, we do not exclude hallucinations, dreams, and so forth. The most analytic definition of 'object'
would be, 'sense-data of given extension and endurance'. Space and
time are implied, but left unspecified: all that is stated is that the
precondition for denoting any experience with an object-word is that
it should consist of extensional and enduring sensory components.

Now every sense-datum extends in that shadow-realm where sense-data inhere. But do sense-data *endure*? For endurance we must assume that whatever unit of measurement we use, the length of time during which a particular sense-datum is given is measurable and not specious. We can readily affirm that such may be the case with respect to particular sense-data, as well as in regard to particular sensory fields. I may perceive 'redness' constantly for a measurable length of time. I may also have a visual field which is constant, if nothing moves within my sight, and I do not move my head and eyes either. Could I say, then, that the particular constant sense-datum 'red' and the particular constant visual field are 'objects'? I suggest that this would be an extension of the term that would lead to misunderstandings, since nothing which I could thus denote with an object-word would necessarily correspond to 'object' in any meaningful sense. One sense-datum, whether it is in the form of a colour, sound, taste, touch, smell, or whatever, is insufficient ground to call it an 'object'. One entire sensory field, on the other hand, is the class of particular sense-data, since the field as such is constant as long as all particular sense-data are; when any sense-datum has changed, the field as such has changed. Hence on the one hand the plural in the above definition of 'object' as 'sense-data of given endurance and extension' must be made into a categorical imperative of its validity: an object is constituted by the conjoint endurance of a group of extending and enduring sense-data. On the other hand, the range of application of the plural must be restricted: it must refer to some, but not to all contemporaneous sense-data. The proposition is more concisely summed up by defining "object" as 'a group of sense-data enduring relatively longer than other sense-data'. Yet this definition is still not perfect. We could imagine a visual field, for example, wherein two red patches endure longer than a green patch. Would I be justified in calling the two red patches an 'object' in contradistinction to the green patch? Evidently I could do so with any measure of justification at all, only if the two red-patches are contiguous, or are connected by contiguous data. Since contiguous visual sense-data are usually varied, we cannot expect that the same data be given contiguously in any one area, and thus, if enduring relatively to the rest, constitute an object. Such may well be the case (as when an object has no shadings in colour and no discernible contours, and light is distributed evenly over its surface), but it is rather rare. As a rule, contiguous groups of sense-data tend to include diverse type of data. Hence when we include into the definition the notion of contiguity, we need not restrict it to sense-data of one given kind. All data of whatever kind, presented in contiguity, can form the group which, when enduring longer than other contemporaneous data, may be called an 'object'.

Contiguity within one sensory field is immediately definable: we can tell contiguous forms, colours, sounds, textures, smells, tastes, by virtue of their structural and qualitative relations. We cannot tell contiguity between data of different sensory fields, however, except through association, presupposing repeated acquaintance with the given data. But such presuppositions are in the form of cognitive *judgments*, which belong to a language of a higher order, and not to the primary-language. Thus, we must exclude such judgments from present consideration, even if they are in the form of spontaneous inferences from given sounds to corresponding smells, sights, tastes, etc. Ordinary objects are indeed constituted by the contiguity of associated data (as when the touch of something hard in the dark calls forth the image corresponding to solidity, and certain smells give rise in the imagination to the sight and taste of food), but such 'objects' are constructs based on past experiences; for it is evident that not only the experiences we have of things prompt us to think of them as objects, but also our judgments of the experiences we have had of them. Thus, most ordinary objects belong to the category of a language of a higher order. This fact does not exclude, of course, that some objects should also belong to the primary-language. But this remains to be proven.

What then, is the correct definition of 'object' on the basis of immediate experience? It is, I suggest, 'enduring contiguous sense-data belonging to one sensory field'. 'Endurance' is *relative* endurance, in reference to other more short-lived data within the same sensory field. Whenever we have a group of contiguous sense-data within one sensory field enduring longer than some other data of that field, we have an 'object'. This 'object' can be denoted with an object-word in the primary-language. But are there such 'objects' given in immediate perception?

If the above outlined findings of experiments on perception are correct, and if the conclusions I am drawing from them are valid, the various constancies of size, shape, speed, movement, brightness, (etc.) are present in our normal perceptual experience, but *not* in the objective content of our experience. When we would realistically say 'I move' or, 'the object moves', changes are introduced into the content of our experience which we normally interpret as movement and not as a changed pattern of sense-data. Yet what we have is in fact a changed pattern of perceptual experience. That we interpret it as movement may be correct, but it is a judgment belonging not to the description of our experience, but to the explanation of our description. Any 'object' assumed as such by virtue of the interpretation of change as movement is representative of a judgment of the data of experience and not of its description. An object can be denoted by an object-word in the primary-language if, and only if, it is given to us as such in immediate experience. However, in order that it be so given, a group of contiguous sense-data within one field must conjointly endure longer than other patterns of data within that field.

The point is that if no constancies are given in the form of sense-data then no 'objects' are given either, for constancy means precisely the conjoint relative endurance of contiguous data within one sensory field. When we interpret changes in our apprehended data as relative movement between us and the event, or between the events themselves, we endow the data we take for 'the object' with the constancies which make us see it as such, and these constancies are in the from of a *presumed,* but not factual, conjoint endurance of contiguous data in a given (though mostly in the visual) sensory field. That 'the object' is a fact (or may be one) is not contested; I only suggest that the object-character of perceptions represents cognitive judgments and implies an act of consciousness, and that, as a result, object-words should be excluded from the truly primary-language. The experimental evidence furnished by the various schools of modern psychology testifies to this effect, for experimental results show that when we think in terms of an object, and give it a name, we are doing so on the presumption that the object has constant characteristics. But, the immediate and factual experience we have of the object does not permit this inference. Under 'laboratory-conditions' every movement appears to cause modifications of the thing we normally think of as a constant, enduring object. Take a red disk at a given distance, and move it away from the observer. Under 'normal' conditions, he would say that the red disk is receding, and not that it has changed. Under 'laboratory' conditions, however, the assumption under which he would normally identify the disk as one self-identical object is rendered inoperative (by giving brief flashes of light, and abstracting the object from its surroundings) and the observer reports that he sees a smaller disk every time the experimenter has moved it away from him. Hence if the assumption of the identity of the object is cancelled out, the constancy of size disappears. If we now say that the experiment has the effect to neutralize the assumption of the sameness of the red disk in the mind of the observer, we mean that it cancels out the judgment which leads to the interpretation of changing sense-data as a receding object. The experiment has the effect, then, of cancelling out the cognitive act which permits the apprehension of changing data as 'the object'. And, since the cognitive act is a judgment of the content of an experience, and the content of experience is furnished by changing data, 'object' belongs to a language of an order higher than the primary. The reports of the observer under laboratory conditions furnish the primary-language L, and the reports of the observer under normal conditions the object-language L_1. Thus, I expect of the primary-language that it contain a description of the above experiment as 'red circle – smaller red circle – red dot'; and of the object-language that it contain the description 'red disk receding'.

If it is hardly possible to conceive of one self-identical 'object' which constantly changes its size, it is quite impossible to conceive of one that changes its shape, speed, and shade of colour in addition. Yet, the constancy of size is only one of several constancies which the observer attributes to his apprehensions under normal conditions and cannot maintain in the laboratory. Take the red disk now, and turn it slowly on its axis in view of the observer. Under normal conditions (i.e. in the object-language) he would say 'red disk turning'. Under laboratory conditions, however (hence in the primary-language) he could only report 'red circle – red ellipse – red line – red ellipse – red circle'. (The fact that the experimenter's assessment of what 'really' takes place coincides with that of the observer under normal conditions signifies no more than the evident fact that the experimenter himself views the process under normal conditions. It is not a guarantee therefore, that this is what *really* takes place.)

The case is similar with respect to the attribution of other constancies. The red disk, when reflecting more light, should become lighter in colour, and this is what the observer would say in the laboratory and therefore in the primary-language. But under normal conditions he would report that it conserves its shade of colour, with the result that this is what he would say in the object-language. The point need not be further belaboured; my assertion – that by attributing constancies to perceived events we qualify sense-data to sense-objects – does not suggest that such qualification is false, only that it represents a cognitive judgment. It follows that whatever sensory experience can be denoted with an object-word can be analysed to sense-data (the objective content of the experience) and to an act of judgment (the attribution of the object-qualities to the objective content).

The conclusion I derive from the above analysis of the implications of experimental psychology's findings for my problem is that no occurrences qualify for being denoted with object-words without recourse to an act of judgment. Thence I am led to assert that there are no object-words in the primary-language, and that whenever object-words are uttered they are uttered in a language of a higher order. The primary-language consists of words describing sense-data in changing conformations which manifest constancies only of the kind which do not correspond to any meaningful concept of 'object' as an *entity* which *is*, in any rational combination of these two terms. There are constant isolated data, and there are constant sensory fields. There are no constant contiguous sets of data within one sensory field, however. 'Objects' may well exist 'in reality' but that is an inference. As far as the pure contents of consciousness (and hence also the primary-language) are concerned, there are none. Thus, what the primary-language can signify are merely patterns of diverse exteroceptive and proprioceptive sensations. Altogether, this language consists of words standing for the apprehended sensations, and these words do not refer to anything objective and organised. They refer to some relatively constant, some more rapidly changing sensory events which manifest no constancies of contiguous delimited data in one sensory field, and thus do not provide for the identification of any group of events by an object-word. It follows that no identifiable particulars will be described in that language, aside from the particular unities of presented sense-data. If we wish to designate this primary-language by a name, we would be justified in calling it 'sensation-pattern-language'. Object-language relates then to sensation-pattern-language as L_1 to L. Russell's assumed equation of the primary with the object-language is thereby contradicted.

III

The point may appear to be of negligible importance, since, as I define it, the primary-language is by no means a language that could ever be spoken or put into use. As far as logical linguistic analysis is concerned, its value consists in making the claim that there is a language which is presupposed by the object-language, while it does not presuppose any further language.

But there are further implications of such a language, and these concern theory of knowledge.[1] Sensation-pattern-language is of value to the sceptic's inquiry into the nature of reality if we assume that the description of immediate experience is (i) incorrigible, (ii) meaningful. Both these statements have been seriously contested. It has been argued that 'avowals' of immediate experience are expressive rather than indicative and hence not factual and propositional, and it has been argued that such statements, even if they are propositional, are falsifiable. I shall consider these contentions as they relate to the philosophical concerns of the sceptic.

Arguing to the corrigibility of statements describing immediate experiences, Ayer assumes that two lines of approximatively the same length are so drawn that they both come within the field of vision.[2] If I am uncertain as to which is longer, an element of doubt is suggested which permits the inference that I may be possibly wrong when I come to a decision. There are cases, Ayer asserts, when it is more plausible to say that the mistake is factual than that it is verbal, arising from confusion as to the meaning of words. Hence in allowing that the observer is uncertain as to his decision, we have drawn a line between the facts and his assessment, or description, of them.[3]

But who can be a better judge of how things look to him than he who looks? Ayer admits that no direct test is possible. But, although the experience is past and cannot be produced for re-inspection, Ayer finds that there may be indirect evidence which, he believes, could 'carry weight'. Speaking of the above mentioned two lines, Ayer asserts, "I may have indirect, say physiological, evidence that their appearance, that is the appearance that they offer to me, has not changed. Or I may have reasons to believe that in the relevant conditions things look the same to certain other people as they do to me: and then the fact that the report given by these other people disagrees with mine may have some tendency to show that I am making a mistake.[4] Now what Ayer claims is that there may be evidence which could 'carry weight' or 'have the tendency to show' that a mistake was

---

[1] For still further implications of this thesis, cf. my study 'Is the Primary-Language an Object-Language?', in *Foundations of Language*, I. (1965) pp. 157–170.

[2] A. J. Ayer, *The Problem of Knowledge*, 'Are mistakes about one's own immediate experience only verbal?'

[3] *Ibid.*

[4] *Ibid.*

made in my statement. But the question is not so much whether there are weighty reasons for suspecting, but whether there are means of *establishing*, that I am actually making a mistake in my description. The weighty reasons Ayer offers concern evidence that the lines have not changed since I last saw them despite of the fact that now they look different to me than they did then (or rather, despite the fact that now I come to a different decision than previously concerning them). The other such evidence is that they seem to look the same to other people, who disagree with my description.

It is clear that if my description is to be corrigible, it can be corrected only in the light of evidence which can falsify it. Thus we need to establish some rule or criterion for showing that the *verifiens* is more evidential than the *verifiendum*. Hence, the *verifiens* must be something which I either do no doubt, or doubt less than my own description. (I assume for the moment that my description is made in good faith, and that I truly believe things to be as I say they are.) Ayer holds that how the same thing looks to me at some other time, together with information I obtain concerning its unchanged condition, is sufficient to induce me to believe that my previous estimate was wrong. I do not contest that it may be sufficient to cause in most cases, such a change of mind. I do contest, however, that this is logically justified. For what is the nature of the evidence? Every information I receive is in the form of some datum of experience. There are some data I can recall, and some I will presumably forget. I must reckon with the possibility that even the data I shall recall will be incorrectly recalled in some respects. I can either offer a description of what I experience now, or wait and describe my experience later. If I choose to wait, I must consider the possibility of error in my recall. Hence my description of my present experience is more evidential (excluding error to a greater extent) than the description of a past experience. I cannot be sure, therefore, that I have been wrong in my previous assessment on the basis of a subsequent inspection of the things I assessed. But suppose that other experiences have led me to conclude that I am in fact re-inspecting the events now which furnished the content of my previous experience. If I come to a different decision than I did before, would I not be justified in saying that I am right this time, and was wrong before? Ayer would tend to say that I would be justified in this, since the evidence 'carries weight'. But he is identifying thereby the inspection of the presumedly unchanged object of apprehension with the experience one could be said to have of it: he takes the content of the apprehension for the thing apprehended. This assumption cannot be verified however. For you may always say that these lines are the same I saw before, and I may always reply that the experience I have of them now is different from the one I had then. *Then*, it seemed to me that that was the case, *now* it seems to me that this is the case. The information I receive about the identity of the data does not falsify this proposition, for it refers to the things which it is presumed I am experiencing, and not to my experiences. In the strict optic of the sceptic what I describe is not the thing itself, but only my experience of it. And hence it can be neither verified nor falsified either by any subsequent inspection, or by any further information. It is not falsified even by 'convincing' information furnished by 'other people', since the information I obtain through them is also in the form of data of experiences, and as such it is not any more evidential than any other data. I do not see that there could be anything definitive about any datum of experience that would make it more evidential and less open to doubt than any other. On the other hand, each datum tends to lose evidentiality proportionately to the time elapsed between its occurrence and its description. Hence no present experience I may have can correct any of my past experiences, though the present descriptions of my past experiences may be so corrected. All present experiences have equal evidentiality, and their evidentiality is at all times greater than that of any past experience. Since, however, past experiences may have been represented by past descriptions which were contemporaneous with the experiences, these descriptions also described 'present' experiences. Thus it follows that such descriptions are not corrigible by my descriptions of my actual experiences, since they have equal status of evidentiality. All I can correct is my recall of past events. But that is not the same as correcting past experiences, stated in the past. In sum, no description at time t_1 of an experience taking place at t_1 can be falsified by any event or judgment at t_2.

To return to Ayer's example, the incorrigibility proposition I advance would stipulate that if I say at t_1 that of the two lines A and B, A is longer than B, and if I say at t_2 that B is longer than A, both are correct, independently of any other fact relevant to A and B, with respect to the apprehension of A and B at t_1 and at t_2.

This conclusion is valid if I sincerely describe what I experience. There could be situations, however, when I am convinced that A is longer than B, but say the converse. In that event nobody who hears or remembers my statement would know what I really experience. The assumption of bad faith would not invalidate the previous argument, however, for my conclusion is not bound to what I actually say, but to what I know. A false statement is misleading for those who hear it, and possibly even for myself in retrospect. But neither other persons, nor memory can function as verifier for the truth of my present experience, and hence it is immaterial that a false impression is left in the minds of others, and in my own mind later. It is not what I say, but what I *know* of my present experiences now, that is true. But the truth of this knowledge is incorrigible.

This conclusion is built on the premiss that sentences describing immediate experiences represent meaningful statements. If they do, I do not see any categorical reason for admitting their corrigibility, though there may be 'weighty' reasons for doing so. These, however, turn out to be more psychological than logical reasons. But we still have to reckon with the objection against the incorrigibility of 'avowals' of immediate experiences which asserts that such avowals are not truly statements at all, and are therefore neither true, nor false. The major exponents of this line of thought have been Wittgenstein (in *Philosophical Investigations*) and Ryle (in *The Concept of Mind*). Ryle argues to the corrigibility of statements such as 'I feel bored' or 'I feel depressed' and concludes that we should not ask 'Fact or fiction?', 'True or false?', 'Reliable or unreliable', but 'Sincere or shammed?'.[1] Such sentences are neither verifiable nor falsifiable: they do not state or deal with matters of fact. Wittgenstein, though coming to the same conclusion, reaches it by affirming that the description of sensations replaces more primitive and natural forms of self-expression. Although such descriptions have the form of statements, they are in fact forms of behaviour. "Words are connected with the primitive, the natural, expressions of the sensation and used in their place. A child has hurt himself and he cries: and then adults talk to him and teach him exclamations and, later, sentences. They teach the child new pain behaviour. "So you are saying that the word 'pain' really means crying?" – On the contrary: the verbal expression of pain replaces crying and does not describe it."[2] Now my difficulty with the arguments of Wittgenstein and Ryle is that they seem to refer only to one aspect of descriptions of experiences, and that there are others, and it is precisely the others that are important in an empirical inquiry in the

---

[1] Gilbert Ryle, *The Concept of Mind*, IV, 4.
[2] Ludwig Wittgenstein, *Philosophical Investigations*, § 244.

context of scepticism. I agree with Wittgenstein that not all language-games are statement-making ones, and that sentences in the indicative form do not necessarily describe states of affairs and express propositions, and hence that certain descriptions of experiences are in fact forms of behaviour. I grant thereby to Ryle that the correct questioning of such sentences is not whether they are true or false, but whether they are sincere or shammed. I do not grant on the other hand that avowals of sensations are the only aspects and values of sentences describing immediate experience. When a child has hurt himself he might well say that he is in pain in order to achieve the effect a younger child or a dog would achieve by making noises indicative of suffering, and when he does so it is more relevant to ask whether or not he is sincere than whether or not it is true what he is saying, for the sentence 'I am in pain' is a form of behaviour. But when such a sentence is uttered, and regardless of whether or not it has a behavioural function, it has (also) an indicative character. For provided the person saying, 'I am in pain', is sincere, 'I am in pain' states a fact, namely, that whoever utters it experiences sensations which he considers unpleasant, and which he subsumes under the category of sensations which he (if he is well acquainted with the language he is speaking) refers to as 'pain'. If he is sincere, he is stating a fact which he experiences and which, as I have shown, is not corrigible by anyone else, or even by himself subsequently to having undergone it. Inasmuch as he says 'I am in pain' when he sincerely believes that he is, his sentence is propositional, and as a proposition, it is incorrigible. But I cannot be sure that he is sincere, for in order to be sure, I need proof, and there are no ways of checking on anybody's momentary sensations. Hence I can only be sure that *I am* sincere (for this I need no proof other than a clear conscience) and thus it follows that only 'I' can be sure of making true and hence meaningful avowals of sensations. Thus it would seem that the clause of incorrigibility applies to avowals in function of factual descriptions of immediate experience, although it applies only with respect to the person in question. As a result, even if we allow that sentences describing *private* experiences are incorrigible, the significance of the 'sensation-pattern-language' in which the descriptions will be made, still appears to be doubtful. Ayer, for one, holds that such a set of incorrigible utterances would not be worth much, for "In any given case it would operate only for a single person and only for the fleeting moment at which he was having the experience in question. It would not, therefore, be of any help to us in making lasting additions to our stock of knowledge." [1] Hence, concludes Ayer, the sceptic's victory is empty. "He robs us of certainty only by so defining it as to make it certain that it cannot be obtained." [2]

A different assessment of the problem is also possible, however. I still allow for considerable importance to incorrigible statements (and hence to the primary-language) by noting that, (i) it states immediately experienced matters of fact and brings us as close to knowing our immediate contact with empirical reality as we possibly can; (ii) it can be regarded as a set of basic (or 'protocol') sentences, and verifiable-falsifiable hypotheses may be put forward to account for the stated facts consistently and meaningfully, much as it is done in natural science.

These considerations designate the sensation-pattern-language as the unfalsifiable, and hence empirically apodictic premiss for the formulation of hypotheses in a syntax-language. The innovation I believe to have offered hereby affects only two points: first, the primary-language is so construed as to exclude all possible falsification; second, the syntax-language is so construed as to be hypothetical with respect to the primary-language, but verifiable by it. As a result, meaningful discourse in an object-language presupposes for coherency a syntax-language of a higher order justifying the use of object-words. If the object-language is verifiable by the primary-language while presupposing a syntax-language, the syntax-language, when formulated, must be verifiable by the primary-language. Hence in the optimum event we would obtain a hierarchy of three languages: a language L describing sensations without the use of syntax; a language L_1 describing the perception of objects with implicit syntax; and a language L_2 explaining how we perceive objects on the basis of sensations, using explicit syntax.

The significance of this three-language model for epistemology emerges when we equate, "description of sensations" with "contents of consciousness", "description of the perception of objects", with "the experienced world", and "how we perceive objects on the basis of sensations", with "theory of knowledge". The three-language model would then include (i) the primary language describing the contents of consciousness; (ii) the object-language describing our experience of the world; (iii) the syntax-language advancing the epistemological thesis. The distinction between the primary-language and the object-

[1] Ayer, *op. cit.*
[2] *Ibid.*

language is equivalent in the sceptic's theory of knowledge to the separation of the *content* and the *act* of consciousness. The sceptic's syntax-language is valid if it explains our knowledge of the world consistently with the actual sense-data given to consciousness, i.e. if it consistently relates the object-language to the primary-language. Such a model, however, belongs to the realm of pure theory. The primary-language, if incorrigible, is also impracticable; the object-language lacks therefore its operational verifier, and the syntax-language becomes conjectural.

When the criterion of the inquiry is 'experientiality', the sole justified conclusion is that the events stated in the primary-language are factual. No proposition concerning the nature of these facts can be made without involving hypothetical statements. Hence *what* experience is, is a hypothetical inference from the *fact* that experience is taking place. At the ultimate level of certainty, we can say no more than that the events described in the primary-language *are*. This statement implies in turn that the *class* of described events *is*. Now this class is none other than the *content*, rather than any cognitive act or process, of consciousness. The proposition 'consciousness is a fact' follows from the evidence furnished by the description of immediate experience in the primary 'sensation-pattern-language'. If nothing else, even the most consistent of sceptics can at least claim this with a clear conscience.

"INTENTIONALITY"

The analysis of the contents of consciousness to utterances in the primary-language led to the conclusion that consciousness is a fact. This, however, is most trivial since it does not entail any other fact; it does not afford the deduction or induction of any fact of 'the world' from the fact of 'consciousness'. What then, you may ask, is the sense of pursuing scepticism to such lengths? It is evident that *some* propositions concerning the events of experience must be capable of being formulated in addition to the fact that they take place if the sceptic's argument is to have value as an empirical inquiry into the nature of reality. If it can have nothing whatsoever to say of reality, the sceptic's enterprise is foredoomed and becomes an intellectual exercise in contradicting realistic notions on grounds of being speculative. No doubt the role of such a critic is flattering, but if it is purely destructive, it does more harm than good. Scepticism must be able to come up with some coherent propositions concerning reality if it is to be worth the trouble of being taken seriously. However, the ready assertion that "coherent propositions" concern 'the world' and thus affirm realism is too hasty and entirely ungrounded. The sceptic does not require the existence of the external world to advance coherent statements concerning the contents of consciousness: he can restrict his inquiry to the evidence and take the experience of 'reality' for the experience of 'consciousness'. The only thing he cannot do is to formulate a principle explaining the *act* of consciousness as apodictic, fully grounded in and derived from the facts of experience, for as we have seen the act of consciousness is (i) unpostulable without involving an infinite regress, (ii) distinct from the content, hence not discoverable in a consistent analysis of the immediate data of experience.

I have dealt with both these points in the previous chapter and thus my task here is to explore the possibilities of determining an act of consciousness in the form of a *working hypothesis* testable against experiential facts. The determination of such a principle will be in a syntax-language which has the purpose of so relating the object-language to the primary-language that the description of objects should become consistent with the apprehension of (or rather the 'mere presence of') sense-data. If the principle is correctly determined, it will afford the formulation of consistent and economical propositions argued from the root-axiom "consciousness" and will thus represent the the "sound" premises upon which this prototype of sceptical arguments may be constructed. As a result, the function of the principle determining the act of consciousness will be purely heuristic: it is to permit the discovery of those facts about consciousness which let us infer coherent conclusions from the analysis of contents.

Since I shall denote the principle having this heuristic function "intentionality", it will coincide with the designation of the phenomenological principle. Before going any further, it should be pointed out, therefore, that the fundamental difference between my concept of intentionality and that of Husserl, is the fact that I treat 'intentionality' as a heuristically functioning hypothesis, rendered necessary by virtue of its function within the argument, while the phenomenological concept of intentionality is treated as an evidential fact *about* consciousness. Husserl prejects the principle of intentionality to his analysis of consciousness and lays himself open to the objection, advanced among others by Ingarden [1], that on his theory we have to assume the specific nature of consciousness in order to conduct the phenomenological investigations, while it is precisely first through the proper practice of such investigations that the nature of consciousness should be revealed. The expectation that the nature of consciousness permitting the analysis of experiential events to coherent structures and things may be discovered in its analysis is implicit in this critique, but in the light of our view of "consciousness" it is unfounded. Of the then arising alternatives – either assuming the specific nature of consciousness as basic and empirical premiss, or adding it to the stated empirical facts as a heuristic, hypothetical concept – I choose the latter, and thus avoid the fallacy of considering my conclusions sound and derived from a true premiss when in fact they are derived from a true, but trivial premiss in significant combination with a hypothetical principle, and are only rendered sound by pre-established criteria.

The major consequences of attributing "intentionality" as heuristic

---

[1] *cf. CM* (German edition, The Hague, 1963) p. 211. Also see pp. 105-108, below

principle to "consciousness" are first, that experience becomes analysable to coherent things and events; second, that the analysed events imply a purely immanent space-time, where the fixed locus of experience is the measure of the space and time of the experienced events; third, that all propositions refer to particular experienced events, and treat of generalities only as classificatory concepts, introduced in order to render the argument schematic and comprehensible. Consequently, (i) consciousness should be analysable to an act in addition to a content; (ii) the act is to render the content coherent and comprehensible; the content should not imply any reality beyond consciousness; and (iii) the coherency of experience should consist of the coherence of particular events. Since what we may thus define are empirical events, and since they do not imply realities beyond consciousness itself, the defined and coherent empirical events are to represent the 'private' knowledge of experience, deduced from intentional consciousness.

This assessment of the heuristic principle's logical status in the argument from consciousness, and of the character of the conclusions to which we can attain on assuming it, does not mean that we are free to postulate any principle having such function and status we wish. The principle "intentionality" is bound to "consciousness" by the consistency and economy of the resulting conclusions. Our syntax-language can contain only such propositions which consistently and economically explain the facts stated in the primary-language as an object-language. Hence we must scrutinize these facts with a view toward finding the principle which offers the most consistent and economical means of explaining incoherent sense-*data* as coherent sense-*objects*.

I

When we scrutinize thes fact of experience we will come upon an immediately evident differentiation between sense-data. The differences are evident in the description of the sense-data in the manner of *naming* them. There will be some data which can be easily and immediately named whenever they occur, regardless of the conformation in which they occur. Other data, on the other hand, may elicit hesitation and difficulties in finding the proper description. We need not think that the reason for this distinction is purely linguistic. Language would no doubt be capable of providing a name for all sense-data that occur, if they would occur at relatively equal intervals, and would otherwise be equivalent in manner of presentation. The difference in the clarity of the description of some data, contrasted with the vagueness pertinent to the presentation of the other, is extra-linguistic, having to do with the manner of apprehension of the datum itself. Inasmuch as 'apprehended sense-datum' is redundant in the context of "consciousness", the 'clarity' and the 'vagueness' of the description concerns the presentation of the sense-data, i.e. the form and manner *wherein* they are given, *when* they are given (which is equivalent to saying 'the form and manner wherein they are apprehended'). At this stage of the analysis we need not make more of this fact than to propose a rough division of sense-data into two major classes: the 'clear' and the 'vague' classes of data.

Within the class of clear data we may take, for example, one which will be described as "redness". The data "redness" is capable of definition in relation to other data of analogous qualities which may be jointly termed "colour". The described datum may not exist for more than a specious moment in the form and manner in which it is presented, i.e. it may constantly change its intensity, shape, position, etc. Yet even during a specious moment of its existence it may be described as a given shade of "colour" with reasonable accuracy. Into this class of data fall the sense-qualities of colour, form, sound, surface, taste, odour, and their sub-varieties. Each of these data may be described with comparative accuracy in relation to other data of its own kind.

What about data of the 'vague' class, then? Evidently, data of this kind are most difficult to describe, and require more explanatory concepts to clarify. Although vague data can be described by recourse to the concepts of organic functioning (such as specific feelings of relaxation, tension, movement, pain, and the like), the difficulty with this kind of description is that it presupposes the physical existence of our body. Now the body is not necessarily a consistent and economic explanatory concept of these data. Before assuming the body we should attempt first to name the data as they come about. That the names we give them are suggestive of kinesthetic and organic sensations and come generally under the heading of proprioception (as opposed to exteroception for the 'clear' data), need not enter any more into the meaning of the data themselves as the organ of sight enters into the meaning of 'redness'. It is precisely then, when we refrain from assuming the physical existence of our body that the vagueness of this class of data becomes evident.

It may be objected, however, that I introduce the vagueness by re-fraining from assuming the body, and hence the vagueness is artificial and arbitrary. But this objection implies the fallacy of rationalism in an inquiry which should be as empirical as coherent discourse con-cerning the facts of experience permits. Consider that it is evident that the statement "my stomach aches" is clearly understandable in reference to 'my stomach'. But what makes us assume that there *is* a stomach that aches? We have no more ground to assume this than we have to suppose that 'redness' exists, or, that there is something 'red' whenever I perceive the datum I name "red". The distinction (imma-terial in the present context) is due to the fact that ontological realism assumes the existence of 'red' as a universal, while nominalism assumes only that 'red' is an aspect of a particular. Since I can suspend judgment on the existence of 'redness' as on that of 'red thing', I can also put into brackets 'my stomach' and speak simply of a datum described as a stomach pain. What I get then, is a pain which is such as the pain I ordinarily suppose is linked to some malfunctioning of my stomach; it has, in other words, a 'stomach-pain-quality'. This, however, is not the same as saying that it is a stomach pain, for it involves merely a quality which is decribed *as* a stomach pain. Hence we could substitute the sign sp in place of 'stomach-pain' and get a sense-datum which is described by the quality sp. This datum is in no essential way different from that of 'redness'.[1] Redness (abstracted from the diverse data presented in the visual field) is a datum described by the quality 'red' (r) just as the stomach pain is described by the quality sp. The difference does not justify the assumption of the body, but it does justify the classification of the former into the class of *clear*, and the latter into that of *vague* data. A datum having the r quality is accu-rately and unambiguously described every time it occurs. The datum having the sp quality is more ambiguous, in that it is more difficult to identify and locate among the diverse data in the stream of experience. It may be that the sp datum is once described as a 'burning' sensation and at another time as a 'piercing' sensation. Seldom, if ever, can it be exactly and definitely described, being suffused with an instrinsic vagueness. Nevertheless, since a sensation such as a stomach pain can be described, and if a datum such as red may be described, both are data of experience present in consciousness, and there is no immedi-

---

[1] It is interesting to note at this point that D. M. Armstrong argues in twelve out of sixteen chapters of his study *Bodily Sensations* (London, 1962) for accounting for bodily sensations in terms of concepts involved in perception. Armstrong shows that thereby the field of philo-sophical psychology may be significantly simplified.

ately binding reason to assume that they are essentially different from one another. While the former is 'vague' and the assumption of the physical body would serve to clear up its definition, if we succeed in defining data such as sp without physicalist assumptions, the concept of the body will become unnecessary, and, in fact, uneconomical as principle of explanation. Therefore, our first task should be to consider in what respects the datum r is different from the datum sp, when the former is considered a representative member of the class of data realistically described as data of the exteroceptive organs, and the latter as representative of the data of proprioception.

The differences I have noted so far concern the manner in which sense-data are named: data of the class of sp is unclearly definable, while data of the class of r is explicit and well determinable. Since I wish to see whether more sense than this can be made of this situation without adopting the realist's position by assuming the existence of a physical body (which entails the assumption of the existence of the physical world as the relevant environment of the body and thus contradicts the basic assumption of this method of inquiry), I shall explore what further differences are entailed by the non-evaluative naming of sense-data in the primary-language. I expect of these descriptions to furnish the basic signposts which, even if they do not strictly imply, at least orient the postulation of the explanatory notions to be admitted into the syntax-language.

I believe to have found such a signpost in the content of the primary-language in noting that the so-called 'vague' data are contemporaneous with certain indistinct 'feelings' or 'emotions' while the 'clear' data are not. I mean hereby that when I name a datum such as sp I am aware of a 'disturbed' or 'dismayed' frame of mind, while the presence of the datum I describe as r is not necessarily contemporaneous with any such feeling. Since I find that the 'emotive' or 'feeling' quality of vague data is present whenever the corresponding datum is, I can establish a relation of identity between them and assimilate the feeling-quality of vague-data as an intrinsic component of its class. The feeling may be one which I note as 'pleasant' or it may be 'unpleasant'; the point is that vague-data appear to be intrinsically emotive. On the other hand, it seems that no such feeling is intrinsically present when clear data are perceived.

Before I explore the value of this basic observation for the construction of a heuristic principle, the objections which could be advanced against it should be considered. It may be said, namely, that clear-data are also infused with feelings, and that this is evident when we consider the case of a suddenly introduced strong light which is accompanied by a decidedly unpleasant feeling, or else of a soft glow which is accompanied by a most pleasant one. The examples could be multiplied, but these indicate the kind of objections which may be advanced against the above thesis.

Let us consider, therefore, whether or not the 'unpleasant' feeling present at the perception of an intense light is intrinsic to the light as visual datum. While it is evident that when a light of unusual intensity is perceived, a decidedly unpleasant sensation accompanies the perception, this fact does not entail that the 'unpleasant' feeling should be intrinsic to the light. If we consider that not every light is necessarily unpleasant and that some may not only be pleasant (as when a strong light is turned down and a soft glow takes its place) but also be emotively 'neutral' (many lights do not call forth any emotive reaction whatsoever), we shall conclude that it is not the light, but its intensity which incorporates the 'feeling' quality. In other words, not visual data, but some fact *about* visual data are provocative of emotive sensations. If this is true of visual data, it is also true of sounds, tactile data, smells and tastes. The point is that the 'pleasantness' or 'unpleasantness' adhering to a percept is itself indicative of a *vague* datum. An intense light can be analysed to 'light' and to the 'unpleasantness' associated with its intensity. A sharp tactile datum can be analysed to a local tactile sensation and the pain occasioned by sharpness. (And so on, in the case of sounds, smells, and tastes.) The perception of any such datum is not bound to a feeling of any kind; it may also be e-motively neutral. When it *is* associated with an emotive sensation, then the latter is a resultant of some property of the datum which calls forth a 'vague' sensation. Hence we may conclude that 'clear' data are not *necessarily* charged with emotive qualities, and when they appear to be so charged, that quality is indicative of a vague datum, associated with the clear one. This thesis is evident when worded in physiological terms. An intense light does not 'itself' hurt; it 'hurts the eye'. An unpleasant taste derives its unpleasantness by association with the sensations inedible or poorly prepared substances produce in the stomach. (There is, of course, an aesthetic element in holding a sight or a sound 'pleasant' in which event it is indicative of 'beautiful', or 'unpleasant', meaning 'ugly'. But these are judgments concerning things with which we have some acquaintance and do not concern the immediate and non-evaluative presentation of the data.) Physiologically, it is entirely tenable, I believe, to assume that exteroception is initially neutral as regards emotive responses, and becomes so charged only when affecting the functioning of the organism. In that event, however, the feeling-quality is in the form of proprioception, even if it is associated with an exteroceptive datum. When we experience pain in looking into the sun, it is not the bright light that 'hurts', but our eyes. That we say, 'the *light* hurts my eye' is due to the observed contiguity of strong light and pain in the eye. That we may come to speak of an 'unpleasant light' as a consequence, shows merely that such contiguity results in the attribution of the observed feeling-quality of the eye to the light under the (implicit or explicit) assumption that the light 'causes' the pain. Suspending physiological terminology, we can only say that there is an observable temporal nexus between certain kinds of 'clear' and 'vague' data, and that as a result clear data become associated with the feeling-quality of vague-data, and vague-data in turn, become associated with the clear definition of contiguous clear-data. The result of contiguity is the attribution of the pain to the light (as its cause), and the definition of the light in reference to the eye which, as organ of sight, is said to hurt, "when...". Hence we have learned something about our eye – but at the cost of projecting physiological assumptions to our evidence; and we have learned something about the light – at the price of lending the quality of pain to it. It is immaterial in this respect that the vague datum is 'pain', and the clear datum is 'light'. We would obtain the same results when we place any vague datum in repeated contiguity with any clear datum: the feeling-quality of the vague data would become associated with the accurate presentation of the clear data, and the presented aspects of the clear data would be attributed (as cause) to the vague data. In physiological terminology the argument may be summed up by asserting that proprioceptive sensations represent a degree and form of organic well- and mal-fuctioning, and consequently vary between pleasure and pain, while exteroceptive sensations register colours, shapes, sounds, odours, textures, tastes, and become pleasurable or painful only when affecting an organ which thus registers them in the form of a pain-pleasure species of proprioception. Since certain exteroceptions produce physiological sensations, such data can become associated with the latter to the point that pain-pleasure qualities are attributed to them whenever they occur.

The conclusion entailed by these considerations is that there is no ground to assume that clear data are charged with a feeling quality on the ground of the objection based on 'unpleasant' perceptions; nor is there a reason given so far to assume that there would be any vague-datum which at any or at all times would be exempt from such a charge. This is the hypothesis; we must now explore its implications.

The first problem to examine is in what these feelings consist. I have said that they can be subsumed under the category which is best described as a species of feeling ranging between pleasure and pain. Such feelings can be defined in many terms, but most of them will conserve some reference to organic functioning. If we are to define these feelings with some term referring to, and hence implying, only psychological functions, we must dispense with the pain-pleasure designation. Such a purely psychologically implicative term, I believe, is "preferentiality".

By 'preferentiality' I mean a quality of a sense-datum which involves something intrinsic in the presentation of the datum making it more desirable than some others. Whenever such a datum is presented, the equivalent of 'pleasure' is registered, but without implying that the datum itself is the cause of some pleasure felt in the organism. The term "preferentiality" implies merely a restricted type of pleasure (or "pleasantness") involving a purely psychological event. Preferentiality means that of two or more data otherwise equal as regards feeling, the one charged with the 'quality of preferentiality' would be obtained *if* there were a choice. ("Pleasure" and "pleasantness" have equivalent functions in this respect.) Provided that 'preferentiality' is a correct term for describing some data, it will apply to vague-data exclusively, for it will apply to data which are charged with the quality of feeling, and we have said that all vague data are so charged and no clear datum is. In pursuing this train of thought we shall come to the conclusion that in the interaction of the two classes of data preferentiality is spreading by associations of contiguity to clear data, and clarity of definition is thus infusing preferential vague data. The final result of the interaction (based on contiguity and resultant associations) is that clear data become infused with preferential qualities and vague data become definable with greater clarity.

Let us press on now with the inquiry into the quality of preferentiality. This is a quality which implies that *if there were a choice* between various data, the one endowed with this quality would obtain. But is there not a choice? Are there no situations in which consciousness can determine in some way which one out of a given and limited number of data is actually presented to it? We could assume that there is no such case without contradicting anything previously affirmed of consciousness. After all, the given quality of a datum emerging in its description in the primary-language does not imply that that datum could conceivably be made either to disappear, or to appear more or less frequently than it actually does. But we are looking for a heuristic principle in the syntax-language for the explanation of the facts stated in the primary language. Since no such principle is strictly implied by the contents of consciousness as stated in the primary-language, we must choose the most suitable one and posit it in the syntax-language for the stated heuristic purpose. The principle will be hypothetical – but then I make no claim to the opposite. The *act* of consciousness is posited as a heuristically functioning principle, chosen on the basis of empirical evidence, without being fully demanded by the character of that evidence. I believe that the principle which can determine the act of consciousness in the light of the above considerations is expressed by the concept of *intentionality*, being, in this definition, the striving of consciousness toward those data which are describable as preferential, and away from those which are (relatively) unpreferred. I shall consider intentionality to be truly an *act* of consciousness, by assuming that if there is a situation in which two or more data may be obtained and at least one of them is 'preferential', intentionality determines that the preferential datum obtains.

The difficulty remains that there may be more than one datum of perhaps equal preferentiality presented to consciousness simultaneously. Which datum will then be intended? Or, will all data be intended contemporaneously? In the former event we must show by what criterion we claim that intentionality is directed toward one datum rather than to another of equal preferentiality, and in the latter we must introduce some rule for limiting the multiplication of contemporaneous, yet diversified intentionalities.

The logical solution is to consider the quality of preferentiality a relational, as well as a particular quality. By this I mean that preferentiality is at all times both a quality of given data, and a dominant quality arising from the interaction of all contemporaneous data. Intentionality is directed to particular data in function of preferentiality as a relational *product*. Thus when several data together determine the emergence of this quality, even if no single datum in the group manifests it, intentionality is directed to the syndrome of qualities emerging in the group. Also, when the relational product of a group is not preferential, although some members thereof are imbued with this quality, intentionality is directed to the group in function of the modification of the non-preferential quality of the group as a whole, even if thereby the preferential qualities of particular members are sacrificed. The intended preferential quality is not, strictly speaking, the quality of any sense-datum, but the quality of all sense-data at any given instance of experience. Since all sense-data together signify the *'state' of consciousness* of the moment, the quality of preferentiality must be attributed, as intendable factor, to that 'state of consciousness' wherein preferential qualities emerge with the greatest force and clarity. The intentionality directed toward this syndrome is the referent of all intentional processes; these are undertaken in function of obtaining what I shall henceforth call the *'intended* state of consciousness'.[1]

II

In defining what I mean by "intentionality" I have refrained from assuming the body. The reason for this lies in the fact that once the body is assumed, the physical world, which is the relevant environment of the body, must be equally assumed. Hence we would arrive at physical realism starting from the premiss "consciousness". This, however, means epistemic reductionism, the fallacy of which I have tried to show. To avoid this fallacy, the argument from consciousness should be restricted (if possible) to the universe of meaning which follows from the root-axiom. Such notions as 'body' and 'external world' should be excluded from the discourse. But this exclusion, though consistent, has most unpleasant implications. It implies solipsism, not, of course, as a categorical denial of the external world but as the proposition that nothing external can be indubitably inferred from the experience we have. Such a position has tempted thinkers, other than the relatively few consistent sceptics, to find evidence in the facts of consciousness for the existence of the external world. I would like here to briefly examine some of the more relevant and influential arguments which are based on the concept of consciousness as basic premiss, but arrive at the external world by some inference from epistemic to physical facts.

The argument for the external world finds a natural support in the differences existing between data of experience. I have been led to

---

[1] This argument will be worked out in 'Deductions', below.

postulate two classes of sense-data to account for differences of this kind, but many thinkers would find that such a division is not radical enough. They demand that the external world be posited as a logical inference from the differences obtaining in the presentation of the various data of experience. I have termed one class of data the 'clear sense-data' and the other the 'vague sense-data'. The physiologist would term them the 'exteroceptive' and the 'proprioceptive' sensations. I maintain, however, that while it is evident that differences are intrinsic between data of these kinds, one can deny that these differences provide a sufficient reason for the postulation of the external world.

The proposition is made here that the two classes of sense-data can be ascribed either to the realm of consciousness (the pure *cogito*) or to the natural world, but that the difference between kinds of data is not a sufficient ground to postulate a natural world *in addition* to consciousness. Thus the possibilities, according to this contention, are: exteroceptive sensations as 'clear' data, proprioceptive sensations as 'vague' data (sceptical interpretation); *or*, exteroceptive sensations as the experience of a self-including-world, and proprioceptive sensations as the sensations of being a self-in-the-world (realist interpretation).

Contrary to this thesis is not only reductionism, but also dualism. But it may be held that dualism is tenable or even indicated in the light of scepticism. To consider this possibility, let us take the argument of Descartes, the most influential epistemologist, and certainly the greatest dualist of modern times. As a methodical sceptic, Descartes formulates his famous 'demon-argument' in supposing that there is "I know not what being, who is possessed at once of the highest power and the deepest cunning, who is constantly employing all his ingenuity in deceiving me. Doubtless, then, I exist, since I am deceived; and let him deceive me as he may, he can never bring it about that I am nothing, so long as I shall be conscious that I am something." [1]

Notwithstanding his methodical scepticism, Descartes also argues to the existence of the external world ('material things'). To this effect, he presents an ontological, a rational-idealistic, and a more relevant *empirical* argument. The last named will concern us here. His empirical argument for the existence of material things (hence for dualism) is stated, among others, in the following passage, "... when I consider the mind, that is, when I consider myself in so far only as I am a thinking

---

[1] Descartes, *Second Meditation* (tr. by G. Veitch).

thing, I can distinguish in myself no parts, but I very clearly discern that I am somewhat absolutely one and entire; and although the whole mind seems to be united to the whole body, yet, when a foot, an arm, or any other part is cut off, I am conscious that nothing has been taken from my mind; nor can the faculties of willing, perceiving, conceiving, etc., properly be called its parts, for it is the same mind that is exercised [all entire] in willing, in perceiving, and in conceiving, etc. But quite the opposite holds in corporeal or extended things; for I cannot imagine any one of them [how small soever it may be], which I cannot easily sunder in thought, and which, therefore, I do not know to be divisible. This would be sufficient to teach me that the mind or soul of man is entirely different from the body, if I had not already been apprised of it on other grounds." [1]

Now the 'other grounds' Descartes speaks of consist of a rational-idealist, an ontological, and, more importantly of a previously formulated empirical argument. The latter concerns his division of sensory data into *world* and *cogito*. It is evident that this division is presupposed in the above passage, since Descartes would not be entitled to speak of the body and its parts if it had not been. Thus the division is prior to divisibility in systematic value, as it is prior in presentation in the *Meditations*. To my mind, the decisive empirical argument brought forth by Descartes in the *Meditations* for the existence of material things is contained in the following passage. "Nature likewise teaches me by these sensations of pain, hunger, thirst, etc., that I am not only lodged in my body as a pilot in a vessel, but that I am besides so intimately conjoined, and as it were intermixed with it, that my mind and body compose a certain unity. For if this were not the case, I should not feel pain when my body is hurt, seeing that I am merely a thinking thing, but should perceive the wound by understanding alone, just as a pilot perceives by sight when any part of his vessel is damaged; and when my body has need of food or drink, I should have a clear knowledge of this, and not be made aware of it by the confused sensations of hunger and thirst; for, in truth, all these sensations of hunger, thirst, pain, etc., are nothing more than certain confused modes of thinking, arising from the apparent fusion of mind and body." [2]

Now when we reject Cartesian rationalist idealism, culminating in the statement that, "all that is true is something, [truth being identical with experience]" [3] on account of being empirically irrelevant, we also

[1] *Idem, Sixth Meditation.*
[2] *Ibid.*
[3] *Idem, Fifth Meditation.*

reject the necessary existence of geometrical forms and of God, and are left with the above passage as the primary substantiation of the existence of the body. Upon closer inspection it becomes evident that this argument is based on the judgment that "hunger, thirst, pain, etc. are nothing more than certain confused modes of thinking arising from the apparent fusion of mind and body". But on what does this assumption rest? Obviously, on the identification of these 'confused modes of thinking' with proprioceptive sensations ('vague' data). For it is on this basis that Descartes differentiates himself from the pilot. If he were a 'thinking thing' and pain, hunger, etc. were not ascribed to him, he would perceive pain when his 'body' is hurt as the pilot perceives damage done to his vessel: by understanding alone. However, the above sensations are 'confused modes of thinking' and as such radically distinguished from, and even counterposed to, modes of understanding. The only analytic ground for this claim is the qualitative difference between hunger, thirst, pain, etc., and the intellectual understanding of the other data of experience. In the final analysis the 'vagueness' of one class of data serves as the empirical-analytic ground for the identification of certain sensations with the body, and the relative clarity of other data provide the ground for the assumption of the realm of material things. Now, if so analyzed, neither the body nor the material things have sufficient reasons for existing; no more than the qualitative differences in sensory evidence can be noted, and sub-classes of the category of 'sense-data' (which is a post-Cartesian term) postulated. For Descartes starts from the assumption of the cogito and the position of universal doubt: from that standpoint all evidence of existence other than that of the cogito is, and remains, subject to doubt. (To doubt the cogito is to doubt the act of doubting – a paradox, since it demands the doubting of doubting, and therefore of the cogito as agent of doubt.) It would be different altogether, had Descartes taken for his root-axiom 'being', rather than 'cogito'. He would then have reason (though axiomatic with respect to the argument) to affirm generalized substances such as his *res cogitans* and *res extensa*. But for the consistent sceptic, arguing from the cogito, no generalization, and no transcendence of private experience, is possible except through conjectural and ampliative inferences.

Concern with the nature of experiential evidence leads to the denial of the apodiciticity of *two* worlds, one subjective and private, the other objective and public. Ferrier, for example, maintained that "sensation in man is found to be, first of all, a unity, and at this time there is no *ego* or *non-ego* at all in the case; but afterwards it becomes a duality, and then there is an *ego* and a *non-ego*."[1] This point (also made by Schiller in a perceptive passage in *Briefe über die Aesthetische Erzeihung*[2]) is of paramount importance for this inquiry. If we take as root-axiom consciousness (as the pure cogito) we can attribute all data of experience to it alone. Thus, we shall not be faced with the impossible task of finding convincing grounds within the inner world of private experience for the postulation of a public external world. We can refer intentionality to a purely immanent matrix, as the act of consciousness affecting its contents. Thus for this sceptical inquiry the notion of intentionality (which we find already in Descartes: "nature . . . teaches me to shun what causes in me the sensation of pain, and to pursue what affords me the sensation of pleasure"[3]) is not an intention directed toward 'the world', but toward the matrix of conscious experience itself.

An important objection against this sceptical position has been brought (among others) by Hartmann,[4] however. He calls this position 'empirical idealism', and shows that in its final conclusion the world is denied, reality does not exist: we know only our own representations (*Vorstellungen*). (Hartmann also calls this the "psychological viewpoint".) The classical sceptics have prepared the ground for it (says Hartmann) without drawing the idealists' conclusions. Classical scepticism begins with the subjectivity of perception, and finds no ground to assert that they grasp an object outside of our representations or states whereby they are known to us. Every evidence to the contrary is exposed to the same objection of being given as representation or as subjective state, with the result that we cannot know whether there are real objects or not. Consciousness is enclosed in itself.

According to Hartmann, modern sensualism develops this line of thought. It inquires into the qualities or things that are 'left over' when the sensory qualities of the perceived things are removed and finds that regardless of whether the 'left-over' is thought to be a set of 'primary qualities', 'extension', or an unknowable substance without spatiality, it is unacceptable, for we cannot know it. Besides, according to modern nominalism the universal is not real, while such a basic

---

[1] J. F. Ferrier, *Lectures on Greek Philosophy and Other Philosophical Remains*, II, 144 (quoted by A. Thomson, *Philosophy*, 1964, I, p. 47).
[2] Letter 25, in *Works*, ed. Goedecke.
[3] Descartes, *op. cit.*, Sixth Meditation.
[4] Nicolai Hartmann, *Grundzüge einer Metaphysik der Erkenntnis*, Berlin, 1949, pp. 144–149.

quality left over after subtracting sensory qualities from the objects of perceptions is a general entity, i.e. a kind of universal. Thus for sensualism also, nothing other than representations and their connections exist: the object of perception is replaced by the product of representation, and the final conclusion is always *esse est percipi*.

The consequences of these considerations are weighty, for they deny the knowability – and in the extreme forms of idealism also the existence – of other minds as well as of other objects. Hence man is left by himself in the world, for this world is nothing but his consciousness. Such a position has never been seriously considered, says Hartmann, but it is nonetheless evident that subjective idealism cannot avoid it as its final conclusion.

Hartmann poses two difficulties to accepting the solipsist conclusion. One is the givenness of objects (and here also other minds are to be understood) as something distinct from the self; and the other is the uncontrollability of the experienced series of events. As regards the first difficulty, Hartmann considers that in the light of solipsism it leads to the conclusion that the production of the object is not known, while the product is. The production of the object is below, or behind consciousness, for objects are arbitrarily given. The subject therefore holds for its own only that of which he can follow the production. He must take the things which reach his consciousness as 'ready products' for something externally given, even if in reality it is his own. This applies also to dreams, hallucination, etc. The other difficulty encountered by Hartmann in the solipsist position is the arbitrary sequence of the processes presented to consciousness. If nothing outside the subject exists, these arbitrary events represent a self-affection of the subject. This, holds Hartmann, contradicts perception, which differs from free fantasy precisely in that it is obviously bound to something which it does not master.

Hence, Hartmann's argument states two points: objects are given as 'outside'; and the sequence of perceptual events is uncontrolled by the subject. His conclusion is that subjective idealism hereby contradicts itself and leads to its own negation. For consciousness must henceforth be seen as split into consciousness and unconsciousness, and the latter is independent and autonomous in regard to the former. Thus the independent and autonomous fraction of consciousness is no longer part of consciousness, but is behind it, with the result that it may be considered real, and if it *is* real, subjective idealism changes into metaphysical realism.

I, in turn, find difficulty in accepting such conclusions from the stated premisses. One conclusion is that objects are given as being outside consciousness; the other is that the things which are given as external objects are presented in a series of patterns which are not under the wilful control of the subject. Hence we have ostensibly external objects in an uncontrolled sequence given to consciousness. Regarding the first objection, Hartmann's thinking is still dominated by a view of perception which has been common until recent experimental evidence upset it, namely, that objects are presented to the percipient *qua* objects. Taking this position, Hartmann seeks to account for the 'production' of the objects, and is forced to the conclusion that it does not take place in consciousness and, if we insist on identifying the world of objects with consciousness, we shall have to create a separate sphere of consciousness for this purpose. However, experimental tests show that the very consciousness which objectivistically 'belongs' clearly to the subject, is responsible for the act whereby constancies qualify fluid sensory patterns into 'objects'. The objective content of perception is not in the form of shaped, discernible objects, but in that of a series of patterns of transient 'sense-data'. The commonsensical proposition, that we evidently perceive objects and not merely their sensory counterparts, is tenable only by the introduction of some heuristic principle accounting for the act whereby 'objects' are constituted from events given to consciousness. That objects are presented as external does not entail the conclusion that the locus of their presentation requires a separate sphere of consciousness: the very act of perception is already responsible for the apprehension of objects. We can thus maintain without contradiction that even though objects appear to be given as external, they are the products of the percipient consciousness. Instead of the separate sphere of consciousness posited by Hartmann as alternative, we can have recourse to the principle of an *act* of perception which – whether it is one or the other of the hypotheses advocated by psychologists and phenomenologists – is a basic property of consciousness itself. Instead of a realm beyond or behind objects, we have an act belonging to consciousness itself. The difference is vital, for the distinct realm implies metaphysical realism (of the kind usually connoted by the term 'objective idealism'), while the act of perception has no implications beyond the nature of consciousness itself.

We are left thus, with an uncontrolled sequence of patterned events ('sense-data') rather than with objects directly. But this sequence is as uncontrolled as the objects have been in Hartmann's argument, and the substitution of sense-data in the place of ready-made objects does not help this position in the least. But let us take an objective look at this proposition. We claim to have a series of sense-data in various temporal and relational (implying spatial) conformations. Does this fact imply the existence of the world? In a sense it certainly implies *something* other than consciousness as a wilful master of its own experiences. We can advance one of two propositions: either that the uncontrolled series of perceptual events implies the existence of the world as well as of consciousness, or that it implies the existence of consciousness alone. The proposition that it implies both the world and consciousness can be maintained if consciousness is conceived as fully under wilful control, in which case the events which it does not master imply something external to it – hence 'the world'. 'Master' and 'control' must be used then in the sense of wilfully directing the course of events, so that this concept of consciousness is equal to the will, given free rein. The precondition of assuming *both* consciousness and the world, is the equation of consciousness with the domain of intentional volition. Few if any contemporary students of mind, be they ever so objectivistic, would agree to this suggestion. Consciousness (when used in the integral sense as the totality of perceptive, cognitive and apperceptive processes, rather than only as the latter) contains several layers besides the fully apperceived and wilfully controlled one. Positing layers or aspects of consciousness other than self-awareness under wilful control, does not suggest doubt as to the structural identity of the diverse layers. Certainly, it does not imply that the regions beyond the will be treated as an *external* domain. Hence, merely on the strength of the arbitrariness and autonomy of the series of perceptions, the existence of an independent world cannot be logically inferred. It is a most ampliative inference to propose independent objects and events on the basis of uncontrolled sequences of sense-data. It is more economical, and more consistent with sceptical inquiry to assimilate sense-data, even in an uncontrolled sequence, to consciousness conceived as an entity which is not under full volitional control and manifests events which it cannot master at will. In other words, an uncontrolled stream of experience implies the fact of an uncontrolled stream of experience, and from thence we can only conclude with optimal economy and consistency that consciousness is afflicted with a stream of experience which it does not wilfully control. That the given stream of experience implies independently existent objects is still subject to doubt: we may say that events, even if they are not such as we want them to be, are still only our own representations. Lack of control means limitation of the affective faculty of purposive consciousness as regards its own experience. In the terminology proposed above it means that "intentionality" is delimited in relation to "consciousness". Nevertheless, the principle "intentional consciousness" is capable of accounting for the stream of experience as the matrix of intentional acts which it intends to draw ever closer into the sphere of volitional control. Intentionality accounts for the constitution of objects and coherent events, and affects the stream of experience as the act of consciousness affects its content. The content need not be regarded as fully independent and seen therefore to imply 'the world'. The processes of perception, cognition and apperception (or 'reflection') may be shown to have entirely immanent connotations.

In pursuing this sceptical train of thought, I see no compelling reason to assume that our knowledge of 'objective' things implies the existence of these things outside consciousness. Thus, I find that also the Husserlian noetic-noematic division of consciousness (unless it is interpreted as a mere distinction between content and act) can be rejected on the ground that the transcendence of consciousness is a contradiction in terms when consciousness is taken as a purely immanent realm inclusive of the world. Now Husserl evolved a type of systematic doubt introduced into the scene of modern philosophy by Descartes. But Descartes did not propose something entirely new, he evolved rather a philosophic attitude which had previously manifested itself in the form of traditional scepticism, sophism and agnosticism and has usually led to the idealist standpoint in epistemology. In developing and systematizing the propositions entailed by this attitude, Descartes made man into a dual entity, a psycho-physical being, and the world into a realm composed of two distinct elements. Either one of these elements could subsequently be championed as exemplifying the true approach to problems of philosophy. But the affirmation of one led to the necessary neglect of the other. Husserl chose the Cartesian root-axiom "cogito" for starting point, and at the same time for basis of his critique of Descartes. He reproaches Descartes with instroducing the "fateful change whereby the ego becomes a *substantia cogitans*, a separate human *"mens sive animus"* and the point of departure for ontological inferences – in short for the change by virtue of which Descartes became the father of "transcendental realism . . . an absurd position".[1] Husserl himself searches in the contents of

_____
[1] Husserl, *CM*, § 10.

consciousness for the solution to the problem. He attempts to find the experiential evidence which is apodictic and first in itself. Such evidence represents absolute indubitability in a definite sense. Evidence, says Husserl, is the grasping of something 'that is', in the mode "it itself", with full certainty that excludes every doubt.[1] But ordinary evidences may subsequently become doubtful, they can perhaps be proven to have been products of fancy, illusions, or merely mistaken apprehensions. This possibility of being doubtful (continues Husserl) can always be recognized in advance by critical reflection despite experiential evidence when we consider the *kind* of evidence that supports our assumptions. An 'apodictic' evidence is not merely a certainty of a specific state of affairs being in such and such a way, but it is more: it is, says Husserl, the absolute inconceivability of its non-being, excluding every possible doubt as "objectless", empty. Thus, an apodictic evidence is not a mere perception, but a grasping of some state of things which, already in advance, is necessarily true and given. This apodicticity cannot be maintained with respect to the ordinary perceptions of the world. Although the world stands continuously before us as existent without question, evidence of the world lacks the superiority of being the absolutely primary evidence, notwithstanding its priority to the "other" evidences of life and to all evidences of the objective sciences. Not only can particular experienced things become subsequently doubtful in the light of (or even disproven by) further evidences, but even an entire unitary interconnection of many things and events can prove to be illusory. To ascertain the absolutely primary and apodictic kinds of evidences, the phenomenological bracketing is to be undertaken. This *epoché* is held by Husserl to be the radical and universal method by which I may apprehend myself purely as Ego, with my conscious life, in and by which the entire Objective world exists as this world is for me: ". . . anything belonging to the world, any spatio-temporal being, exists for me – that is to say, is accepted by me – in that I experience it, perceive it, remember it, think of it somehow, judge about it, value it, desire it, or the like." [2] Now Descartes indicated a similar position by his concept of *cogito*. Husserl accepted this concept as a pure transcendental one, without assuming the dualist position. "The world is for me absolutely nothing else but the world existing for and accepted by me in such a conscious *cogito*. It gets its whole sense, universal and specific, and its acceptance

---

[1] Husserl, *CM*, § 10.
[2] *Idem*, § 8.

as existing, exclusively from such *cogitationes.*" [1] These considerations lead Husserl to posit, "the being of the pure ego and his *cogitationes,* as a being that is prior in itself, is antecedent to the natural being of the world – the world of which I always speak, the one of which I *can* speak. Natural being is a realm whose existential status (*Seinsgeltung*) is *secondary;* it continually presupposes the realm of *transcendental being*".[2]

Thus Husserl, in the typical attitude of the epistemic reductionist, assumes that the world as it is experienced is secondary to the pure transcendence of the ego and that the ego is antecedent to the natural world. Since he affirms at the same time that the non-apodicticity of the evidence of the world need not be taken to indicate a full proof that, in spite of its continual experiencedness the non-being of the world is conceivable, a counterposition of transcendental ego – natural world obtains, wherein the former is primary, and the latter secondary.

Husserl arrives at the position of reductionism by wishing to apply consistently his method of systematic doubt, and yet not to doubt absolutely the existence of the world. The difficulty with his position is that it can bring in the world only at the cost of inconsistencies and implicit circularity. I have argued that fully consistent scepticism cannot bring in the world at all, and thus does not lead to 'epistemic reductionism'. Husserlian phenomenology is a good case in point, and Ingarden's critique of Husserl's mature work, the *Cartesian Meditations*, is a good example of the criticism which may be advanced against epistemic reductionism. (It should be noted that Ingarden himself would not wish to attack the phenomenological method, but his criticism of the 'transcendental reduction' exemplifies – whether he would wish it or not – a valid argument against Husserl's brand of epistemic reductionism.) I shall refer, therefore, to Ingarden's remarks concerning the *Cartesian Meditations*, and substantiate my claim by means of a purely immanent critique.[3]

The difficulty of Ingarden relevant to my point is the division of constituted objectivity (*konstituierte Gegenständlichkeit*) and pure constituting ego (*reine Subjektivität*) – meaning, in ordinary terminology, the distinction between the experience of 'the world' and of 'consciousness'. Of the various criticisms advanced by Ingarden, explicit reference will be made here to two arguments. One concerns

---

[1] *Ibid.*
[2] *Ibid.*
[3] Page references are to the German edition (The Hague, 1963) which includes Ingarden's critical remarks.

the *content* of consciousness, and the other the *concept* of consciousness in Husserl. Concerning the content of consciousness, Ingarden finds difficulty in accepting Husserl's statement *"Zum eigenen Sinn alles Weltlichen gehört diese Transzendenz"* [1] (in Cairns' translation, "this transcendence is part of the intrinsic sense of anything worldly"), for, argues Ingarden, we may conclude from this that everything which is not distinguished by this transcendence, is non-worldly. But with that assumption we would decide what is non-worldly, i.e. purely subjective. This is undoubtedly concordant with Husserl's intention, affirms Ingarden. But can this division of transcendental constituted objectivity, and pure, constituting subjectivity, be upheld in the light of Husserl's apodictic evidence? First, we have the distinction between all things constituted in manifold experiences (*Erlebnisse*), and pure subjectivity (in the form of a pure constituting consciousness). Then, it is said, much that is constituted, belongs to 'the world'. Can we say then, that 'to-the-world-belonging' (*zur Welt gehörig*) is *only* that, which is also constituted? If a decision concerning this point is made from the purely methodological point of view, we arrive at a 'metaphysical' postulation of an *existential* difference between 'the constituting subjectivity', and 'the world'; for the constituting subjectivity is assumed (methodologically) as given in apodictic evidence, while the same cannot be affirmed of the constituted objectivity. This differentiation may, in fact, be true (concludes Ingarden), but it must be the mature resultant of transcendental viewing, and cannot be posited when introducing this method. The possibility of transcendental viewing (*Betrachtung*) must not be supported by a conclusion which presupposes this possibility.

The second relevant criticism of Ingarden makes a similar point with respect to the concept of Husserl's transcendental consciousness. The difficulty is raised by Husserl's use of *'auch'* ('also', 'likewise') in the sentence *"Ich als natürlich eingestelltes ich bin auch und immer transzendentales Ich"* [2] ("as an Ego in the natural attitude, I am likewise and at all times a transcendental Ego"), to which Ingarden objects on the ground of the inconsistency of identifying these two 'Egos' as one and the same, without further specification. The constituted Ego (writes Ingarden) is not the transcendentally constituting Ego, even though one is tempted to assume an identity between 'I' as the pure Ego, and 'I' as the real Ego of the psycho-physical individual.

---

[1] *CM*, § 11; Ingarden's critique pp. 210, 211.
[2] *CM*, § 15; Ingarden's critique pp. 213, 214.

If one does so, however, one encounters the problem of explaining how one and the same Ego can be a constituting, pure 'I', and a constituted, real 'I', seeing that the attributes of these Egos are mutually exclusive and thus cannot be included in *one* thing. Only if one would take the constituted real 'I', as well as the whole constituted world for an illusion could the difficulty be avoided in that only the pure Ego would be said to exist, and the real Ego considered merely a fiction prescribed by its experiences. But, affirms Ingarden, Husserl would energetically protest against this idealistic interpretation.

Now the difficulty explicated by the first point of Ingarden consists of differentiating between the world and the ego on the basis of experiences given to consciousness, while his second point raises the difficulty of ascribing 'pure' as well as 'constituting' consciousness to the same entity. The first objection may be formulated here as the circularity inherent in assuming that one part of the experiences given to consciousness are experiences of 'the world', and that the other part is not. This division of world-self (self, functioning here as 'consciousness' in the epistemological context) should be discovered in the course of investigations wherein the 'worldliness' and the 'non-worldliness' of experiences is clarified. This division, however, is not the result of an analysis of consciousness, but is axiomatically prejected to the argument in the form of a methodological assumption which, however, is never verified by the application of the method. My personal assessment of the issue is that it is not verified, for it is not *verifiable*: no datum given to consciousness categorically implies its 'worldliness'. To call some data transcendental and constituted, and others pure and constituting is to advance a hypothesis which is neither verifiable nor falsifiable in an analysis of the data themselves.

The second difficulty encountered by Ingarden refers to the incompatibility of speaking of consciousness in both an epistemic and a physical context. The term "consciousness" connotes in my eyes an epistemic fact, but, if so interpreted and accordingly defined, it could connote a physical fact. It cannot stand for both, however. But this is what Husserl assumes (and what Ingarden criticises) when he speaks of 'I' as an Ego in the natural attitude (hence a physical consciousness – or rather 'mind') and 'likewise and at all times' (also) a transcendental Ego (i.e. a pure epistemic consciousness). The universe of meanings of the two are entirely disjunctive, and their identification is a basic fallacy of the phenomenological reduction. It is a fallacy which it shares with all forms of reductionism, for the reduction of physical facts to epistemic facts presupposes the identification of the psycho-physical mind with the purely experiential consciousness. A truly consistent universal doubt cannot operate on the assumption of a transcendence of experiential events given to "transcendental consciousness" without circularity and inconsistency

In a consistent 'argument from consciousness', transcendental consciousness cannot be a legitimate postulate, for nothing can be found in the analysis of the contents of consciousness which would warrant the notion of transcendence. Since, however, the mere existence of consciousness is trivial and unfruitful, the sceptic is compelled to add the principle of an *act* of consciousness whereby the events given to consciousness could be explained as the events of 'the world'. It is entirely fallacious, on the other hand, to assume that adding a principle to explain the contents of consciousness is warranted by the analysis of its contents, and it is equally fallacious to believe that when such a principle is added the events it explains signify the external world presented in the form of sensory data. The act of consciousness has to be a hypothetical and heuristically functioning principle which explains our apprehensions, and not the world itself. 'Intentionality', in *my* definition, is a purely epistemological, and not an ontological concept. Intentionality neither 'points beyond itself', nor does it transcend the objects of experience: it is immanent to consciousness and to the objects of experience. The synthesis of the matrix of experiences and intentionality yields 'intentional consciousness' and not, as Brentano, Husserl and Descartes affirm, consciousness *and* the world. Intentionality and sense-experience are distinct terms, but they do not imply two distinct types of entities, the 'subject', and the realm of 'objects'. "Intentionality" does not imply consciousness counterposed to the world, for – as Levinas said, "intentionality is not the fact that an external object enters into relations with consciousness, nor that in consciousness itself a relation is established between two psychic contents – one encased in the other. The relation of intentionality has nothing of the relations between real objects. *It is essentially an act of endowing with meaning (Sinngebung)*".[1] Sense-experience in relation to intentionality is the content of consciousness in relation to the act of consciousness. Both terms are necessary, for pure intentionality is objectless, void, a mere principle without application to empirical matters of fact, and sense-experience in itself is no more than a series of unorganized, incoherent events. When we

[1] E. Levinas, *En Découvrant l'Existence avec Husserl et Heidegger*, Paris, 1949, p. 22.

equate 'content' with 'sense-experience' and 'act' with 'intentionality', our knowledge of *things* – although they appear to be endowed with an existence of their own – can be given a consistent and economic explanation as intentionally constituted sense-objects. Knowledge is private for the sceptic: it refers to his sense-data constituted into coherent events having the appearance of 'the world'.

PRIVATE KNOWLEDGE
FROM INTENTIONAL CONSCIOUSNESS

"Intentional consciousness" denotes the sceptical prototype thesis from which our knowledge of things given in, or implied by, our experience is to be deduced. Before undertaking the investigations leading to these deductions, I shall emphasize again that the thesis has been designed to satisfy the criterion of experientiality, and the deductions must now also satisfy those of consistency and economy. The conclusions of these investigations cannot signify other than *private* knowledge, and by 'private' I do not mean knowledge that is incommunicable, but one that does not admit evidence (in the light of the adopted criterion) of any mind or object existing independently of its experience, to whom or which information could be communicated.

I. PASSIVE INTENTIONS/CONTEMPLATIVE KNOWLEDGE

Ordinary sense-perception, we have seen, cannot be equated with the mere apprehension of 'objective sensations', i.e. with the simple presentation of sense-data. Perception involves the combination of isolated sense-qualities and the synthetic apprehension of sense-objects, events and qualities. In order to understand how isolated sense-data may be perceived as these familiar objects of perception, we must add the *act* to the *content* of consciousness. The principle applicable to this problem is the conception of intentionality expounded above. According to this view, the constancies of sense-objects and their qualities, as well as the dependable regularities observed in perceptual experience, are due to the affective intervention of intentionality in the stream of presented sense-data. Perceived constancies and regularities presuppose active cognitive processes which abstract certain data from the stream, synthesize them, and constitute coherent objects with constant qualities and relational characteristics. The ever-changing patterns of sense-data are hereby structured into objective events which recur, and are identifiable on the basis of their qualities and characteristics: they manifest the constancies and regularities we find in ordinary perceptual experience.

The objects thus constituted testify to the potency of the act of consciousness to modify its contents. When the act is identified as intentionality, then intentionality must be held capable of providing the necessary changes in the field of apprehension which qualify the dynamic patterns of sense-data into sense-objects and events. The naturalistic assumption is that ordinarily perceived objects represent 'objective' quanta and qualia in the external world. Yet this assumption is an ampliative inference, for sense-data, even when synthesized into the form of objects and external space-time events, remain sense-data in specific combination, and do not strictly imply the 'physical left-overs' which are the events in an external space-time realm after their perceptual qualities have been deducted. Every proposition concerning physical events entails a proposition about sense-data, but no proposition about sense-data entails any proposition about physical events. In the sceptical view physical events imply sense-data, but sense-data do not imply physical events. For the present investigation, the objects of perception are purely epistemic entities: they have the form of objects, but do not presuppose objective counterparts external to the space-time dimension of consciousness. I shall consider the mutual relevance of clear and vague data alone, to be the functional ground for the intentional constitution of constant and coherent sense-objects. According to this thesis, all components of experience interrelate, and the 'intended state of consciousness' may be obtained if not present, and preserved if present, when all further elements of experience are jointly preferential. Now this state can obtain only when all data are such that they permit, by virtue of their interrelations, the presence of a dominant quality of pleasantness ("preferentiality"). It follows, then, that the means to establish and preserve the intended state is to structure the patterns of actual data to yield that conformation which determines the presence of preferentiality. The so structured stream of experience can be said to correspond to the intentionality of consciousness.

Evidently, data can only be structured when the relevance of the items included in the present conformations to the 'intended state' is known. The condition of effective intentional action is the *knowledge of the relevance* of particular data to the intended state. This knowledge is obtained by constituting the contiguous and mutually implicatory sense-data into identifiable and individual sense-*objects*, known on the basis of their relevance *qua* objects (i.e. as the totality of the sense-data therein included) to the intended state of consciousness. Unorganized simultaneous and successive patterns of events cannot be known in relation to the intended state, for their identities cannot be established. Hence, the evidential relevance of any event as it emerges in its relation to the intended state cannot be the ground for knowing its relevance when it recurs; for, in fact, no particular sense-datum recurs, or at least, none is knowable as recurrent. The forms of constancy must be lent to data, and these constancies (those of shape, size, brightness, speed, etc.) must permit the constitution of identifiable patterns of sense-data which are held to recur when a similar pattern, constituable into an 'object' such as the one that has been previously constituted, is given. Hence recurrent sense-objects with recognizable features emerge. These objects have a specific relevance to the intended state, by virtue of their relation to other data in the stream of experience which, forming a continuous chain of events, conduce ultimately either toward the intended state (signified by an increasing total feeling of pleasantness) or away from it. The more preferential data are included in any given temporal section of experience, the more the intended state is approached; and the more preferential relations an object has, the more relevant it is for this state. Thus, not only the qualities of preferentiality inherent in the data constituting the given object but also its relations designate the object's 'value' for intentional acts. An object with relatively little doses of inherent preferentiality may be most relevant to the intended state by virtue of its relation to objects which are eminently preferential.

At this point the distinction between the *actual*, the *operational* and the *possible* values of sense-objects must be introduced. I shall call the object's "value" its relevance to the intended state. This value is attributed through the act of consciousness in function of the objective of the act, namely 'the intended state'. Hence an object which is favourable for the attainment of this state has a *positive value*. An object which is unfavourable for this state has a *negative value*. Each object has one *actual value* graded between the fully positive, and the fully negative value. *Operational value* defines the value the object has by virtue of its relations when these relations are affectable by intentionality and the potential value of the object is operationally realizable in place of whatever actual value it possessed. Finally, the object's *possible value* defines those of the object's relations to other data (and to other objects constituted of data) which it manifests usually, but not necessarily (I mean those relations which cannot be affected through intentionality, and thus the value of which cannot be operationally realized). When we take the *actual* value of the object as the mode of existence of that which is in fact given as actuality; the *operational* value of objects as its capacity to pass to a different state; and its *possible* value the modification of the object without intentionally testable necessity, then these values will relate to one another somewhat like Aristotle's *energeia*, *dynamis*, and *endechomenon*.

'Contemplative Knowledge' is knowledge of the actual value of objects. It deals neither with operational potentiality nor with theoretical possibility, but only with actuality itself. In 'passive' intentions each object is defined positively or negatively according to the preferential qualities it manifests upon presentation. Hence, by "passive intentions" I mean those acts of cognition which involve the actually presented sense-data and do not penetrate beyond the realm of actuality into that of potentiality by means of practical operations or theoretical inferences. Knowledge limited to actually presented data has a character which may be denoted 'contemplative'. It does not pry into the nature of the events; it is content with organizing them so that they form coherent objective occasions of experience. In contemplative knowledge, acquired through passive intentions, each object has a given degree of positive or negative value, and it is discerned in the stream of experience whenever the pattern of sense-data manifests a particular local conformation which jointly has the form as well as the preferential value of what has been previously cognized as that object.

II. ACTIVE INTENTIONS/OPERATIONAL KNOWLEDGE

Passive intentions are 'passive' only in relation to 'active' ones. Taken in themselves, passive intentions are active (they are, in fact, 'acts' of consciousness) since they effectively structure the stream of experience, and, lending constancy to abstracted and synthesized data, constitute recognizable sense-objects. In contrast to these activities of consciousness, explained by reference to 'intentionality', active intentions affording 'operational knowledge' [1] introduce a new dimension of activity. This new dimension arises when passively acquired 'contemplative knowledge' is supplemented by practice and experiment.

To account for 'practice' without presupposing a world wherein the acts themselves are practised, we must bracket the assumption of 'organs' in 'effector organs' and take purely that sense-datum which results upon the use of effector organs, and which may simply be called 'effector sensations'. Typically, 'effector sensations' (organs) are activated at will and result in behaviour which is communicated to the knower in different ways. The lifting of an arm, for example, involves at least the following two types of evidence (i) the sensation 'lifting my arm'; (ii) the observation 'my arm is going up'.[2] Now (i) is a direct communication of the willed movement, and (ii) is its verification through changes in the perceptual field. It has often been pointed out [3] that the latter is more reliable, since in the so-called 'phantom-limb cases' (to which already Descartes referred as introducing an element of doubt) the sensation of 'lifting my arm' is present, but not the observation 'arm going up'. And, it is added, the observation can be confirmed by other persons, with the result that we can say that no movement has occurred, even though the sensation 'lifting my arm' has been present. This argument has validity *provided* the incorrigibility of sentences describing immediate experiences is acknowledged. When we deny that 'outside' evidence can verify or falsify our judgment of our experiences, we are left either with a *concordance* between the sensation 'lifting the arm' and the sense-data signifying 'arm going up', or a discordance between these data. Association through frequent repetition makes us believe that when the former occurs, the latter follows. But if the latter does not follow, an exceptional inconsistency obtains in the relations of already known epistemic events: there is the unexpected failure of certain data to materialize despite expectation to the contrary based on past experience. If we do not admit the physiological explanation of the event (i.e. the clinical theory of 'phantom-limbs') all we can meaningfully say of it is that a past regularity has been unexpectedly cancelled. Henceforth it will be unjustified to assert the absolute contiguity of these particular elements of experience.

---

[1] "Operation" refers here to the operations of the act of consciousness with respect to its contents, and has no connotation involving a physical body.

[2] This example is taken from Wittgenstein's *Philosophical Investigations*, I, 621.

[3] By William James, among others.

Nevertheless, the type of sense-data connoted by the 'lifting of the arm' is only exceptionally without effect on the events in the stream of experience; normally, sensations of this type – which I call 'effector sensations' – procure noticeable changes in the customary order of presented sense-data. The remarkable feature of such effector sensations is that they appear to be accessible to volitional control. The combination of volitional control and habitual effect on other sense-data grants intentionality the possibility of 'willing' changes in the stream of experience. Use of effector sensations to effect such changes is the feature which distinguishes 'active intentions' from 'passive' ones, and justifies the former's denomination. Active intentions make for the acquisition of 'operational knowledge' based on, and thus benefiting from, the already acquired 'contemplative knowledge' of the actually presented objects and events.

Since operational knowledge may be functional in attaining to the intended state of optimum preferentiality, and since it depends upon the controlled use of effector sensations, the latter can constitute effective instruments in the service of intentionality.

The use of effector sensations qualifies each passively constituted object from having one actual value, to being endowed also with an operational value. Its one value is the value of the object as actuality: it is positive or negative, but always such as is given in experience. Its second value emerges upon the application of effector sensations to the object. This is the value of potentiality, inherent in the object as actuality, and realized when the object is operatively modified. Hence objects acquire a new dimension: through active intentions they are known not only as actualities, but also as potentialities, discerned through the use of effector sensations.

The operational value of an object is known through trial and error: it may or may not emerge when effector sensations are applied to it. In fact, one of three results might obtain: (i) the object remains unaffected (in realistic terms we would say "the object is outside our physical reach"); (ii) the object is positively modified; (iii) the object is negatively modified. Effector sensations are functional for intentionality in the event that the object comes into category (ii). But since the categories themselves may be established only by experimentation involving the use of effector sensations, functional use of these sensations depends upon a process of trial and error. In that process the correct use of effector sensations becomes clarified with respect to the contemplatively known objects of experience. Whenever such objects are presented and are known through 'passive' intentions, 'active' intentions can be introduced in order to positively modify the negatively (or less-than-fully-positively) relevant object. Such practice is based on the expectation that when effector sensations are applied to certain objects, these will be modified as they have been in the past. (This is the case when the lifting of the arm produces belief in the effective grasping of things within the arm's reach.)

'Operational knowledge' acquired through 'active intentions' penetrates further into the nature of actuality than does contemplative knowledge through passive intentions. Operational knowledge embraces not only actualities, but also potentialities, and in addition to affording knowledge of sense-data as objects endowed with qualities relevant to intentionality, provides also the 'performance-knowledge', involved in realizing known potentials inherent in a presented object in the event that the object's operational value is more positive than its actual value.

III. THEORETICAL INTENTIONS/INFERENTIAL KNOWLEDGE

The acts of consciousness I have called 'passive intentions' define one value for each sense-object; those I denoted 'active intentions' define several values. The single value of constituted objects represents their contemplative knowledge; this is knowledge of actualities. The several values of constituted objects signifies their operational knowledge, and this means the knowledge of actualities as well as of potentialities. But the scope of operational knowledge is limited to the knowledge of those potentialities which become actualized when the given objects are purposively modified. Therefore, knowledge is limited by passive intentions to the things which are actually given to consciousness, while active intentions afford knowledge also of those things which may be 'made' of the things given. In distinction to these relatively limited forms of knowledge, the kind of knowledge afforded through 'theoretical intentions' directed at the stream of experience, has a considerably wider scope. 'Inferential knowledge' includes things which are not given to consciousness in the form of sense-data and constituted sense-objects, but which reside in the given data and objects as pure, even if theoretical, possibilities. Thus the objects known through theoretical intentions are postulated and not inspected entities; but the postulated entities are not assigned an existence independent of their apprehension, but are considered to *inhere* in apprehended actualities as calculated, theoretical possibilities. The postulated objects are sense-objects which are possibly, but not necessarily actual (i.e. 'sensed'). Thus, the postulates of theoretical intentions are not 'objects', but the values of objects. These values are the values of theoretical possibility, as contrasted with the values of actuality and operational potentiality. Inferences refer to the *possible values of actual objects* inferred from knowledge of their actual values and of the relation of their actual values to their operational values. The possible value is not necessary, in the sense that it does not necessarily occur whenever intentionality is effectively directed toward it, but is contingent upon the correlation of events in the stream of experience. Inasmuch as regularities between constituted objects are apprehended, and these regularities are operatively tested, they can provide the premiss for inferences from actuality and potentiality to pure possibility. Therefore, inferential knowledge is based upon the knowledge of regularities in the stream or experience, and knowledge of these regularities means knowledge of the events of actual and potential experience. If all data could be known to interrelate with a measure of regularity which could be formulated as a law determining the principle of interrelation, the actual value of each object could serve as premiss for the inference of its possible value. Since the range of pure possibility exceeds that of operationally realizable potentiality, the intended state can be envisaged in a wider set of circumstances through inferential knowledge than through operational knowledge. When we consider that knowledge of a wider scope of possibilities includes some events within the chain of possible relations which may include operationally realizable potentialities, we shall see that inferential knowledge can provide the framework for the intentional use of effector sensations to attain to the intended state on the basis of a *greater* variety of actual conformations of sense-data than non-theoretical operational knowledge can. Hence theoretical intentions directed toward most temporal cross-sections of experience are ultimately capable of affording knowledge conducing to the envisagement and the purposive attainment of the intended state. Inferential knowledge embraces (in its most evolved form) the actual, operational, and possible values of all constituted objects. It embraces thereby all values of all sense-data provided we assume that all sense-data are constituted (and constitutable) into sense-objects. Should sense-data exist which are neither constituted into objects nor capable of being constituted into objects, these data would be unidentifiable and hence not known. Thus, there is no contradiction in holding that inferential knowledge may, in its most perfected form, embrace all that is knowable. And knowing the knowable is not a tautology, for not all that is knowable needs to be known, even if the unknowable not only is not, but cannot be known. Theoretical intentions may be directed at all things which *can* be known, and what can be known is the actual, the operational, and the possible values of constituted sense-objects. Inferential knowledge – as operational and contemplative knowledge – is motivated by intentionality, and conduces to that conformation of sense-data which manifests the optimum level of preferentiality and thus represents, what I have called the 'intended state of consciousness'.

THE PRINCIPLES OF SCEPTICAL KNOWLEDGE

According to this prototype of consistently sceptical arguments, the acts of knowledge are intentionally motivated, i.e. knowledge is the product of "intentionality" directed toward "consciousness". This applies to the passive, active, as well as to the theoretical forms of intentionality. In all its forms, intentionality functions to render the content of consciousness coherent. By passive intentions the coherency of the content is limited to the actual values of sense-objects; through active intentions the range is extended to cover their operational values, and in virtue of theoretical intentions the realm of the purely possible values is added to the actual, and to the operationally realizable potential values. All inferences are from actuality to possibility and the intention directed toward the data of experience motivates each inference. This intention consists in the clarification of the data in order to attain to the ultimate end of optimal preferentiality. I do not claim that the intentional knowledge intrinsic to science, art, and religion makes those fields of endeavour interested; merely that some such end must be considered the referent of all knowledge in the sceptic's argument. Insofar as inferences from actual sense-data are made, these concern the task of coherently organizing experience and thus inferring the conditions for that state which is the intrinsic objective of intentionality. That 'state' is the focus of all intentional cognitive processes and, inasmuch as all coherent knowledge is intentional knowledge, it functions as the ultimate referent of all coherent knowledge.

In order to clearly determine the principles of 'knowledge' in the context of sceptical argumentations, this 'intended state' has to be closer examined. Now, the definition I had offered of it was that it is optimally preferential. Intentionality, I said, is implied by the presence of this preferential quality.

Preferential data are not isolated items of experience, however, but form part of the great chain of interrelated events which makes up the stream of experience. To intend 'preferentiality' as a dominant quality of experience means to intend those configurations of those data which together permit this quality to emerge with the desired clarity and intensity. Since the quality of particular data *and* their specific configurations determine the resulting effect, an element of flexibility obtains. When we conceive of the contents of experience in any one temporal section as consisting of an enumerable series, then not merely are the items included in the series determinant, but their contiguity as well, and consequently, intrinsically different items may yet add up to the same results if their configurations compensate for their differences. Hence, differences in the quality of particulars may be compensated by differences of configuration and, conversely, different configurations can give the identical final product provided their principals have correspondingly different qualities. Sense-data are relevant to intentionality not only in isolation, but also relationally. The intended *product* of sense-data in relational conformations is the quality of preferentiality: when it is dominant, it constitutes the intended state of consciousness. Since 'preferentiality' is a product, it is determined by diverse particulars in diverse configurations. It follows, then, that obtaining the 'intended state' does not presuppose the acquisition of one particular set of data in one specific system of mutual coordination. An 'intended state', rather, can be any configuration of any presented data which affords the optimum preferentiality.

Thence we may conclude that the intention directed toward the stream of experience concerns the particulars in function of relations, and relations in function of particulars. Particulars and relations change in time and the change itself is effected in space. But the space-time here involved is immanent to consciousness; the changes of the stream of experience which constitutes the matrix of intentional acts are within the dimension of consciousness.

"Intentionality acts upon the events in the space-time of consciousness" is another way of saying that the content of consciousness is the matrix of the act. Together they constitute the continuum which makes up reality, as the sceptic knows it. In his view the states of consciousness are fluid, being the syndrome of constantly changing configurations of sense-data. The intended state itself is fluid, since it corresponds to the possibilities of attaining to optimum preferentiality through the intentional space-time modification (or preservation) of actual experience. The 'state' which I have designated as the focus of intentionality and the referent of knowledge, is not a static concept of predetermined characteristics, but is itself a constant ideal accompanying the transfigurations of the items of experience in the space-time dimension of consciousness. The intended state is inherent in each inner space-time point as the ideal which it either satisfies or frustrates, and which lends the motivation for preserving or changing the data in that locus. It is not an isolated ideal of particular data, but the common ideal of all data conjointly; the intentionality pervading a given datum is determined not by the quality of that datum alone, but by its relations to all other sensory data in the system of internal space-time coordinates which makes up the content of consciousness. Furthermore, the relation of the intended state to the given data is not determined once and for all, but changes with the changes in the general pattern of actual data. The ideal is relative to the possibilities, and the possibilities are acted upon according to their relevance to an ideal which they imply.

Consider now the nature and composition of 'intended states'. They represent the syndrome of all contemporaneous sense-data in all their quantitative diversity and qualitative richness. They are not a mere mosaic of particular sense-data, and their character is correspondingly complex. While particular 'vague' data are qualitatively (i.e. 'emotively') charged, that charge is simple. It is such that the given datum is describable (and hence definable) in terms of either positive or negative value. But we are now dealing with the syndrome of all intrinsically charged data and with the sum of all the charges which emanate from these to 'clear' data which do not possess them intrinsically but acquire them in the course of interrelations. Hence the qualitative 'feelings' obtaining in a given state of consciousness are infinitely more complex than those that obtain in any member of the class of 'vague' sense-data alone. These qualities are not those of a given basic, evidential and absolutely primary datum of consciousness, but result from (and hence are the products of) the interrelational coalescence of all such fundamental qualities. Any such complex feeling is not a primary datum of consciousness, but an ultimate product, not a basic and apodictic cause, but a highly contingent effect. Complex feelings, or "emotions" [1] were not included among

---

[1] To distinguish complex qualitative products from simple preferential charges of particular data I shall use "emotions" for the former and "feeling" for the latter.

(and not discussed with) primary facts of experience; they can be consistently and satisfactorily explained by reference to our more economic basic premisses: intentionality directed to sense-experience. In this view, emotions are essentially the products of the relations of diverse data-conformations in the stream of experience to the intentional acts. The facts of experience are prior to the awareness of the qualities which result upon their presence: emotions refer to known sense-data and acquire their substance from them. This consistent sceptical position has been summed up by Hume with the words: "To hate, to love, to think, to feel, to see; all this is nothing but to perceive."[1]

(Noteworthy evidence for the assumption that complex emotions, representative of abstract psychic states, are secondary to concrete experiences, is provided by the well known semantic law according to which words connoting abstract events have been evolved from those having concrete connotation. In the words of Bonfante, "It is quite evident that there is in all languages, concurrently with the transformation in mental habits, a general tendency to go from the concrete to the abstract, not vice versa (or very rarely so). A semantic change such as to weigh > to think (Fr. penser, It. pensare) is easy and understandable; an inverse passage, of the type to think > to weigh, is strange, and, as far as I know, unheard of."[2] Of course 'abstract' means here not only emotions, but all awareness of 'subjective' and 'psychological' states. On the other hand, 'concrete' refers to empirically experienced objects and events. Thus, the claim for the priority of sense-data – as the ultimate components of empirical experience – is justified by the above semantic law, even if the range of what is secondary may include notions which are meaningless in the context of a sceptical argument.)

In summary I would like to remark that the quintessence of this 'argument from consciousness', and certainly its major raison d'être, is the fact that it shows (with some degree of conviction, I hope) that the principal facts of human experience can be consistently and economically integrated into a general system of explanation based on the premiss that valid evidence is only that which is communicated to consciousness in immediate experience. The criterion "experi-

[1] Hume, Treatise, Part II, Sect VI.
[2] G. Bonfante, 'On Reconstruction and Linguistic Method', Word, I, 132. Cf. also the convincing series of examples collected by Ludwig Klages in his Von Wesen des Bewusstseins (München, 1955) to demonstrate that the majority of words having subjective connotations are based on such concrete experiences as are those of space, movement, vision, activity, materiality, temperature, etc. Although Klages' examples are in German, a similar series could most likely be collected in the majority of civilized languages.

entiality" jointly with the criteria "consistency" and "economy" determine an ego-oriented type of systematic conception of reality which, though calling for a heuristic principle to render it coherent, does not require the presupposition of any residue 'behind' or 'beyond' sensory experience. The facts are sense-data, and sense-data require neither a subject nor an object in order to be. Sense-data *are*, and if they are, there is consciousness. Only the principle of a cognitive act is required to render the sense-datum theory sufficiently coherent to permit the explanation of the diverse forms of human experience.

If it is at all possible to formulate a prototype of a systematic argument from consciousness, and if, when formulated, its premises and criteria are incapable of disproof, the sceptic deserves to be heard. While his argument may not be satisfactory to common sense and it may not meaningfully penetrate to those regions of 'the natural universe' where realism is still at home, it is undeniable that it is beyond reproach in the light of its own basic assumptions. In that event, however, it represents an entirely valid approach to the problem of reality.

PART III

REALISM: THE ARGUMENT FROM BEING

"BEING"

The task of the following 'argument from being' is precisely the contrary of that of the previous 'argument from consciousness'. Here I shall be concerned with the general and with the particular only as exemplifying the general. I shall take as my root-axiom the concept "being", meaning by it the notion which the realist entertains of the particular existents of the natural world. The premiss-criterion is adequacy at present, and it is adequacy, together with consistency and economy that constitutes the touchstone of conclusions derived from "being". 'Being' is axiomatic with respect to the inquiry; it is assumed without question.

But just what *is* "being"? Many different conceptions of this principle have been proposed in the history of thought, and some have little more than the verbal expression in common. I shall delimit the meaning of 'being' in two ways. First, by taking into account only those of its possible meanings which permit its use as root-axiom, i.e. which do not pretend to have logically deduced or induced this concept from any more ultimate or more evidential fact. Second, I shall consider it to be such that it applies to all things that are, and could conceivably be, in the world. This concept of being must be *axiomatic*, and *universal*. So defined, it can function as the premiss for an argument exemplifying the position of consistent realism, which we may subsequently collate with the argument exemplifying the viewpoint of the consistent sceptic.

If "being" is to designate all things that are, it must apply to man as well as to animals, to atoms as well as to stars. This is a large order; in fact, its formulation directly contradicts the type of philosophical problems which I have previously considered. According to the sceptic, there can be no concept of such generality, or rather, no such concept can be meaningful and demonstrable. Here, however, I am not concerned with the sceptic's objections, for I do not make use of his criteria. As realist, I consider myself free to explain that which I believe I have reasons to think exists, and to explain it adequately, consistently, and economically. Hence I shall start by saying that there is a space and a time which is independent of the knowing subject. The things that are, are in that external space-time, and exist therein independently of being perceived, or of being inferred from perception. There would be no contradiction in saying that X exists, although I do not perceive it; 'X' is merely the class of existents of which I have no experience. I do not consider it meaningless to speak of entities which I do not experience, for sense-perception refers now to physical objects existing in the absence, as in the presence, of the sense-objects given in experience. I have to use 'being' as a universal predicate in the present realistic argument, notwithstanding the fact that its positive use will be analytic and its negative use self-contradictory: within the framework of realism, 'being' is a necessary predicate of all things that exist.

Applicability is not a guarantee of sufficiency, however. The concept 'being' must be such that it is both applicable to, *and* sufficient to explain, the basic and essential facts about the things that are. At first sight the mere fact of spatio-temporality would appear to be sufficient to account for most entities on the micro-physical and the macro-physical level, and to come across difficulties only when touching upon biological phenomena. The problem is focussed sharply in anthropology by the question whether mind can be accounted for in terms of a principle of 'being' applicable to all other entities, and when so accounted for, will that principle be sufficient?

Whitehead, who has accomplished what is probably the major ontological synthesis of modern philosophy, summarized and criticized the problem by saying "The enormous success of the scientific abstractions, yielding on the one hand *matter* with its *simple location* in space and time, on the other hand *mind*, perceiving, suffering, reasoning, but not interfering, has foisted onto philosophy the task of accepting them as the most concrete rendering of fact. Thereby, modern philosophy has been ruined. It has oscillated in a complex manner between three extremes. There are the dualists, who accept matter and mind as on an equal basis, and the two varieties of monists, those who put mind inside matter, and those who put matter inside mind." [1] Whitehead himself sought to put neither mind inside matter

[1] *SMW*, ch 3

nor matter inside mind, but to explain the two consistently. In Whiteheadian metaphysics the notion of 'being' is the 'actual entity' (or the 'actual occasion') and this notion is applicable to all things that are, up to and including man. With respect to the categories of Whitehead's metaphysics, that notion of being is both applicable to, and sufficient to account for, all varieties of entities, regardless of whether they possess consciousness or not. The things that are, are for Whitehead in a space and a time that transcend each particular while including him. The knower, whether he be a man, or any other 'actual entity', is part of the whole and participates in the being of the whole.

Hartshorne has developed this line of thought and has gone so far as to assign 'experience' and, in principle, 'mind' to what is ordinarily and commonsensically termed 'material' 'physical', or 'inorganic' phenomena. Notwithstanding its insistence on panpsychism, Hartshorne's thesis is consistent with a thoroughly explicated, uninhibited physical realism, for it follows up the basic assumption of the realist that all that exists is necessarily real and not necessarily essentially diversified. (Dualism and pluralism are only partially realist, and, since they result from the conviction that monism is insufficient, they are tenable only if monism *is* insufficient.) Hartshorne convincingly states the case for uniting physical and organic nature in one encompassing Whiteheadian kind of scheme. "One may stop at one's own sensations or perceptions, and treat the rest of the world as logical construction only (solipsism); one may stop at human perceptions, and treat all other animals, with the rest of nature, as logical construction only (humanistic phenomenalism); one may stop at the vertebrate animal or the single cell or perhaps the virus unit and regard all below this level as mere conceptual construction, presumably from our human perceptions (animalistic or vitalistic phenomenalism); one may not stop anywhere, but may take all physical processes to involve, or even (for at this point the distinction becomes empty) to consist of, feeling, sensations, or other sorts or aspects of experience – experience as not merely human, not merely animal or vitalistic, but as forming a still vaster array of diverse levels (sub-atomic, atomic, etc.) of which animal experiences are but the higher or more complex of those known to us." [1] Hartshorne asserts, "the point is not merely that we do not know exactly where, ultimately, to draw the line, but that an equally

[1] Charles Hartshorne, 'The Social Structure of Experience', in *Philosophy*, April and July, 1961, p. 99.

good (bad) case can be made for drawing it almost anywhere – at the limits of humanity, the vertebrates, the amoebae, viruses, genes, molecules." [1] And he concludes, "Our inability (so far as we are unable) to imagine modes of experience as different from ours as atoms are different from human beings is only – an inability; it is not a positive insight into the meaningfulness of "mere, insentient matter." [2]

I commend Hartshorne's argument on the grounds of physical realism (since in line with the basic assumption of the realist it eliminates categorical differences between existing phenomena) and not on the reductionist grounds that the unity of 'other minds' and 'mere matter' is demonstrable in an analysis of experience.[3] If an equally good case can be made for drawing the line between 'mind' and 'matter' anywhere, and if this assumption presupposes physical realism, then if physical realism is presupposed, we can draw the line anywhere. And it follows then that we are not justified in drawing it so as to arbitrarily exclude any part or aspect of physical reality. It is for this reason that realism appears to me to entail a notion of "being" which must, at least as a basic, methodological assumption, embrace all there is, or is thought to be, of reality. This thesis presupposes physical realism, and it follows from it. It does not presuppose an analysis of experience, and it does not necessarily follow from it (I have argued in fact, that it *cannot* follow from it). Hence my concern is to explore the feasibility and adequacy of a universal concept of being without acknowledging reasons for justifying it by recourse to the facts of experience. Consequently, unlike Whitehead and Hartshorne, I shall not attempt to adduce experiential proof for the unity of ontic existents, but shall consider the adequacy, consistency and economy of the scheme explaining this unity a sufficient guarantee of its truth.

At present, my first problem is to define the most general characteristics of that concept of being which is applicable to, and sufficient to account for, all things that may conceivably exist.

I shall note that, while 'beings' exist in space and time, their ex-

---

[1] *Ibid.*, p. 100.

[2] *Ibid.*, p. 102.

[3] Hartshorne argues to the latter point in affirming that "We know other minds by analogical extensions of our direct participations in the feelings, thoughts, or experiences, of some instances (cellular, inner-bodily, perhaps divine) of other mind; we know matter by a mode of such extension in which the participation is so vague or attenuated with respect to qualities of feeling, and so heightened or sharpened with respect to spatio-temporal relationships, that it easily appears, and for many purposes is as if, we were dealing with bare "extended substances", devoid of any life or experience of their own." *Op. cit.*, p. 111.

istence is delimited, and thus they occupy finite sections of the space and of the time there is. Each entity extends to some extent in space, and endures to some extent in time. While it does so, it exists, i.e. it 'has being'. When either its spatial extension or its temporal endurance is denied, the entity can no longer be said to exist; at least, such an existence would no longer correspond to the realist's notion of what "being in the world" signifies. If we would maintain that an entity exists, although it has no spatial extension, we must think of something like the Cartesian *res cogitans* or of another concept of consciousness in some idealist context, or else of the concept of universals in an ontologically realist metaphysical system. None of these assumptions could be said to constitute the stock-in-trade of the realist I have in mind – he would label them 'logical entities' or 'epi-phenomena', applied to and derived from existing things, but not themselves existing. For the consistent realist, an entity exists only if it extends in space and endures in time. Evidently, it cannot extend in space unless it endures in time (even if only to some infinitesimal length of time) and if it endures in time, but does not extend in space, it is a purely logical or geometrical entity. Inasmuch as 'being' can be only a space-time existent, and all space-time existents are delimited (other than, in certain views, God), no entity, of which the realist could say that it exists, could exist longer than the finite span of its extended-endurance.

This proposition furnishes the clue for the definition of a sufficient concept of "being" through the determination of the principles involved in 'being a being'. We may consider, namely, that being is not merely a fact, but is also an act: 'being' is both a noun and a verb, and that 'be*ing* being' is the full description of "being". Being is to be; each being *is*, as long as it is spatially and temporally present in the world. If being is both a fact and an act, being is not only 'to be', but to 'want to be': here the psychological term "want" is made to function in place of a general concept standing for active behaviour. But there is no direct connotation of a teleological principle in the notion of 'be*ing* being'. The act of being does not necessarily presuppose an ultimate goal, but can concern merely the prolongation of the existence of that which exists already. A basically similar idea has been advanced by Spinoza as the principle of *conatus*, which, in his metaphysical system, stands for the attempt of each body to preserve its existence and furnishes the essence of all individuals. When every existent entity is ranged on the same fundamental level of reality, each individual is *facies totius universi,* and the act of being, as a kind of *conatus,* applies to the fact of being whenever and wherever being is factual. I shall denote this act of being (the present counterpart of Spinoza's *conatus*) the "ontic function" and attribute it to all entities of which it is meaningful to say that they exist. (The criterion of 'meaning' is adequacy, at present, and not experientiality.)

The advantage of this concept of 'ontic function' is that it is justified, in the realistic view, with respect to all areas of existence. In a very fundamental sense all things resist annihilation by balancing external and possibly destructive influences through an internal distribution of forces. This balancing of external and internal energy holds true of atoms and of galaxies, of amoebae and of men. From the viewpoint of the given entity, the effective counteraction of external influences represents a striving for the preservation of existence. Since existence means extended-endurance, 'ontic function' implies extension in function of endurance, and endurance in function of extension.

Given this simple and yet universal principle, it should be possible to integrate mental phenomena into the range of events in the natural universe by conceiving of it as the ontic function of man. More specifically, this implies that the human organism is so constructed that, like all other entities, it extends in function of endurance, and endures in function of extension. The ontic function is manifested in the human mind, since we may say without contradiction that the human body is so organised as to possess a brain and a nervous system, and that the brain and the nervous system permit the organized system to endure. Conversely, the endurance of the body is a precondition for having developed (and still further developing) this complex form of organization, with the result that the endurance of the body (its highly evolved cognitive apparatus) is the result of extension, and extension affords continued endurance. Thus "mind" becomes compatible with "matter" and we are assured of the applicability and the sufficiency of the concept of 'being'. Mind is a special form of existence, but not a categorically different one: it is merely the expression of the universal ontic function on the level of humanity.

Yet ontic function has wider implications even if it is carefully delimited as a general concept without unduly speculative specifications. It suggests that if any existent functions in order to be, then its function is partially dependent on the external conditions of its existence. Conversely, the function of the entity must be capable of affecting whatever conditions determine its extended-endurance. Unless we wish to postulate transcendental entities (such as universals or God) the conditions determining the entity's existence are furnished by other entities, i.e. by other things that *are*. Whatever is, is a condition influencing the being of whatever other things there are. It follows then, that the function of any existent – its 'ontic function' – is to so condition its environment as to permit its existence within it. "Environment" refers ultimately, to the totality of existent things, and directly, to those things which are in the immediacy of the given entity. Thus the notion of ontic function brings with it either a notion of relational interdetermination of things, or the postulation of transcendent things imposing their 'form' or 'will' upon the existent things. Purely as regards economy, the former would be preferable. Hence *if* this notion of being can be explicated and maintained as applicable to, and sufficient to account for, 'being' on all levels of inquiry, it can serve as the basic premiss of a realist philosophical scheme.

"PROCESS"

Space-time being is a root-axiom which, in one form or another, the modern realist is compelled to accept. Not much more than that it extends and endures can be said of any entity, without involving contestable assumptions, however. But if entities exist, they exist in space and time, and if they exist in space and time, then the complex problems of space, time, relation, law, universals, particulars, and their related problems emerge and have to be considered. Now, space-time being is a root-axiom, but the scheme whereby space-time being can be coherently and logically consistently explained, is not: such schemes are already syndromes of heuristic principles which permit the substantiation of the realist notion of being. The distinction is important insofar as realistically there is little to argue about the spatio-temporality of entities but much about the explanation of their extension and endurance. In an 'argument from being' only the notion of space-time being and its immediately correlated concepts and principles are axiomatic; all further discourse is heuristic, helping to clarify this root-axiom by integrating the various problems which it raises into a coherent and consistent scheme. I suggested as such a root-axiom the notion of 'be*ing* being', meaning thereby that being is both an act and a fact. This follows from the basic assumption of realism since, if the world exists and if it consists of appearing and disappearing entities, then the existence of the given things implies not only a fact, but also an act: it is the act whereby entities exist as long as they actually do.

The implication of an *act* by the *fact* of existence in a changing universe could be denied if we would nihilistically hold that the ultimate state and final goal of all things is non-being. In that event, the processes and conditions whereby things do not exist would imply a nihilistic *conatus*. However, in adopting such notions we look at the reverse side of the picture offered to us as participants in the universal process, holding that it is our non-being which would make us a part of the true nature of reality. Such views (reminiscent of the principles of *Nirvana*) are logically tenable, but contradict the fundamental implication of 'experience-in-world' namely, that the world exists and that existence is its normal state of being. The assumption that being is significative of an act and non-being of the absence of an act, accords better than nihilism with the realistic assumption that perceived things are ontic, physical entities. Therefore, the concept advanced here of 'ontic function' is indicated as corollary of a root-axiom which, in some form or another, is accepted in all typically realist philosophical systems. The fact that the character and specific features of such systems are greatly divergent, should be primarily due to the heuristic principles which thinkers postulate in order to apply their root-axioms to the various objects of inquiry.

I

The scheme for the heuristic analysis of 'being' in the widest realm of reality may, I propose, be subsumed under the heading "process". 'Process' stands for one heuristic set of principles, not for the only one. In this chapter I shall consider the meaning of "process" and the principles and problems entailed by its adoption.

The first problem involves the concept of empiricism in realist philosophy. I suggested that realist empiricism is different from sceptical empiricism and that the difference is due to the respective basic assumptions. Experience is a meaningful concept in both sets of basic assumptions, but for scepticism the world is given in experience, while for realism experience is given in the world. The sceptic as well as the realist can be a proper empiricist in that both can undertake a rigorous scrutiny of experience in their respective contexts. Thus, notwithstanding the different frameworks, experience must be accessible in both approaches and such notions as 'subject', 'object' and 'datum of experience' have to have precise meanings in both. Therefore, the first task in the present scheme is to define the notions 'subject', 'object' and 'datum of experience' in the realist context.

I shall recall that in the sceptical argument the above terms referred to consciousness: 'subject' and 'object' were fused in its content, and were analysed to constituted sense-objects and their processes of constitution by means of the principle 'intentionality' directed by the 'subject' to what thereby became a world of 'objects'. Objects were epistemic sense-data-constructs, having no being of their own. In contradistinction to this sceptical view, it would seem that in the realist optic 'subject' is radically differentiated from 'object' and that sense-data must somehow 'float' between the apprehending subject and his physical environment. But, when we have a second look at the concepts of subject and object entailed by consistent realism, we shall find that subject is not contrasted with object, for they both form part of the one encompassing realm of existent actuality. To quote a significant phrase of Whitehead, "the primary situation disclosed in cognitive experience is 'ego-object amid objects' ".[1] Hence for the realist, the experience of a subject connotes interaction with others like himself. The very notion of "subject" is an arbitrary abstraction in consequent realism, but it is one without which no deduction of experience from realist schemes can be made. Realism is based on the assumption of the solidarity of all objects and on the subsuming of notions of 'subject' under the heading of objects (as one object among many). But if 'experience' and 'knowledge' is at all to follow from such schemes, we must be able to pick out one object from the many, treat it as subject, and show how it relates to (i.e. how it 'knows' and 'experiences') the others. The consequence of such arbitrary abstraction is that the components of experience will seem to refer to a subjective *and* to an objective genus of events. This is a deceptive conclusion, however, for if the subject is not essentially different from objects, but is made into 'subject' by an arbitrary analysis from its particular standpoint, then its experience is part of the general texture of experience in the natural world. There is no reason to assume that some components of the subject's experience refer to essentially subjective, and others to essentially objective events. There could be subjective events only if the subject is not an ultimate 'individual', so that events *within* the entity we take for our subject could be analyzed to further entities. Then, however, each further entity could again be taken for a 'subject', and thus a further group of 'subjective' and 'objective' events could be introduced. If, on the other hand, the subject is an ultimate 'particle', then there are no events which could be properly designated as *within* it, for unanalysability is synonymous with the absence of parts, and the absence of parts prohibits the presence of internal events. Hence if the subject is ultimate, it has no subjective experiences, and if it is not ultimate, its experiences are further divisible until we reach the ultimate.

[1] *SMW*, Ch. 9.

The problem is one of individuality in the context of a realist and relational ontology. Only an individual can be a subject, and unless specific criteria of individuality are introduced, there are no individuals in a relational scheme other than ultimate particles and the ultimate totality. The former have no internal relations, and the latter has no external relations. In both cases the distinction between subjective and objective experience becomes meaningless. It follows that the data of experience had by 'one object among many' refers to its apprehension of the others. This in turn implies that sense-data connote in the realist context the influence of the many upon the one in the natural universe. Sense-data (if we wish to use this term) are neither a property of the subject nor belong entirely to objects; they represent *for* the subject the effective presence *of* objects. In other words, they are the events which signify relational interdetermination for particulars.

This is the realist role of sense-data and it is interesting to note that over the past centuries the meanings of such terms have been slowly, but apparently relentlessly, changing in context from scepticism to realism. While Locke, Hume and the early empiricists have used their own equivalents to "sense-datum" in reference to arguments from consciousness, in modern science and scientific (or 'scientistic') psychology and philosophy 'sense-datum' is usually employed in the context of realistic arguments. Although it is usually said that the concept "sense-datum" has been in use under various names since the seventeenth century, or even from ancient times, it is generally believed to have originated with Moore and Russell. Hall clears up this point in an informative note on the subject [1] in which he shows that neither Moore nor Russell have originated the term, nor claim to have done so. Hall traces the term to several works published toward the end of the nineteenth century (thus pre-dating Moore's *Some Main Problems*, 1910/11, and Russell's *The Problems of Philosophy*, 1912), notably to those of James, and possibly of Fraser.

The first systematic treatment of what is often referred to as the 'sense-data problem', is probably by Locke, who uses the word "sensation" to describe the ideas which we obtain when our senses are affected by external objects.[2] "Sensations" are counterposed to "reflection" which, for Locke, is the ideas we receive when we perceive the operations of our minds on ideas already received. Sensation gives

---

[1] Roland Hall, 'The Term "Sense-Datum"' in *Mind*, January, 1964.
[2] In *An Essay Concerning Human Understanding*.

us such ideas as we have of colour, tastes, sounds, and so on, while reflection provides us with ideas such as willing, doubting and thinking. Both these types of ideas come to us through experience, but sensations dominate, since many if not most of our ideas come to us through the sense-organs. But sensation together with reflection gives us all the ideas that human beings can possess. Innate ideas are emphatically denied: knowledge is based on experience alone. Now Locke distinguishes between 'simple' and 'complex' ideas. A simple idea is uncompounded, contains only uniform appearance, and is unanalyzable; it is essentially the statement of 'sense-datum', as that term is understood in its epistemic reference. Simple ideas can be combined, repeated, compared, and complex ideas made of them, but they cannot be invented. All simple ideas are communicated in sensory experience.

The semantic equivalent of Locke's 'simple ideas' having their source in 'sensation' (i.e. in sensory experience) is Hume's notion of 'simple impressions'. All the information gathered by the mind, writes Hume[1], is composed of impressions and ideas. The only difference is the force and vivacity with which impressions strike us: the force of ideas is pale in comparison. Ideas and impressions can be simple and complex. Complex impressions and ideas arise by combinations of simple ones. Simple impressions are prior to simple ideas for they precede the latter in their appearance in the mind, and they are also more vivid. Hume comes to the conclusion that all our ideas come from experience, there being no innate ideas. The ground for this conclusion is ultimately the notion of simple impressions, which are the ultimate features of experience. These, too, correspond therefore to the epistemic meaning of the term "sense-datum".

Neither Locke nor Hume wished to maintain solipsism, however, although Hume was more sceptical concerning the certainty of our knowledge of the external world than Locke had been. For Locke the criteria for solving this problem were given in the distinction between primary and secondary qualities of objects. The primary qualities are found to be inseparable from bodies regardless of their condition. The secondary qualities, on the other hand, reside in the perceiving subject. Primary qualities include solidity, figure, number, mobility and extension; secondary qualities include sounds, colours, tastes, odours, and the like. The latter are explained as resulting from the experience of primary qualities by a percipient subject. The objects, as they are by themselves, affect the subject and produce those

[1] In Book I of *A Treatise on Human Nature.*

qualities which inhere purely in the subject. Thus the conclusion emerges that primary qualities represent the aspects of objects which really belong to them, while secondary qualities represent aspects of the objects which are properties of the subject. Together with his rejection of innate ideas, Locke tacitly assumed the existence of the natural world, but he was not able to uphold this assumption without allowing for the non-empirical knowledge of necessary truths.[1] Hume realized this difficulty, and adopted a more sceptical viewpoint. For Hume a careful and profound study of human nature results in complete scepticism, although he claims that nature prevents us from carrying this scepticism to its final and destructive conclusion. Yet Hume does not maintain that the independent existence of objects is more than a matter of belief. The factors which make us connect events in apparent causality in experience are responsible for our opinions concerning the external world, and in theory we must realize that the evidence is inadequate to permit us to affirm our beliefs as statements of fact. While Hume diverges from Locke in the degree of scepticism of his final conclusion, both thinkers treat what we now would call 'sense-data', as the ultimate, unanalyzable, uneliminable building blocks of human knowledge. This meaning of sense-data is essentially sceptical: it refers to the 'world' as it is given to us in experience.

In the 'argument from consciousness' I have pressed the implications of this concept of sense-data to their utmost sceptical conclusion. Sense-data formed part of the space-time realm of consciousness, and did not imply the natural world. The sceptical meaning of sense-data (as 'sensations', or 'impressions') does not furnish proof of external reality. Whatever is experienced is constructed out of 'simple' data which, in consequence, form the matrix of experience. This matrix is such that it enables us to construct 'complex' ideas and impressions, but there are no 'physical left-overs': we can no more deduce an 'external' world from the complex ideas than from the simple ones. Therefore, the sceptic's sense-data refer to events in the space-time of consciousness and have to be recognized as space-time point events *in* the dimension of consciousness. This view is not an arbitrary falsification of the standpoint of the early empiricists, but a logical result of their attitude, pressed to its fullest conclusion. (That they did not do so explicitly, may have been due to the fact that, as Hume pointed out, such a conclusion loses force in daily life since the

---

[1] *cf. An Essay Concerning Human Understanding*, esp. Book IV.

sceptic goes on living and acting as though he were a realist. It is also likely that both Locke and Hume held complete scepticism [even if justified] to be merely destructive.)

In time, the sceptical notion of sense-data gave way to a realistic notion according to which a sense-datum is an element in objective existence. The switch did not mean a loss of continuity, however, for the very same basic concepts were gradually reinterpreted in a new context. While the early empiricists saw experience primarily 'from the inside' and defined its elements accordingly, modern realists and scientists see (presumably the same) sense-data 'from the outside' and treat it concordantly with the viewpoint they adopt. Sceptically, sense-data have usually been thought of as factors in the relation of knower and known. The subsequent evaluation of this relation as one between stimulus and response (of which there are indications already in Locke) led to the ascription of stimulus to the external, and response to the internal, world. Sense-data were thus referred to an external world, apprehended in an internal one. Further shift in this direction tended to deny the internal world as a vital factor altogether. The modern empirical natural sciences tend to regard sense-data as space-time points events external to the locus of their presentation, being not only indicative, and, by implication representative, of external events, but being these events themselves. Sense-data now function as points of a compass which, when correctly read, help one to orient himself in a world which he knows to be given, but wherein he would like to find his way with certainty. Like the points of a compass, sense-data are reduced from qualitative richness to uniformity, felt differences being explained by quantifiable points of reference (space, time, relation, system of coordinates, etc.). Sense-data have progressed from being elements of pure experience, to elements of experience in relation to objects of experience, to arrive finally at being the means of verification for relational events concerning external entities which, either in part, or entirely (as science's 'theoretical objects'), transcend sensory experience.[1] The realistic scientist and philosopher of science has replaced sense-data as epistemic facts with sense-data as physical facts. Consequently, it is as physical facts that "sense-data" has to be used in the present 'argument from being'.

---

[1] I am indebted for information concerning the current scientific use of 'sense-data' to A. T. Tymieniecka, who kindly put the manuscript of her study on this subject at my disposal.

II

After these preliminary definitions, we can commence the determination of the principles of "process" appearing to be most consistent and economical with respect to the root-axiom and its corollaries. The major premiss for the inference of the principles of process is the notion of *change:* existence is delimited for all entities and thus all entities are subject to changes in their pattern of existence which reach, ultimately, to the determination of their coming into being, and to their cessation of being. The conditions which make for the factual being of an entity are changing, with the result that the entity, as an ontic individual, finds its ontic function directed at modified environments. Its ontic function is then to resist change insofar as change would tend to annihilate the entity. Fundamentally, the notion of "process" implies not only change, but also changing entities and, inasmuch as the changing entities are 'be*ing* beings', "process" implies both change and resistance to change. Change itself is vacuous; unchanging being is static. But "process" involving change and resistance to change can provide those conceptual tools which may permit the elaboration of the notions entailed by the realist basic assumptions in the light of contemporary science and philosophy.

Change and resistance to change are consistently unified under the assumption that being is both an act and a fact, i.e. that the full description of 'being' is 'be*ing* being'. Neither being as fact nor being as act is new to philosophy, but most of the great metaphysical systems of the past have tended to accentuate one at the expense of the other: there were the great 'atomist' and 'materialist' systems which, from the time of Democritus, emphasized the facticity of the ultimate constituents of reality, and there were also the Heraclitean type of cosmologies which accentuated the flux and fluidity of events, taking the concrete individual more as act than as fact. It is surely unjustified to claim that any great system of thought concerning the nature of physical reality has entirely neglected either of these two important aspects of the problem of being, but there have been significant differences as to which is the more important one.

For most contemporary thinkers, however, the history of philosophy is a lesser factor in the decision concerning this question than is contemporary natural science. And among the various specialized inquiries of the latter, physics is likely to have the greatest influence on thinking upon these topics today. But contemporary physics is very different from the physics of even two hundred years ago, and these differences affect the relations of accent on fact and act. Newtonian physics and Euclidean geometry dominated scientific thinking until recently, and both of these systems were based on an implicit belief in the placid facticity of the physical entity. It is only with the coming of non-Euclidean geometry and the quantum and relativity theories that physics appears to have abandoned its traditional assumptions concerning entities as solid, movable masses, acted upon by energetic principles. Being was mostly a fact for Newton, but it is almost entirely an act for the contemporary physicist. Physics is eminently functional on the basis of this assumption, but, if it does not entail a more factual conception of the physical entity, by no means does it exclude it. As far as the physicist is concerned, the world may be thought of as constituted by a substantive-energizing principle, manifested as energy and mass, and particle and wave, but it is incumbent upon the philosopher, concerned about making sense of the implications of modern physical theories, to come up with some general notion of substance capable of rendering modern physics' acts into ontic facts. Undoubtedly, such undertaking exceeds the task of philosophy as the positivists and the logical and linguistic analysts conceive this task to be; but it is directly indicated as a meaningful endeavour for the thinker who professes realism and does not hesitate to explore the metaphysical implications entailed by his convictions.

The physical realist, if he is scientifically minded, will neither attempt to contest science's competence to indicate the principle facts concerning the nature of the universe, nor will he be satisfied to let matters rest where science leaves them. He will consider it important, however, only to supplement, and never to contradict, scientifically recognized facts. His major task today is to find the bridge between the discarded mechanistic conception of 'matter' and the ontological implication of the mathematical vectors for 'energy' and 'mass'. He also has to grapple with the problems of causality, determinism and probability, but his foundation is provided by a kind of substantialism which supplements, but does not contradict contemporary physical theories.

Pure change is vacuous; inert matter is untenable. The modern scientific world-view suggests a realm of dynamic actuality, where 'dynamic' means the principle of change, and 'actuality' the principle of a substance which is both subject and superject of change.

Of recent thinkers, it is Whitehead, I believe, who has come closest to fulfilling the philosophical task I expect the scientific-minded realist to fulfill. Although there are times when Whitehead assumes a role ill fitting the one I ascribe to him here (as when he engages in what I have called 'physical reductionism'), the general tenor of his thought is sufficiently consistent with scientific, physical-realist and objectivist philosophy to permit me to base much of this prototype of realist argumentation on his organistic metaphysic.

III

I would first of all like to explore the characteristic of the White-headian metaphysic which concerns the emphasis on relations, as opposed to attributes. In championing a process-cosmology, White-head found it necessary to modify the Cartesian conception of 'attri-bute' into one of 'relation': "for Descartes the primary *attribute* of physical bodies is *extension;* for the philosophy of organism the primary *relationship* of physical occasions is *extensive connection.*" [1] Descartes speaks of *attributes*, Whitehead of *relations;* the Cartesian notion of physical bodies attributes *extension* to them, the Whiteheadian notion posits their *extensive connection*. It appears that 'attribute' relates to 'relation' as 'extension' to 'extensive connection'. An attribute is that without which a thing is unthinkable and for Descartes *extension* is the ultimate attribute of corporeal reality and *thought* is the ultimate attribute of spiritual reality. A relation, on the other hand, does not involve one thing, or one type of things, but several things in their mutual nexūs. The things which the relation involves are already presupposed, with all their necessary and possible at-tributes. Thus 'relation' presupposes 'attribute', and we find the same presupposition of the Cartesian 'extension' in the Whiteheadian 'extensive continuum'. "We diverge from Descartes by holding that what he has described as primary *attributes* of physical bodies, are really the forms of internal relationships *between* actual occasions and *within* actual occasions." [2] But, importantly in my eyes, re-lations do not refer to purely logical entities or hypothetical space-time points, for Whitehead often and explicitly repudiates the notion of 'vacuous actuality'.[3] In proposing the concepts 'subject' and 'superject' there is not only an explicit protest against the

[1] *PR*, Part IV, Ch. I. Sec. IV.
[2] *PR*, Part IV, Chapter III, Sect. V.
[3] e.g. *PR*, 'Preface'.

'bifurcation' of nature and actuality, but also the attempt to conserve unity without sacrificing either the substantial individual or the dynamic relation. A subject is essentially an individual, and a superject represents the focal point of dynamic influences. "There are elements only to be understood by reference to what is beyond the fact in question; and there are elements expressive of the immediate, private, personal, individuality of the fact in question. The former elements express the publicity of the world; the latter elements express the privacy of the individual. An actual entity considered in reference to the publicity of things is a 'superject'; namely, it arises from the publicity which it finds, and it adds itself to the publicity which it transmits. It is a moment of passage from decided public facts to a novel public fact . . . An actual entity considered in reference to the privacy of things is a 'subject'; namely, it is a moment of the genesis of self-enjoyment. It consists of a purposed self-creation out of materials which are at hand in virtue of their publicity." [1] Yet 'subject' and 'superject' are theoretical distinctions, necessitated for the purpose of schematization. In reality both terms refer to each entity, affirms Whitehead. "An actual entity is at once the subject experiencing and the superject of its experiences. It is subject-superject, and neither half of this description can for a moment be lost sight of . . . 'subject' is always to be construed as an abbreviation of 'subject-superject'." [2]

The unity of the concepts of 'relation' and 'substance' is also evident in Whitehead's assessment of the interaction of a given entity with its environment. The endurance of the entity and the features of its environment must be harmonious, for "any physical object which by its influence deteriorates its environment, commits suicide".[3] 'Physical object' stands for subject-superject, and in its capacity of superject it influences its environment, and in its capacity of subject it commits suicide if that influence is detrimental to its own endurance.

Process implies the organic relation of particulars to the totality, and the problem of explaining the particular as distinct from the totality is taken up by Whitehead in the Category of the Ultimate. This category includes the notions 'creativity', 'many' and 'one'. 'One' stands for the "singularity of an entity". The term 'many' "conveys the notion of 'disjunctive diversity' ", and 'creativity' is

[1] *PR*, Part IV, Ch. I, Sect. V.
[2] *PR*, Part I, Ch. II, Sect. IV.
[3] *SMW*, Ch. 6.

the "ultimate principle by which the many, which are the universe disjunctively, become the one actual occasion which is the universe conjunctively".[1]

The Category of the Ultimate describes the 'creative advance' of the world from disjunction to conjunction, accentuates the principle of 'novelty' and embraces all actual entities in process. "The novel entity is at once the togetherness of the 'many' which it finds, and also it is the one among the disjunctive 'one' which it leaves; it is a novel entity, disjunctively among the many entities which it synthesises." [2] In view of this description of creative advance, it would seem that the atomism of traditional metaphysics has been definitely repudiated. This, however, is not the case. While Whitehead claims that "this Category of the Ultimate replaces Aristotle's category of 'primary substance' ", he asserts, "the ultimate metaphysical truth is atomism". It is fairly clear, however, that Whitehead's atomism does not accord well with his cosmology and his insistence on the 'fallacy of misplaced concreteness'. H. N. Lee has shown that the philosophy of organism may be considered to incorporate the extensive continuum as its decisive aspect, while the atomism affirmed by its author is in fact a disturbing and eliminable element.[3] But for us, this is a digression. Important for our purposes is that Whitehead's 'actual entity' is in process and that it is a subject-superject. As superject, the actual entity derives its actuality (or 'being') from the coordinate nature of public facts, and we are invited to consider other entities as its relevant environment. As subject, the actual entity manifests an element of purposive self-creation, and thus it implies that as individual, it is a functional entity. Its function is a property of the entity as subject, and it is conditioned by its environment, in regard to which the actual entity is a superject. Whitehead's concept of function coincides on major points with my concept of 'ontic function'. To function, in Whitehead's words, "means to contribute determination to the actual entities in the nexus of some actual world". "An entity is actual, when it has significance for itself. By this it is meant that an actual entity functions in respect to its own determination." ". . . Self-functioning is the real internal constitution of an actual entity. It is the 'immediacy'of the actual entity. An actual entity is called the 'subject' of its own immediacy." "The final phase in the process of

<hr>

[1] cf. PR., Part I, Ch. 2, Sect. II ('The Category of the Ultimate').
[2] Ibid.
[3] cf. H. N. Lee, 'Causal Efficacy and Continuity in Whitehead's Philosophy', Studies in Whitehead's Philosophy, New Orleans and The Hague, 1961.

concrescence, constituting an actual entity, is one complex, fully determinate feeling. This final phase is termed the 'satisfaction' . . . Each element in the genetic process of an actual entity has one self-consistent function, however complex, in the final satisfaction." [1]

The function of an entity is its self-determination *qua* subject. The function which contributes determination to the entity in the nexus of 'some actual world' is the determination of that entity *qua* superject. But every entity is both subject and superject. Analysed to the functions of other entities as convergent upon the one in question, the entity is the superject of its external determinations ('experiences'). The syndrome of external determinations is one aspect of the determination of the entity, when by "determination" we mean the factors that make the entity what it is, at any given time. External determination is the pole of change acting upon the pole of constancy. The self-determination of the entity is conditioned by external determinations, and the external determinations affect the entity in function of the potency developed by self-determinations for processing influences. External determinations signify the relevant environment of the entity; self-determinations, its own intrinsic nature or potency. In a complete analysis, the entity is seen to be determined by the interaction of its internal function with the function of others.

The function of mind is to assure the extended endurance of the entity; it is that function which is directly implied by the notion of space-time being. The mind functions *for* the entity *by* organizing and processing the syndrome of influences converging upon its space-time locus. Hence mind is a specific manifestation of the ontic function; it presupposes reality, while it is not presupposed by it. This view follows directly from the scheme of philosophy of organism as developed by Whitehead (although Whitehead speaks of "consciousness" where I speak of "mind"). "The principle I am adopting is that consciousness presupposes experience, and not experience consciousness. It is a special element in the subjective forms of some feelings. Thus an actual entity may, or may not, be conscious of some part of its experience. Its experience is its complete formal constitution, including its consciousness, if any." [2] Hence any given entity experiences its environment, and the experience (termed 'feeling') of some entities is in the form of a conscious awareness of the facts of experience. How the syndrome of influences converging upon a given

---

[1] *cf. PR*, Part I, Ch. II, Sect. II ('The Categories of Explanation').
[2] *PR*, Part II, Ch. I, Sect. VI.

particular become differentiated into sensory qualities has been worked out by Hartshorne, on the basis of Peirce's and Whitehead's philosophy. Hartshorne asserts that "the first appearance of a given quality at a certain stage in evolution is not a pure 'emergence' (though it has an emergent aspect) of the quality, unrelated to the previous state of nature, but intelligible in much the same fashion as the appearance of a new organ." [1] Thereby a continuum of undifferentiated and indeterminate 'feeling' can become objectified into particular sensory qualities through 'consciousness', which is merely a "special element in the subjective forms of some feelings". Thus mind is given an explanation that accords with the categories of the process-cosmology, and conscious experience is integrated into the scheme as a property of one entity in universal nexus with the rest.

There is a consistent and an inconsistent aspect to Whitehead's determination of the concept of consciousness. Consistent is his view that mental activity presupposes a process wherein all existents interrelate, and of which it is one special element. Such a view follows logically from the root-axiom 'being'. Inconsistent, on the other hand, is Whitehead's attempt to demonstrate that this view of consciousness follows from the data of immediate experience. Use of the term "consciousness", suggestive of the Cartesian and epistemological view of mind, is perhaps indicative, but certainly not conclusive, of the reductionist function of this concept in philosophy of organism. (It may be that "consciousness" is assessed by Whitehead as I assess "mind".) More conclusive is Whitehead's critique of Hume's thesis on sense-impressions according to which all items of experience are separable, and are only linked together by a belief in the occurrence of certain events when given impressions are contiguous and succeed one another in experience. Hume defined "cause" as "An object precedent and contiguous to another, and so united with it in the imagination, that the idea of the one determines the mind to form the idea of the other, and the impression of the one to form a more lively idea of the other." [2] Such an impression, said Hume, is 'perfectly extraordinary and incomprehensible'.

Whitehead's objection is significant. "If we hold with Hume, that the sole data originating reflective experience are impressions of sensations, and also if we admit with him the obvious fact that no one such impression by its own individual nature discloses any information as to

---

[1] Charles Hartshorne, *The Philosophy and Psychology of Sensation*, Ch. 8.
[2] Hume, *Treatise*, Part III, Sect. XIV.

another such impression, then on that hypothesis the direct evidence for interconnectedness vanishes." [1] The temporal disjunction of Hume's sense-impressions are supplemented by Whitehead through a specific view of experience wherein the interconnectedness of the *percipienda* is a factual datum. The alternative of this conception of experience is seen to lead directly to what Santayana calls (and Whitehead emphatically quotes) the 'solipsism of the present moment.' [2]

The solution Whitehead proposes is the postulation of a notion of experience according to which the past arches over into the future, through the present. The conceptual tool for developing this notion is 'causal efficacy'. "Causal efficacy is the hand of the settled past in the formation of the present".[3] Experience is not instantaneous, but thick enough to contain the immediate past in process of perishing, and the future in process of becoming. This, however, does not follow from an analysis of experience.

One of the results of this doctrine is that it implies the assumption of *absolute* space-time. The alternate solution, namely *relative* space-time, implies instantaneous entities: if time consists of temporal relations among particulars and space of spatial relation among particulars, particulars are instantaneous, having no duration and no extension.[4] One and the same particular cannot be in two places, nor presented on two occasions. Particulars are the measure of space and time and are thus themselves changeless, temporally as well as spatially. But, we cannot hold that instantaneous entities may be empirically *known*, for whatever is perceived, has duration. On the other hand, if entities have duration, then they are no longer the measure of time, and it is difficult to see how their spatial relations can be the measure of space. Hence they exist *in* time and space, and are relative to the space-time framework. This framework means the 'absolute' space-time, wherein spatio-temporal events take place. Space and time do not change with the events, but encompass them. Events are spatio-temporal, and result in space-time structures, but space-time itself is a constant and unchanging framework for occasions.

There is an alternate solution to the problem, however, which involves the re-interpretation of Whitehead's 'actual entities' as 'quantum-monads' that do not endure, but merely inherit the form of

---

[1] *AI*, Ch. 15, Sect. I.
[2] *Symbolism, Its Meaning and Effect*, Ch. 28.
[3] *Idem*, Ch. 50.
[4] For an exposition of this argument see, Reinhardt Grossman, 'Particulars and Time', *Essays in Ontology*, Iowa City and The Hague, 1963.

their predecessors, and are thus instantaneous.[1] But even if this should be possible, it would not change the extreme rationalism of the problem, since neither conception is directly reducible to experience – not even to the experience of 'physical facts'. Relative space-time involves instantaneous entities, failing to meet the criterion of the Principle of Acquaintance. Absolute space-time allows for enduring entities, but places them in a framework which is not dependent upon any particular, and hence it implies that space and time are independent of spatio-temporal particulars. The question can be reduced to the consideration, which of these concepts accords better with philosophy of organism? I believe that absolute space-time is the more indicated solution.[2] This assumption is underscored when we consider the character of philosophy of organism and the character of instantaneous entities. The former does not tolerate the principle of simple location (termed the 'Fallacy of Misplaced Concreteness') while the latter reduces ultimately to entities given in distinct space-time loci. An instantaneous entity has simple location, and although its endurance is merely specious, the succession of hereditary forms preserves the simple location of successive entities. This notion is incompatible with the assertion that "in a certain sense, everything is everywhere at all times. For every location involves an aspect of itself in every other location. Thus every spatio-temporal standpoint mirrors the world."[3] Instantaneous entities would render the nature of reality irrevocably atomic. While Whitehead's atomism stands in strange contrast with his emphasis on continuity, when the latter is taken as the decisive feature of his metaphysics, absolute space-time and enduring entities are the indicated concepts. The problem of the philosophical determination of space and time is complex and the often inconsistent propositions advanced by scientists make its resolution difficult.[4] As far as the present principles are concerned, however, there can be no doubt that of the two rationalistic evils, absolute space-time and instantaneous entities, the former is the lesser one. Neither can satisfy the Principle of Acquaintance, while if we posit the notion of 'space-time being' as the ultimate and unanalysed premiss of realist-constructionist metaphysics, absolute space-time is at least implied while relative space-time is not.

[1] Ivor Leclerc proposed this interpretation in 'Individuals', *Philosophy*, January 1963.
[2] In *Symbolism, Its Meaning and Effect*, for instance, Whitehead makes clear himself, that he has no use for time as pure succession (*cf.* esp., pp. 34–35 and 44–45).
[3] *SMW*, Ch. 5.
[4] It is to be noted that the question of absolute and continuous, or relative and discrete space-time is still entirely open in contemporary theoretical physics.

IV

In process, each entity has an 'ontic function' (or *conatus*) and in that respect all entities are alike. But the function of entities is specified to great diversity, and the specificity of function has to be accounted for. I shall term the *specific* ontic function of a given entity its 'nature', and consider that its 'nature' mirrors the universe from the spatio-temporal standpoint of that particular. The entity's nature is a product of interaction between itself and its environment, and it can be conceived in terms of quality as well as in terms of quantity. Although modern empirical science thinks in terms of quantity and permits qualities to enter only as still unknown quanta, the very same conception of an entity's 'nature' as resulting from and manifested in interaction with its environment, may also be qualitatively defined. Though qualitative definition is less frequent today, a remarkable passage from Bacon (quoted by Whitehead in *SMW* Ch. 3) testifies to its logical feasibility. "It is certain that all bodies whatsoever, though they have no sense, yet they have perception, for when one body is applied to another, there is a kind of election to embrace that which is agreeable, and to exclude or expel that which is ingrate; and whether the body be alterant or altered, evermore a perception precedeth operation; for else all bodies would be like one to another." Bacon's qualitative formulation of the nature of bodies in interaction signifies one extreme of a long philosophic tradition which has ranged between purely quantitative, purely qualitative, and a combination of qualitative and quantitative explanations. Aristotle saw greater complexities with his wide vision and distinguished three sorts of change: qualitative change (alteration), quantitative change (growth and diminution), and change of place (locomotion). Bacon conceived of change in terms of qualities in the 'perception' of objects which "embrace that which is agreeable, and . . . exclude or expel that which is ingrate", while modern empirical natural science tends to see all change in terms of quanta, measuring alteration, distance, energy, direction and size.

But, regardless of how we conceive change, the nature of the body exposed to change is manifest in the process of change itself. The nature of objects will appear to be qualitative if the interaction is so evaluated, but may be seen as quantitative, or as a combination of both. For the purposes of this argument the quantitative or qualitative definition of the nature of objects is of secondary importance; decisive is that objects change according to an element of self-determination and to an element of external determination. Change, in other words, concerns bodies of definite characteristics undergoing definite influences, due to their relations with other bodies of equally definite characteristics. Thus the 'nature' of an entity is simply the function it reveals in interaction with others. It is in the 'nature' of the hydrogen molecule to behave like water when combined with two oxygen molecules, and in the 'nature' of the Earth to describe an elliptical path around the Sun. The factors concerning these 'natures' may be quantified as well as qualified. Which is preferred is irrelevant to the validity of the statement that given extended entities behave in a specific manner and that this manner is due to the interaction of the factors which they incorporate with those incorporated by the interactive partners.

A 'natural entity' (an entity endowed with a 'nature' which is proper to it) is not necessarily a simple individual, but may also be a *compound* individual. It may be a concrescence of items which does not reduce to them, i.e. which acts differently as a whole than as the sum of its parts. A collection of water molecules is merely a certain extension of water, but the specific collection of molecules found in an amoeba is already more than the sum of its parts: it behaves as an amoeba and not as molecular phenomena. The same applies to biological and psychological, as well as to chemical and physical phenomena. But regardless of whether we take a 'society of occasions', a 'society of societies', or a 'simple individual', we shall not find entities either lacking in an inherent nature, or being endowed with categorically different natures. Complexity of structure determines the specific form of the entity's nature, but does not determine whether or not it possesses a nature. The simplest of all entities, the relatively widely spaced hydrogen atoms found in the 'background stuff' of the universe possess a nature, and what is more, their nature includes as potential all the natures of the entities in which they can participate at a future time. This concept of 'nature' is theoretically applicable to all entities, regardless of complexity of structure and organization.

Analyzing the problem of existence from the viewpoint of one entity results in the assertion that it incorporates in its nature all the natures of all existents in the cosmos. It is not enough to define it as a bundle of the influences acting upon it, for all influences have specified characteristics and they imply entities having those characteristics. Characteristics cannot float about between entities, but must inhere in them – lest a purely speculative theory be required to account for them. The central issues are the contentions that being implies extension in space-time, and that the identifiable characteristic of the existent entity is not the change which it undergoes, but the constancy which it preserves. This constancy is a function: a function of space-time extension or, simply, a *function of being*. Every entity shares this function, in that all ontic entities extend in space and endure in time. Their inherent nature, together with the character of all entities, determines their actual space-time locus. The specificality of an entity's 'ontic function', i.e. what I here term its 'nature', is determined by the past of the entity: by its 'historical route' which designates the interactions of the entity with all other entities and lends it its present form and character. In the words of Whitehead, ". . . physical endurance is the progress of continuously inheriting a certain identity of character transmitted throughout a historical route of events. This character belongs to the whole route, and to every event of the route." [1] The 'nature' of the entity is the product of a series of events which have been objectified in past interactions, and have become 'stubborn facts' affecting the extrinsic relations of the entity and conditioning its intrinsic nature.

The process-theory rejects notions of unchanged entities independent of space-time specification. Rather, each entity is held to be that which it is through a series of events consisting of the convergence of cosmic influences upon its historical space-time loci. The interaction qualifies the relations and the nature of the entity, and yields those quanta and qualia with those relational features which the entity at present has (regardless of whether these features are known by an observer). But, since the specification of an entity is a space-time process, its meaningful discussion requires the explication of the directly indicated notions of space and time.

I have suggested that absolute space-time is the indicated framework for modern realist metaphysics. This means that all events take place within the framework of a public space by which they can be measured, and in a public time which determines their simultaneity or succession. Absolute space-time furnishes the concepts for comparing particulars, and integrating them into an organic whole. The whole into which they are thus integrated is the organic society of societies which encompasses all things that are. It is the cosmos, the 'maximal compound individual'.

[1] *SMW*, Ch. 6.

Absolute space-time is the public space-time of all particulars, meaningful if we assume the position of a universal intelligence, free to roam the natural world uncommitted to any one standpoint. Absolute space-time exists for the intelligence liberated from the commitments of one spatio-temporal body and its specific locus. Such an intelligence is a rationalistic abstraction, presupposed by the heuristic principle and warranted by the realist basic assumptions. From its viewpoint the notion of absolute space-time may be maintained; therefore, in this prototype of realistic reasoning we can legitimately inquire into the status of particulars in absolute space-time.

In 'process' each particular has a location which is not 'simple' but cosmic, in that it incorporates the aspects of the totality from that particular viewpoint. Correspondingly, the totality incorporates that locus as one part of its organic wholeness. No part is independent from any other by virtue of being a constituent of the encompassing totality which is more than a mere aggregate. The space-time common to all particulars determines the constitution of each particular, and becomes specified according to the locus of that particular within the whole. Consequently the particular acquires that nature which corresponds to its own *private* space-time, representing a specific standpoint within *absolute* space-time; absolute space-time being the *public* space-time of particulars.

The factor of time, which is determinant for the particular, is relative to its historical spatial loci. 'Time' refers to the hypothetical instant when the process began. That instant has had only spatial relations: it has not known differentiated entities, but only one common substantial substratum which has included in potential the capacity for specification. When the first, unenduring instant has been succeeded by a second, the two have formed a duration. In that duration the spatial nexus of the entities have undergone change corresponding to their relative distance from one another. (In physical terminology: the haze of background stuff consisting of hydrogen atoms has manifested the first stirrings toward the formation of vortexes which were later to compress and lead to the formation of stellar systems.) The element of time has added a measure of specification to the particulars existing at the beginnings of process; duration has specified the entities themselves according to their extrinsic spatial nexus. Hence duration has become an intrinsic factor in the nature of each entity. Space, however, has remained extrinsic to it, functioning as the means of temporal specification. Had all entities been distributed evenly in space at the beginning of the process, we could not account for differentiation between them under this hypothesis (nor could we logically account for that differentiation under any current scientific hypothesis). We must assume that spatial unevenness was present at the instant when the process began. Another way of expressing this is to say that the process began *when* unevenness of distribution – due to a cause which could never be deduced from the observation of the process itself – was introduced. Thereafter time had the role of specifying particulars according to their increasingly uneven spatial distribution. In the process each particular gained a locus in space, and corresponding to the relational influences converging upon its locus, also a temporal standpoint distinct from that of all other entities. As a result, in process, each particular has its own private space-time. Private spatial loci given dimension in time (i.e. given endurance) result in differentiated particulars. Relative differences are due to the element of time being added to that of space: space and time jointly determine the specific nature of each entity. The spatio-temporal differentiation of particulars takes place within one public space-time realm: absolute space and absolute time. Thus it comes about that although each particular is at a different temporal locus from all others, it is yet simultaneous with them. 'Simultaneity' means measuring with the space-time of the cosmic 'whole' of which all particulars are constituent parts; by the cosmic yardstick all particulars coexist in one space-time. 'Different temporal loci' means measuring by the yardstick of the given particular; from its standpoint we look at a world composed of particulars, differentiated among themselves corresponding to their locus in time. We then observe that the difference of each particular is due to its spatial locus determining a different temporal locus within the process.

We obtain this conclusion when we construct (theoretically) a clock, which keeps time according to the total rate of change taking place in the range of absolute (public) space-time. *Alpha* is the beginning of the process; *Omega* is its end, *qua* process (final entropy).[1] If we then assume that we can follow the process throughout its total range of space and time, we can observe the changes it undergoes. (Analytically, these changes refer to changing particulars.) We can thus obtain an average rate of change from *Alpha* to *Omega*, and can grade our clock to record this 'public' rate of change. Thus we will measure,

[1] As regards the finiteness of process, this scheme presupposes the evolutionary theory, rather than the theory of continuous creation.

in a sense, the absolute time of the cosmos. We can then construct individual clocks for each particular and measure its rate of change *against* that of all change in the process. Differences will occur between the time of change of the particulars and the public rate of change according to the distribution of particulars in space. We can chart the private temporal loci according to observed diversities by referring to the absolute time of the cosmic clock. At all times the differences will balance, since the absolute time is the public time, and the total rate of the change is the average rate of change of particulars. We will then come to the conclusion that particulars, existing each in its own space and time, are nevertheless simultaneous: the decisive question is merely which clock we are reading. The cosmic clock shows all particulars as simultaneous, spaced within a common absolute dimension of time; the individual clocks show each particular as existing in its own time.

Measuring by the clocks of particulars we shall find that temporal specification involves and differentiates spatial nexus. Private space implies private time, and private time implies private space. The process-existence of an entity specifies its individual being and its individual being in turn specifies its process-existence. Differentiated entities behave differently in process; if they did not, all entities would be undifferentiated and purely passive agents, and activity would have to be introduced as a distinct principle. Such vitalistic assumptions degrade entities to mere passive 'matter', and superimpose upon them a formal principle. The transcendentalist explanation works, but is uneconomical. It is unable to account for evolution as a property of that which evolves, and brings in a principle (strongly resembling a will) which makes things into what they are. It is as though an inert mass was being purposively moulded. The more efficient explanation lies in the attribution of active nature to particulars, assuming that all particulars are structural unities, specified by the space-time process of the cosmos. Thus, each entity is acted upon by all others and in turn acts upon every other. The action is concordant with the actual specifics of the acting entities. The reaction qualifies the active influence in accordance with the nature of the entity acted upon. The *reaction* of one entity is the *action* of that entity seen from the standpoint of *another:* each entity acts by reacting. Expressed more concisely, the influence exerted by each entity is in accordance with its nature, and, since its nature is specified by exposure to the influences converging upon its standpoint in space over the duration of its existence, 'acting in accordance with intrinsic nature' means having extrinsic relations in the form of formative interactions. The extrinsic factor of space and the intrinsic factor of time are fused in the 'nature' of the entity. Its nature is dynamic: it is part of the dynamic cosmic process. It is part of a great chain of interaction which qualifies it, and which simultaneously qualifies all other parts of the process. Diversity is the result as regards the particulars, and functional interdependence as regards the parts of the whole. Diverse particulars are functionally interdetermined parts. The answer to whether they are diverse, or harmonious, depends upon our viewpoint. Diversity is seen from the viewpoint of particulars, functional harmony from that of the whole. But, diversity and functional harmony are not contradictory; unity is not necessarily internally homogeneous. Similarly, the private space-time of particulars and the public space-time of the whole are entirely compatible. Private space-time signifies the specific and diversified nature of dynamic particulars; public space-time signifies the consistent harmony of all particulars within the dynamic whole.

This conception of space-time differentiation permits the inductive generalization of the principle of ontic function. This function is simply one which all entities have regardless of their private space-time. The function is shared by all entities, for it is equivalent to the above developed conception of the dynamic 'nature' of particulars. The function is the manifestation of that nature in reaction to extrinsic influences concordantly with the 'historical route' of the entity: entities have functions corresponding to their evolutionary history. Insofar as the evolution of particulars in the process lies in the direction of complexity, their function will be adopted to the requirements of the compound individual. Viewed from the standpoint of the compound entity, it will appear to be correspondingly complex. Yet, it is basically the function of all entities, and it harmonizes with them.

Relative progression in the direction of the evolution of the process depends upon the spatial relations of the entity in its past and present. When the entity is located in a position which provides favourable terrain for interaction, i.e. where influence from others may be directly utilized for the maintenance of the entity, the entity progresses more rapidly than entities in a spatial locus which does not furnish the proper coordinates for evolution. I assume hereby that the ontic function of the entity (specified by its spatial relations to a particular temporal level) is *evolutionary*, and by that I mean that it is concordant with the direction of change in the process as a whole. Change in turn, is definable as the progression from simplicity to complexity of structure and is manifest in particulars as the specific rate of progression (measured by their private clock) from simple individuals to compound individuals. Evolution determines simple individuals to form organically interconnected parts of compound entities, and compound entities to form similarly interdetermined parts of societies of compound entities, to reach ultimately to the maximal compound entity – the 'ultimate individual' – i.e. the cosmos as a whole. Entities in poor environments lag behind this general progression, and are analysable to a private progression-time which is below that of the level of general complexity in the universe. Entities in favourable environments overtake the average level of evolution and, their complexity being greater than that of the average level in the universe, their progression-time exceeds the one shown by the cosmic clock. Simple entities are in the relative past, complex entities in the relative future.

But analysis to 'individuals' is a theoretical and arbitrary abstraction, for all entities are parts of greater entities and, ultimately, of the maximal entity, the universe itself. The distinction concerns only the particulars we wish to abstract from process and examine in themselves. Thus, certain individuals so abstracted can be analysed to a society of organic compounds, and these can be denoted 'compound individuals'. Other individuals can be analysed to lesser components, and some will turn out to be simple, having no parts. (The latter, as far as our knowledge of the nature of the universe goes, are the subatomic particles.) But, when we abstract a human being, we can analyse him to atoms, molecules, cells, tissues and his various organs. Together, they constitute the individual we call 'man'. Singly, each of these constituents is an entity, interfunctioning within the human being and conjointly affording the ontic function on the human level. But this is not to deny that the components themselves have ontic function. Each cell may be considered a 'being' in the same sense that we consider man a 'being'. In turn, the environment of the human individual together with him as particular entity, constitutes a higher totality, a society of the compound individuals 'men', which is itself a compound individual, but of a higher (i.e. of a 'social') order.

Each of these 'orders' or 'levels' of individuality can be measured and distinguished by reference to differences obtaining between the cosmic and the particular clocks. 'Advanced' is the individual whose clock shows a time typical of a future epoch, 'backward' the one whose clock shows a time typical of a past epoch. All entities coexist in absolute (public) space-time, and are available for the scrutiny of a hypothetical cosmic intelligence. They are disjunctive as particulars, although their disjunction concerns only their space-time locus and not isolation and abstraction. Each entity is at all times everywhere, but it is everywhere by virtue of its relations; and it relates in space and time. 'Disjunction' and 'conjunction' are different theoretical concepts to account for the solidarity of all elements of the process in view of its diversity as consisting of particular events, and its unity as one encompassing whole.

V

Among the various specific problems raised by the determination of the principles of process, two further problem-complexes stand out. These are the *problems of universals*, and the *problems of law and relations*.

With respect to the problem of universals (which I shall consider first) two clear-cut positions are possible, with diverse shadings in between: realism and nominalism. Realism concerns the assertion of the reality of universals, nominalism their denial. Due to the poverty of philosophical terminology in this respect, "realism" is counterposed to nominalism in ontology and to scepticism or "idealism" in epistemology. Yet realism has an entirely different meaning in the first use than in the second. As a matter of fact it has meaning in the first sense only if it is admitted in the second: some degree of epistemological realism must be given in order to consider that the problem of whether universals are *ante rem* or *post rem* is at all meaningful. Full scepticism will deny the meaning of ontology and by that token also the meaning of the problem of universals.

While a degree of epistemological realism is a precondition of ontology, it does not decide the question of ontological realism. The most naïve epistemological realist may be an ontological nominalist (indeed, will tend to be that), while a moderate sceptic, such as a reductionist, may opt for realism. But the opposite combinations are equally possible, though perhaps less frequent. On the purely ontological level no argument has been forthcoming which would have settled the problem definitely.

Consider the simple and classical ontological root-metaphor, 'this is red'. Realists tend to assert that this sentence refers to two entities (or two kinds of entities) one of which corresponds to the meaning of 'this' and the other to the meaning of 'red'. They claim that 'red' and 'this' stand in the relation exemplified by 'is'. This assertion is contested by the Principle of Acquaintance which demands that ontological description refer to entities with which one is directly acquainted. Russell says, "one is tempted to regard 'This is red' as a subject-predicate proposition; but if one does so, one finds that 'this' becomes a substance, an unknowable something in which predicates inhere, but which, nevertheless, is not identical with the sum of its predicates." [1] One cannot be actually acquainted with a red entity except as red and as entity together. In fact, one is neither acquainted with the 'bare particular' which is the entity without consideration of 'red', nor with the character of redness without some entity of which it is asserted. Thus we have two unanalysable entities of different kinds which, while explaining the proposition 'this is red' as logically consistent with all further ontological propositions through the individual-character analysis, do not let us conclude that the elements to which the entity has been thus analyzed are empirically knowable.

If realism is faced with serious objections on epistemological grounds, nominalism is open to criticism on the basis of inapplicability to many typically metaphysical problems. A set of metaphysical principles such as those postulated for 'process' imply the existence of universals in some sense. A series of distinct particulars could account neither for the categories of the scheme nor for the organic interdetermination of simple or compound individuals. Under the thesis of pure nominalism the definition of 'individual' would come up against insurmountable difficulties in philosophy of organism, since particulars are denied simple location, hence they cannot be 'pointed at' nor analysed to something 'here-now'. While realism can be criticised on the basis of the Principle of Acquaintance, nominalism can be criticised on its limitation of applicability to process-metaphysics. In an important sense, the objection to nominalism is on grounds of adequacy, and to realism on those of experientiality. As the present investigation must satisfy the criterion of adequacy, regardless of whether it does or does not satisfy experientiality, we may assume the realist position. But, we must note that the realism of the process-metaphysician is not the realism of the traditional ontologist; universals and particulars lose the sharp distinction they have in Platonism. As one entity is, in a sense, in every other, so is the universal in each particular, and all particulars constitute, by exemplification, the universal. This position

---

[1] Russell, *An Inquiry Into Meaning and Truth*, Ch. 6.

has been defined by Whitehead in a trenchant passage in which he repudiates the terms 'universal' and 'particular', holding them misleading in the context of his process-metaphysics.

"The antithetical terms 'universals' and 'particulars' are the usual words employed to denote respectively entities which nearly, though not quite, correspond to the entities here termed 'eternal objects', and 'actual entities.' These terms, 'universals' and 'particulars', both in the suggestiveness of the two words and in their current philosophical use, are somewhat misleading. The ontological principle, and the wider doctrine of universal relativity, on which the present metaphysical discussion is founded, blur the sharp distinction between what is universal and what is particular. The notion of a universal is of that which can enter into the description of many particulars; whereas the notion of a particular is that it is described by universals, and does not itself enter into the description of any other particular. According to the doctrine of relativity which is the basis of the metaphysical system of the present lectures, both these notions involve a misconception. An actual entity cannot be described, even inadequately, by universals; because other actual entities do enter into the description of any one actual entity. Thus every so-called 'universal' is particular in the sense of being just what it is, diverse from everything else; and every so-called 'particular' is universal in the sense of entering into the constitutions of other actual entities." [1]

Elsewhere, Whitehead writes, "reality is the process. It is nonsense to ask if the colour red is real. The colour red is ingredient in the process of realisation." [2] What is 'real' then? Real, for Whitehead, are (among others) 'eternal objects.' Now, this will appear as a surprising fact when we consider that eternal objects closely resemble universals, and are in fact their organistic counterparts. Would not a notion of substance as dynamic, self-determinant actuality better accord with the scheme of philosophy of organism? If so, then why are eternal objects so emphatically introduced?

It is possible that a thinker owes much to influences of which he himself is not fully aware. It may be that Whitehead's profound admiration and study of Plato and his appreciation of the Platonic 'ideas' had much to do with the introduction of 'eternal objects' into his own philosophy. But this is conjecture. The fact is that the essentially Platonic 'eternal objects' are present in his metaphysic,

[1] *PR*, Part II, Ch. I, Sect. V.
[2] *SMW*, Ch. 4.

notwithstanding the repudiation of universals as such. Now it is evident that the other great traditional solution to the problem, Aristotle's 'primary substance', which is "neither asserted of a subject, nor present in a subject" is not directly applicable to Whitehead's scheme either, for, as Whitehead says, "The principle of universal relativity directly traverses Aristotle's dictum, '(A substance) is not present in a subject'. On the contrary, according to this principle an actual entity *is* present in other actual entities. In fact if we allow for degrees of relevance, and for negligible relevance, we must say that every actual entity is present in every other actual entity. The philosophy of organism is mainly devoted to the task of making clear the notion of 'being present in another entity'." [1] Yet, it seems to me that making this notion clear does not imply the reification of universals. Rather, it implies a notion of substance which can be predicated of every entity; one that is *causa sui*. If substance remains purely actual, the sum of actual substantive events gives us the universe: all there is to reality. Such a contention follows, as a matter of fact, directly from Whitehead's own definition of the 'solidarity of the universe': "The perceptive constitution of the actual entity presents the problem, How can the other actual entities, each with its own formal existence, also enter objectively into the perceptive constitution of the actual entity in question? This is the problem of the solidarity of the universe. The classical doctrines of universals and particulars, of subject and predicate, of individual substances not present in other individual substances, of the externality of relations, alike render this problem incapable of solution. The answer given by organic philosophy is the doctrine of prehensions, involved in concrescent integrations, and terminating in a definite, complex unity of feeling. To be actual must mean that all actual things are objects, enjoying objective immortality in fashioning creative actions; and that all actual things are subjects, each prehending the universe from which it arises. The creative action is the universe always becoming one in a particular unity of self-experience, and thereby adding to the multiplicity which is the universe as many. This insistent concrescence into unity is the outcome of the ultimate self-identity of each entity. No entity – be it 'universal' or 'particular' – can play disjoined roles. Self-identity requires that every entity have one conjoined self-consistent function, whatever be the complexity of that function." [2]

[1] *PR*, Part II, Ch. I, Sect. V.
[2] *PR*, Part II, Ch. I, Sect. VI.

The "doctrine of prehensions, involved in concrescent integrations, and terminating in a definite, complex unity of feeling" needs no reified universals, for it can be more consistently explained in reference to actual objects, following Whitehead's own statement that "to be actual must mean that all actual things are alike objects . . . and that all actual things are alike subjects". Yet, Whitehead postulated the notion of eternal objects and insisted that they enter into the acts of prehensions of each actual entity. Now this notion introduces an element of indeterminacy which accords badly with the notion that all prehension terminate 'in a definite, complex unity of feeling', since, for the purposes of this termination, a substance containing the element of formal determination within itself appears more suitable than the notion of real 'eternal objects'.

The suggestion is made here that Whitehead introduced the notion of eternal objects in the reductionistic effort to render his scheme concordant with the facts of immediate experience. There are several cogent passages in Whitehead's writings which support this hypothesis.

Already in *Science and the Modern World*, Whitehead expressed concern over the tenability of the concept evolved into the notion of the 'solidarity of the universe' in the light of immediate experience. The solidarity of the universe implies exclusively internal relations, which present the difficulty that "In so far as there are internal relations, everything must depend upon everything else. But if this be the case, we cannot know about anything till we equally know everything else. Apparently, therefore, we are under the necessity of saying everything at once." [1] Whitehead avoided this difficulty in postulating the 'abstractive hierarchy' of eternal objects. "The difficulty inherent in the concept of finite internal relations among eternal objects is thus evaded by two metaphysical principles, (i) that the relationships of any eternal object A, considered as constitutive of A, merely involve other eternal objects as bare relata without reference to their individual essences, and (ii) that the divisibility of the general relationship of A into a multiplicity of finite relationships of A stands therefore in the essence of that eternal object." [2] By 'isolating' eternal objects, Whitehead appears to seek (and believes to have found) a logical starting point for his description of process and of reality. The scheme of 'abstractive hierarchies' seems to be based upon the necessity of finding an identifiable group of events which

[1] *SMW*, Ch. 10.
[2] *Ibid.*

may form the starting point for the inference of further events. While actual entities cannot provide this starting point, since they are consolidated by virtue of their internal relations into a universal whole which must be known before any actual entity could be known, eternal objects *are* isolable and thus the development of the scheme may be anchored on them. It is evident, however, that this difficulty is real only if we insist – as Whitehead does – that the scheme must be inferred from concrete, irreducible facts of experience. If we can abandon this requirement, we render the difficulty spurious. Eternal objects become superfluous then, in function of their isolability.

In *Process and Reality* however, eternal objects also function as the 'principle of indetermination'. But even in that capacity, they can be shown to be a result of Whiteheads' attempt to reduce his cosmology to immediate experience. It is stated in the *ninth Categoreal Obligation*: "The concrescence of each individual actual entity is internally determined and is externally free." [1] The second function of eternal objects within the philosophy of organism is to explain this freedom as the principle of indetermination with respect to actualities. "An eternal object is always a potentiality for actual entities; but in itself, as conceptually felt, it is neutral as to the fact of its physical ingression in any particular actual entity of the temporal world. 'Potentiality' is the correlative of 'givenness'. The meaning of 'givenness' is that what *is* 'given' might not have been 'given'; and that what *is not* 'given' *might have been* 'given'.[2]

The eternal object is 'conceptually felt' as such, but, " 'conceptual recognition' must of course be an operation constituting a real feeling belonging to some actual entity." [3] Conceptual recognition would appear to be a form of internal relationship binding all actual entities. Yet it is not that, for internal relations are determinate and eternal objects are indeterminate in relation to actual entities (i.e. to their realization as actualities). "The point is that the actual subject which is merely conceiving the eternal object is not thereby in direct relationship to some other actual entity, apart from any other peculiarity in the composition of that conceiving subject.[4] But, the solidarity of the universe leaves no room for relations which are not actual and are contingent with respect to actualities. Consequently, determination of final feeling in the mechanism of the process-cosmology, and

[1] *PR*, Part I, Ch. II, Sect. III.
[2] *PR*, Part II, Ch. I, Sect. III.
[3] *Ibid.*
[4] *Ibid.*

indetermination in the conceptual recognition of eternal objects (which, as Whitehead says, represent the term for 'Platonic forms' devoid of misleading suggestions) are internally contradictory.

However, Whitehead's postulation of eternal objects becomes understandable when we take into account his concern to explain his scheme consistently with the following facts of human experience: "... in the case of those actualities whose immediate experience is most completely open to us, namely, human beings, the final decision of the immediate subject-superject, constituting the ultimate modification of subjective aim, is the foundation of our experience of responsibility, of approbation or of disapprobation, of self-approval, or of self-reproach, of freedom, of emphasis. This element in experience is too large to be put aside merely as misconstruction. It governs the whole tone of human life ..." [1] The freedom of human beings as presented in moral experience is transposed by Whitehead through inductive generalisation to a principle of cosmology. "The ultimate freedom of things, lying beyond all determinations, was whispered by Galileo – *E pur si muove* – freedom for the inquisitors to think wrongly, for Galileo to think rightly, and for the world to move in despite of Galileo and inquisitors." [2]

The primary function of Whitehead's eternal objects thus appears to be an epistemological one: to support the empirical pretensions of the metaphysical scheme through providing a logical and ostensibly empirical starting point for its construction and by helping to account for the feeling and appreciation of human freedom. Therefore, 'eternal objects' function analogously to 'causal efficacy' insofar as both are to permit the reduction of the metaphysical categories to the facts of immediate experience. The introduction of causal efficacy has as its consequence the critique of Hume's division of sense-impressions as leading to the 'solipsism of the present moment', and the introduction of eternal objects results in a dichotomy of the otherwise exemplarily consistent concept of process, by the notion of 'dipolarity'. "Thus the process of becoming is dipolar (i) by reason of its qualification by the determinateness of the actual world, and (ii) by its conceptual prehension of the indeterminateness of eternal objects." [3] Here the *determinateness* of concrete actuality is counterposed to the *indeterminateness* of universals in the guise of eternal objects. If external

[1] *PR*, Part II, Ch. I, Sect. IV.
[2] *Ibid.*
[3] *Idem*, Part II, Ch. I. Sect. III.

objects have been introduced, partly in order to provide a starting point for metaphysical schematization, partly to account for the experience of human freedom, then they represent the conceptual tools for Whitehead's attempted reduction of his metaphysical categories to the facts of experience. The question now to be considered is whether or not eternal objects are eliminable by replacing their function with that of more overtly and consistently realist concepts.

My impression of Whitehead's philosophy of organism is that it is entirely independent of principles of indetermination; that, on the contrary, it directly suggests determinism. Organic philosophy is the doctrine of prehension, says Whitehead, and prehension means concrescent integration terminating in a definite unity of feeling, regardless of the complexity of the feeling and of the function leading to the feeling. The actual world is determinate, and I see no reason other than a reductionist one to introduce an other-than-actual world of indeterminacy. Instead of this world and its eternal objects, the conception of a substance harbouring the formal determination of change is indicated. Such a Spinozistic one-substance theory incorporates the notion of universals as the principle of formal, determinate change, by virtue of which things are *what* they are. It also incorporates the notion of 'matter', by virtue of which things *are*. It manifests a delimited process *causa sui* and thus implies the postulation of principles which are the eternal and infinite grounds of this limited process. Universals are inherent in self-determinate substance.[1] The analysis of actualities to subjects and predicates, to characters and individuals is a mistatement of the problem. The problem is to conceive of the category of 'being' as composed of substantive entities self-determined within their universal nexus, expressing the full determination of the solidarity of the universe in their identity, and abstractable from the cosmos merely by an arbitrary act of analytic scrutiny. The notion of universals as principles distinct from particulars, even in the guise of eternal objects which are realized in particulars (but are distinct from them nevertheless) casts a dualistic shadow on the consistency of process-metaphysics. Since the notion of determinate form and recurrent identity demands the postulation of concepts resembling universals, the best we can do is to 'fold' them into the concept of substance which becomes, by that token, the principle of activity, in addition to being the principle of actuality. "Dynamic Actuality" is to characterize the substance which is the

---

[1] I have expounded this idea in *Essential Society*, Part I.

ground for the incontrovertible *fact*, and the purposive *act*, of every being. 'Be*ing* beings' as particulars, can be abstracted from this notion of 'Dynamic Actuality' only arbitrarily, and this fact may be aggravating to thinkers who believe in the possibility of empirically descriptive metaphysics. But, for the purposes of a consistently realist philosophy this problem is spurious.

VI

The second problem-complex I wish to examine concerns the notion of 'law' and 'relations'. 'Dynamic Actuality', as the substance incorporating universals lending formal determination to particulars, provides the conceptual tools for tackling the problem raised by law. The problem is a typically philosophical one, for, though numerous inquiries operate on the basis of an assumption of law, none of them (as Bochenski points out [1]) make it their concern to inquire just what 'law' *is*. In addition, the laws used by the specialized disciplines (including the empirical natural sciences) tend to be *ad hoc* principles adopted because they provide adequate explanation of certain, delimited groups of phenomena. The concept of law itself, and the concept of a universal law expressing the solidarity of all partial explanations of reality, poses a philosophical, more specifically a *metaphysical* problem.

Law in the metaphysical sense, is not an epistemological principle, such as intentionality in Husserl, or belief in the causal interconnectedness of things given in perception in Hume. Law must express the principle of interconnectedness reigning in the ontic world but including the perceiving subject as 'one among many'. These laws are not 'created', in any sense of the term, by the mind, spirit or intellect, but can only be *known* by the cognising faculties.

Whether or not such laws may be directly inferred from the most immediate facts of experience, and when so inferred, whether they apply to the facts of experience or to facts of the physical world, does not greatly bother the consistent realist, since he argues from an axiomatic notion of objective being. Hence whatever laws he discovers apply to 'physical facts' rather than to 'epistemic facts', and he assumes that if he finds epistemic correlates for his theoretically postulated physical objects these are sufficient to prove the latter's existence. The question that occupies him – and hence us, at present – concerns the status of these laws. There are two major possibilities arising from

---

[1] *cf.* Bochenski, *Wege zum philosophischen Denken*, Freiburg im Br., 1961, Ch. 1.

the adoption of the corresponding two major standpoints. One is Immanentism, and results in the notion of law as *immanent law*. The other is Transcendentalism, and gives rise to the notion of *imposed law*. The decision as to which of these kinds of laws should be asserted may be influenced by empirical considerations as well as by acts of faith. Whitehead, we have seen, was led to espouse eternal objects and the position of Transcendentalism in that particular respect (though in few others) due to concern over the empiricism of his scheme. The case is the converse in theology, where concern over matters of belief leads to the position of Transcendentalism and to the resulting notion of imposed ('divine') law. Since I am not particularly concerned to demonstrate the empiricism of this scheme, holding such effort to be futile if attempted through a direct reduction of the physical facts with which we must deal to epistemic facts, and since I am not led by consideration of acts of faith either, my problem is to decide whether *immanent* or *imposed* law accords most consistently and economically with the realist process-cosmology I have outlined above.

Consider first the case for imposed law. The notion of imposed law presupposes the doctrine of external relations in addition to the doctrine of internal relations. External relations involve transcendental entities as the ultimate constituents of reality, understandable in abstraction. The ultimate truth with respect to any such entity is that it requires nothing but itself in order to exist. But, this classical metaphysical doctrine must be extended in modern process-cosmologies to include the realm of entities bound and determined by mutual relations. Hence in addition to a set of entities determined as to their nature and characteristics by interactions, imposed law requires the postulation of another set of entities (or one such entity, e.g. God) which are not determined by others, but require only themselves to exist. On the other hand, they do determine the mutually determined set of entities. Hence the relations binding the interdetermined entities are internal relations, and the relations binding the interdetermined entities to the ultimate entities are external relations. External relations determine the permanent aspects of changing things, acting – in the guise of universals, characters, Ideas, eternal objects, or the like – as formative principles of actuality. They are imposed as the Law of Nature, upon observable nature. But these imposed laws stand behind or beyond actuality, and are not part of it. As Whitehead remarked "you cannot discover the nature of the relata by any study of the Laws of their relations. Nor, conversely, can you discover the laws by inspection of the natures. The explanation of the doctrine of Imposition both suggests a certain type of Deism, and conversely it is the outcome of such a Deistic belief if already entertained." [1] That such imposed laws cannot be discovered by the inspection of the nature of any particular does not constitute a reason for abandoning them, for we argue at present from an axiomatic objectivist premiss. But that these laws may be redundant, since they have to be postulated *in addition to* immanent laws, could be a valid objection. Thus the problem amounts to whether or not purely internal relations are sufficient in the context of process-cosmology? The answer is given by consideration of my notion of 'Dynamic Actuality'. Therein, formal determination and formed substance are fused into one universal principle, self-determined, and thus determinant of all its parts conjointly. Analysed to particulars, Dynamic Actuality gives us dynamically actual individuals, bound and determined by internal relations. There is no transcendence of actuality – all that exists is actual, inherent in actuality as a potentiality realizable in the course of process. The standpoint upon which Dynamic Actuality is based is purely immanentist, and it results in the postulation of immanent laws, determining internal relations. The maximal compound-individual – the universe as an organic totality – has no relations with other entities, for it embraces all relations. Thus within that totality, all relations are internal and no reference is made to entities or principles which would transcend the whole.

The fact that, when analytically abstracted, any given entity (with the exception of the simple individual) can be seen to manifest relations which determine its nature intrinsically and relations which determine its nature extrinsically, need not mislead us, for references to 'intrinsic' and 'extrinsic' are due to arbitrary analytical abstraction. From the viewpoint of the analysed entity the relations *constituting* its nature are internal and the relations *conditioning* its nature are external. But all these relations are immanent within the 'maximal compound entity' (the cosmos as a whole) and are consequently immanent to the process itself: they are determined by *immanent* laws.

Dynamic Actuality is self-determined; each of its parts is determined by itself conjointly with all other parts. The notion of immanent law law is sufficient to determine the relations binding any part of Dynamic Actuality to every other, and the case for immanent law is strong enough to disqualify the notion of imposed law in a realist scheme which values economy as highly as consistency.

[1] *AI*, Ch. 7.

PUBLIC KNOWLEDGE FROM ONTIC PROCESS

I developed the above prototype of realist reasoning through a critique of Whitehead's philosophy of organism from a standpoint justified by the thesis that all attempts at reductionism are bound to failure and that, as a result, elements of realist-metaphysical thought introduced merely to permit the reduction of the system to the facts of immediate experience are eliminable, since their function is spurious and superfluous with respect to the scheme itself. Hence I have criticised the principles of 'eternal objects', and 'imposed law' and the latter's corollary 'external relations', and attempted to replace the former by an arrangement of universals which permits the formulation of the concept of substance as self-determined Dynamic Actuality, and the latter by the notion of immanent law and internal relations, implied by the notion of Dynamic Actuality. Through the heuristic principle of 'process' I analysed and explored the realist's notion of space-time being and determined the concept 'ontic function'. My purpose now is to define the kinds of knowledge implied by space-time existence in an ontic process.

The kind of knowledge we can derive from the scheme will be *public*, since it is always the experience of one entity interacting with others that furnishes the matrix of knowledge. Thus all data of knowledge attributable to entities on whatever level of existence, will consist of the apprehension of physical facts in the form of epistemic events. There is an *a priori* certitude, by virtue of the realism basic to the scheme, that whatever is apprehended refers to or indicates real events in the real world external to the locus of its apprehension: there *is* a physical 'left-over' beyond apprehension. The act of apprehension is always by a real entity, i.e. by "one ego-object amid objects".

Another point to be emphasized is that knowledge will be assigned to entities in function of their experience and their experience assessed in relation to their level of existence, measured by the progression-time shown by their private clock. Hence knowledge will be deduced from the scheme, and only the scheme can serve as its verifier. There will be no attempt to make the postulated forms of knowledge check with the facts discovered in an analysis of immediate experience. No reduction of the physical facts to epistemic facts will be undertaken, for I consider such reduction futile and – if the scheme of verification I propose works – also unnecessary. The premiss-criterion is adequacy, and the conclusions are 'proven' if they follow consistently and economically from the root-axiom "being" explored and explicated through the heuristic principle "process."

THE CATEGORIES OF ENTITIES

Entities can be identified and their private space-time within absolute (public) space-time determined, by recourse to the concept of the one determinate and self-consistent function they manifest. The function is universal in essential nature, but is specified corresponding to the space-time of the given entity. As universal function, ontic function is striving toward extended-endurance, i.e. toward the stabilization of the entity's actual structure. There are several grades of function to be distinguished, ranging from the function of a subatomic particle to the function of galaxies and including the range of biological evolution such as we witness on earth. The grading of functions according to level implies progression by leaps from level to level. This is false, and is a corollary of the rigidity of classificatory schemes. The function is continuous, manifesting an unbroken line from the simplest entity involving the least mass, to the most complex, possessing the greatest mass. This is not to say that all parts of the continuity of evolving entities are available to inspection: parts of the continuity have to be deduced from the observed evolutionary phenomena of the process. These phenomena are generalized in the thesis that whatever differences in function (or 'nature') are observed, are historically reducible to homogeneity in the primordial state. The stuff of the universe is homogeneous, but is capable of specification into a diversified continuum. The continuum can be qualitatively, as well as quantitatively conceived. In process-metaphysics both quality and quantity are fused into the concept of space-time diversity from homogeneous beginnings. Quality means measuring with the yardstick of a particular on the basis of its direct experience of others: it means measuring particular spatial relations according to the immediacy of the temporal standpoint. Quantity signifies transcendence of subjective temporality and measurement with the universal yardstick of a cosmic intelligence; it means abstraction from the immediacy of particular space-time standpoints, and represents a view of such standpoints in relation to the whole, i.e. through the concepts of an objective totality with its own space-time, which relates to the private space-time of particulars as the absolute to the relative.

Physical Entities

It is asserted on scientific grounds that certain species of elementary particles (that is, those units of 'substance' or 'stuff' or 'wave' which at the present time appear to be indivisible) engage in associations with other elementary particles whereby a total effect results which endures in space and time. It is within these total effects that the elementary particles emerge, according to the role they play within that primary entity. An entity is known by the qualification of the effect of another entity and the resulting qualification of the other entity through the influence of this qualification. In other words an entity is known by its relations, wherein its nature is functionally manifest. When it ceases to have constant relations with its associates, the entity appears to lose its identity; it has to be discovered in the context of other relations. However, there is no way to establish the personal identity of the particular as having changed from the former, and now discontinued set of relations, to the other, new and actual set. To all appearances (and as far as experimental experience goes) it is a new particular. Hence an entity can be said to endure as an individual only as long as it has stable relations; thereafter it continues to be a part of the cosmic process which is self-enclosed, from which nothing can escape, and to which nothing can be added, but it is lost as an identifiable particular. Hence the determination of the duration of an entity depends upon the stability of its relations. These in turn depend on the associations which the entity finds in its environment. Associations among mutually compatible entities counteract tendencies to alter relations (hence to lose identity) by providing an environment favourable to the historical nature of the entity. We can conceive of the atom as such an association on a basic level. An example is provided by the association of a positively charged nucleus with electrons of negative charge, resulting in a 'neutral atom'. The neutral atom is immune to influences from certain electric fields which would otherwise produce radical changes in the relation of its elements. Its elements – the sub-atomic particles – are stabilized by the association and the stability is expressed by the nature of the atom as an organic whole. Within that whole, the particles are in relatively stable association; that is, their frequencies, courses, spatial dimensions and temporal inter-relations are so arranged as to promote the stability of the atom. Therefore, the atom may be conceived as an 'organism', for it is more than the sum of its parts: the sum of the electrons, protons and neutrons composing an atom would not endure as an atom does which fuses them into unity. The unity of the atom is its 'ontic function', the specified 'nature' whereby it exists in space and time. Hence the atom may be predicated a 'being' on a specific level of existence, with an identifiable nature and localizable position.

This basic description is an abstraction from the complex descriptions and hypotheses of nuclear physics. Owing to its high level of generality, it fits the various, and internally sometimes contradictory theories of micro-physics and field-theories. But the description also applies to astronomical objects. Stellar bodies may be shown to enter into associations which maintain the stability of each body at the point where it could no longer exist without the support of other stellar formations. All stellar formations favourize stability, and oppose (with varying efficacy) disruption and explosion.

The extremes of the scale as regards size, provide examples that show that stability is through association and that an association is more than the sum of its parts: it is the parts in mutual balance. The association signifies an entity with a new, more stable and more highly qualified nature. It has a function which is different from the function of its parts in isolation; it is the product of these functions fused into specific relationships which jointly promote space-time existence to a greater extent than could any other relationship of those particular entities. This is the ontic function of the compound entity, composed of the association of the simples. It applies to phenomena on the micro- as well as on the macro-physical level.

Biological [1] Entities

Biology deals with greater complexity of organisation and of function than physics does. It is clear that all biological species are composed of

---

[1] I shall use "biological" for what would otherwise be termed 'organic' or 'life' phenomena, since neither 'organic' nor 'life' introduce meaningful distinctions between this and any other type of entities under the categories of this scheme.

complex compound individuals, analysable to several layers of particulars in mutual interdetermination, each manifesting its own ontic function harmoniously with the ontic function of the analysed totality, i.e. the biological entity as such. The function of the biological entity is the preservation of its existence and is thus analogous to the function of physical entities.[1] That the function of biological entities involves great complexity signifies merely the fact that the conditions of existence of the biological entity are much more delicate and presuppose correspondingly more accurate functionality; it does not mean that the functionality of biological entities is categorically different from the functionality of physical entities, and that restricting the concept of 'ontic function' to one of these types of entities is warranted. As long as it can be shown that biological species manifest a behaviour pattern tending to preserve their existence, the concept of 'nature' as the evolutionarily specified from of ontic function is applicable to them, for 'ontic function' means precisely the striving for the stability of organic structure and thus for the extension of its span of existence.

In studying the behaviour of biological species a striking fact emerges: their behaviour pattern is as much tuned to the needs of personal survival as to the survival of the species (the latter in the form of acts of reproduction, and caring for the offspring). In the context of this scheme, this is a sign in the behaviour of the individual of a 'higher compound individual' of which it is a part. The higher compound individual embraces several members of the given biological species, and its function concerns the assurance of the stability of relations between the members. In this, not the personal identity of the members, but their function within the collectivity is decisive. Any individual may be replaced by another, if the successor assumes the function of his predecessor within the whole. Hence one aspect of the function of the 'higher compound individual' (the 'herd', 'school', 'flock', etc.) is to assure the replacement of individuals. This takes the form (from the viewpoint of the individual members of the collectivity) of the instinct for reproduction. The other aspect of the function of the higher compound individual is the stabilization of relations between the existing members, and this is felt by the members in their various instincts for social behaviour and collective action.

---

[1] Some behaviourists (e.g. Ashby, Taylor) would agree to this proposition, since they consider the living organism a 'multi-stable system', the principal feature of which is its striving towards stability.

Psychological Entities

All that has been said of biological entities applies also to 'psychological' ones, but the latter have extra specifics in addition. Psychological entities are 'societies of societies'; they are extremely complex and their ontic function is correspondingly accurate and highly qualified. Under 'psychological entities' we can only understand man; though it is not excluded that other species of this level should exist somewhere in the universe (the statistical chances are extremely favourable under any hypothesis assuming the universal invariance of laws determining particular events), the postulation of other-than-human 'psychological entities' is purely conjectural. In order not to exclude this possibility, however, I shall use "psychological entities" to define existence on the human level, rather than *a priori* limiting this category by explicit reference to our own species.

The two main aspects of the ontic function of biological entities is evident in psychological entities in the form of an instinct for self-preservation on the one hand, and in the instinct for reproduction, social action and collective identification on the other. The former leads to the conclusion that man can be analysed to a compound individual in his own right; the latter that his analysis directly implies the existence of a higher compound individual which is designated with the word "society". However, since society is also a means for assuring the optimum conditions of existence of the individual, to some extent social action comes under the heading of the ontic function of man, as an individual 'psychological entity.'

Human nature is an expression of the universal ontic function specified to the nature of the psychological entity: it is the product of temporal relations (being evolved in the course of the history of mankind from lower forms of biological phenomena), and it is the product of spatial relations (evolution having been made possible by the relatively favourable environment of the species throughout its general history). The specific manifestation of the ontic function in psychological entities is their 'psychic' quality, i.e. the phenomenon of *mind*. As I shall show, "mind" can be realistically interpreted as the expression of the universal ontic function in the nature of psychological entities.

THE CATEGORIES OF KNOWLEDGE

The present 'argument from being' seeks to outline the concept of ontic function as a universal attribute of entities relationally specified. Any entity having this function is a 'being' and, by definition, all 'beings' have ontic function. Now the specification of the function is through spatial relations determining the entity's 'nature' through time spent in process. What all entities have in common is the ontic function in its universal essence; what differentiates entities is their spatio-temporal position reflected in the specification of their 'natures'.

The different categories of existence have corresponding types and patterns of experience. 'Experience' is taken as the Whiteheadian "feeling", representing the "prehension" of a given entity of the rest by virtue of the solidarity of the universe. Each particular determines, and is determined by, every other, and this mutual determination results in the specification of the natures of particulars. What an entity can be said to 'know' will be in function of what experiences he actually processes for his own advantage. In other words, the 'knowledge' of entities will be deduced from the external influences a given entity must process in order to exist as it does. Hence 'knowledge' will be deduced entirely from the principles of the here advanced 'argument from being'.

The knowledge of each category of entities corresponds to the experience which makes it what it is. Physical existents can be said to have a *basic existence*, in the sense in which biological entities have *projective existence*, and psychological entities *reflective existence*. I shall define the meaning of these terms in the course of these deductions by determining the principles which govern existence in the various categories.

Knowledge in Basic Existence

The definition of knowledge in what I shall call 'basic existence' follows from the most general aspects of the present scheme, since specification is at the lowest level here: basic existence is persistence by virtue of processing the influences converging upon the private-space-time of the entity sufficiently to permit its continued extended endurance. In a sense all ontic function consists of this, but levels of complexity must be allowed to exist. Basic existence is existence by virtue of the least complex of ontic functions; thus, it applies to 'physical entities'.

Consider that each entity describes a 'historical route' which takes him over a compact series of space-time loci. Physical entities are concerned with their actual space-time locus, and not with any potential ones. An 'actual' space-time locus is one where the entity is here-and-now; a 'potential' space-time locus is one where the entity can be in view of the possibilities offered to it by the interaction of its own nature with that of others. In a sense, basic existence is functional with respect to the instantaneous present. The influences acting upon the physical entity at its private space-time are specified according to their relevance to the structure of the entity at that spatio-temporal locus. Influences are processed to promote internal structural stability in the 'here-and-now' actuality, regardless of the future consequences of acquiring stability at this point. Basic existence implies that the processing of an external influence through the functional nature of the entity takes no account of its own influence upon the other entities with which it interacts. It exists 'for-itself' in the present time and at the present place. Hence basic existence implies that the entity does not functionally modify the pattern of influence to which it is exposed, but merely processes it according to the possibilities offered by its functional nature in order to promote its actual stability. The result of the specification is a reaction of the entity on its interactive partners. This reaction is the influence of the entity upon the rest of the universe; it signifies its effective functioning within the process. In basic existence the nature of the entity is its reaction to the sum of the influences acting upon it in view of its actual internal structure.

The physical entity exercises an effective influence upon its partners in interaction, but this influence takes no account of the partners: the physical entity ignores its effect upon others, it is concerned purely with the effect of others upon itself. Hence (in principle) there can be no case where an influence which is detrimental to the actual stability of the physical entity would be functionally processed as an internal effect contributing to the entity's stability at some future time. An influence, if detrimental at the actual space-time locus, is reacted to as detrimental, notwithstanding the possibility that it may be highly contributory to the stability of the entity in the pattern of influence obtaining at another (future) space-time locus of its existence. Basic existence is the product of the past of the entity conjointly with the past of all other entities, but limited to the present of the given entity, and, as far as that entity is concerned, to the present of all other entities as well.

A physical entity is exposed to the influence of all existents in the universe as are all other entities in every category of existence. Thus its experience could be said to consist of the perception of the natures of the rest of the existents. But when we consider this statement we shall see that 'perception' is used in an unpermissible sense. For a physical entity cannot be said to perceive things to which it does not react, and it reacts only to influences relevant to the immediate facts of its endurance. An atom can be said to perceive atomic processes in its direct environment, but not psychological processes on another planet. Yet the atom is exposed to all events at all loci of the cosmos at all times. But its actual experience, namely that experience, which can be said to enter into its constitution perceptively, consists only of those data of the cosmic syndrome which actually affect the atom in a manner determining its existence *qua* an identifiable persistent individual. Hence the *knowledge* of any physical entity can extend merely to those influences which are relevant for its endurance at the present time and place.

'Knowledge' is an evident misuse of the word by the linguistic criterion of ordinary language, but it is entirely indicated by the consistency and universal scope of the realistic 'argument from being'. If it is meaningful to speak of the 'experience' of an entity, it is also meaningful to speak of that entity's knowledge *as* the acquaintance of the entity with the data of its experience. Such acquaintance could only be denied if the entity in question is held to be fully immune to determination by the influences constituting its experience. Inasmuch as that assumption is not made, the factors which actually determine the entity can be said to be *known* by it : they enter into the constitution and become part of that entity. Consequently the 'knowledge' of a physical entity (and the basic aspect of the knowledge of all existent entities) extends to those relationally communicated events which enter into the constitution of the given entity and determine its existence. The knowledge of the physical entity takes no account of the sources of the influence, only of their presence. It extends fully to the entity in question, and to the rest of the process-existents merely by virtue of the experience whereby their natures become objectified in the constitution of that entity.

Knowledge in Projective Existence

Basic existence is existence in the context of actuality. The relevant experience of a physical entity concerns its own present at its actual locus; the future, and the spatial loci in which it may find itself in the future are matters of contingency for the functional nature of the physical entity. Control over the future means control over the influences which will be exerted upon the entity at another, not yet actual, phase of its existence. Control over these influences is possible if present influences converging upon the space-time of the given entity are specified not merely concordantly with the requirements of its actual existence, but also in view of the requirements of existence that will arise in a time and place not yet occupied by the entity. Such control means a reaction to influence which is not exhausted in the ontic function of preserving spatio-temporality at the actual present, but extends to a consideration of the entity's future existence. Function such as this is typical of *biological entities*, which by that token can be said to manifest *projective existence*.

If basic existence means processing external influences concordantly with ontic functionality extending to the present, projective existence signifies processing external influences concordantly with ontic functionality extending to some degree beyond the present, into the future. Such existence involves the 'projection' of the past to the future, in the form of a function gained in a historical process, to the process as historical. It differs from function in the context of actualities, which is function acquired in a historical process, but which treats it as momentary. When existence is *projective*, and not merely *basic*, the element of time (which is the factor of the evolution of particular natures as manifest in the relational process) is projected beyond the present on the basis of the past. The relative clock of the particular is speeded up in anticipation of fresh space-time loci, and of fresh influences converging upon these loci.

The pattern of influence to which the entity will be exposed in the projected space-time locus is not discontinuous with the present pattern, but is the logical resultant of the interaction of the entity and other entities. Continuity is assured by the intrinsic nature of the entity; that nature, if it takes into account its own future position, can contribute to the modification of the pattern of influence to which it will then be exposed. *Present* influence is to promote *future* stability on the basis of experience gained in the *past*.

Let us consider this proposition. Projective existence, I have said, is typical of biological entities. Empirical evidence (in the realist context) is to the effect that biological entities manifest some concern over their future, whether as a result of intelligence or instinct, and this concern influences their actual behaviour pattern. Thus a biological entity does not behave purely in a manner which is conducive to its momentary existence, but tends to undertake acts which have their justification in meeting a requirement arising in the future. This point is evident when we allow for degrees of projection, and need not be further elaborated. The problem is rather to determine what kind of 'knowledge' is implied for a species of existents which, due to their advanced evolutionary level (i.e. high progression-time in the process), manifest complex functions in meeting their own complex requirements of existence?

I shall use 'knowledge' in the sense I defined it with respect to basic existents: as an entity's perceptive experience of external influences. When the biological entity is taken as one pole of an interaction the other pole of which is the rest of the universe (from which it has been abstracted with analytical arbitrariness), then the experience of the biological entity, as that of all conceivable existents, is *of* the natures of all process-existents presented as a specific syndrome of influence converging upon its private space-time. Yet, just as the physical entity cannot be said to 'know' the rest of the universe through our acceptance of this statement, so must this acceptance entail a limited knowledge for the biological entity. In fact, each entity will be said to 'know' only so much of this cosmic influence as effectively enters into its constitution and determines its actual existence. The difference between a basic and a projective existent in this respect is that the former is determined by the mere perception of the physical facts in its immediate environment, while the latter is determined by a considerably wider series of events. Some of the events perceived by the physical entity fall away (thus the minute processes of micro-physics, which have but a small, or at any rate, an indirect, effect on biological entities), while the vast area of biologically relevant facts opens up for the biological entity as a genus of facts which effectively determines its constitution. The biological entity can be said to 'know' these facts. The knowledge of the biological entity is wider, therefore, than the knowledge of the physical entity, while it does not entirely include the latter. Often only the compound product of a series of facts becomes biologically relevant, and the knowledge of the biological entity extends then to the product, but not to its components. At other times particular facts may be biologically entirely irrelevant and in that case the entity has no knowledge of these facts.

But not merely has the scope of knowledge of biological entities been changed and widened – also their type of knowledge is different from physical entities. The facts known by the biological entity are known not only as actualities, but also as historical processes. They are known as events which have their grounds in the past and their consequences in the future. Before taking a closer look at the implications of such knowledge, however, I would like to show that this assumption follows from the heuristic principles I advanced.

A biological entity is a compound individual composed of smaller, and micro-organisms (such as tissues, cells, macro-molecules, atoms), and the superimposition of further organic totalities on already existent organic entities constitutes, in the light of this scheme, evidence of the advanced temporal standpoint of the biological entity. The biological entity is more advanced as regards the public time of the universe than its constituents and it has a correspondingly more delicate constitution. When the biological entity ceases to exist *qua* biological entity, (i.e. when it 'dies') the constituents of the entity continue to exist as physical (and bio-chemical) entities. But the totality which has constituted the biological entity is a mere aggregate of physical entities when the self-consistent ontic function identifying the biological entity has ceased. A direct result, and at the same time evidence of the cessation of that function, is the decomposition of the components of the biological entity into numerical, but no longer functional, aggregates of physical entities. Thus the ontic function of the biological entity is empirically as well as logically more complex than that of physical entities. Hence the 'final satisfaction' wherein the biological entity 'prehends' the 'solidarity of the universe', and 'objectifies' it in its own constitution (to use Whiteheadian terms) is the result of a far more complex function than the corresponding 'final satisfaction' of a physical entity. In fact, the complex constitution of the biological entity (its nervous system and brain) directly implies a function which provides for responses not only to actual, but also to future influences, as the latter are manifested in, or are implied by, actual experience. The more complex the entity, the more complex its constitution, and the more it exercises and is dependent upon the anticipatory type of ontic function.

Now such a function is in the form of an anticipation of events to come, through the projection of the past experience of the entity to its future; it is a result of the historical nature of the entity, acquired in interaction with its evironment. Through such interactions the entity, by virtue of the perception of changes occasioned by environmental influences in its own constitution, develops an ontic function in the form of a 'nature' which is capable of operationally processing ingressing influences corresponding to the conditions of endurance for the entity. When anticipation of the future is a condition of endurance, then the corresponding function is performed, and it *can* only be performed on the basis of historical experience.

Projective existence is typical of the wide realm of entities dealt with in biology, but is the most explicitly exemplified by man: a biological entity, endowed with 'psychic' properties. The processes involved in the projective existence of biological entities may be studied by analysing the reasoning processes used by man whereby he anticipates future events on the basis of past experience. The equation of all forms of psychological activity with anticipation of future events would be fallacious, but there are elements in human reasoning which exemplify the processes present in less evolved biological species, inasmuch as they are typical of an *anticipation* of future events on the basis of past experiences manifested (to some degree) by every biological entity.

Each entity is exposed to a set of influences which, together with his own internal constitution and externalized ontic function, determines its existence. For man, as for biological entities in general, the influence includes biologically relevant facts. (For man it also includes psychological facts.) In the anticipatory function of projective existence this pattern of influence is evaluated not merely as *given* facts, but as *historical* facts. Man treats his environment in terms of sources of influences which are not merely momentary and unforeseeable, but as a series of grounds having future consequences and as a series of consequences having past grounds. The scope of knowledge is thus deepened, extending to the past and to the future in addition to the actual present. Reasoning from an actual event as ground of its anticipated consequence involves projection of past experience into the future; reasoning from an actual event as consequence of a past ground means explaining the present in terms of a past by which it is determined. Both are forms of inference and both, though rationalized *only* by human reason (as far as our knowledge of the universe goes), exist in, and are implied by, the behaviour of primitive biological entities as well.

Anticipation is based on knowledge acquired in the historical experience of the entity by taking actuality as a consequence of a past ground. On this basis a theory concerning the facts in question can be formulated and applied as inference from present to future events.

Consider that in a fundamental sense, all deduction of empirical fact is based on some previous reduction, so that every reasoning from ground to consequence presupposes previous acquaintance with grounds of which the present is a consequence. But knowledge of the present as consequence of a past ground is effective in practice only if used as an instrument to predict the future as a consequence of the present (evaluated as its ground). But, reasoning from known consequence to a surmised ground is a fallible and hypothetical procedure, requiring the inductive generalization of a hypothesis of ground reductively verifiable by inspection of a section of actuality, *qua* its consequence. If the present consists of events which recur, and if the scope of the hypothesis is sufficiently inclusive, then upon its verification (i.e. upon the experience of the present in the context of logical resultants from past events), the hypothesis is capable of functioning as a means of predicting future events from present ones – inasmuch as *some* present events are analogous to those which have been considered as the ground of consequences given in actuality: the invariance of the hypothetical ground as present actuality is a precondition of the prediction of future possibilities on the basis of hypothesis.

Given these preconditions, hypotheses concerning the nature of reality can be operationally tested. By this I do not mean only controlled scientific experiments, but would include all forms of practical endeavour whereby the nature of any sector or part of environmental reality is operationally known. Operational definitions are prior as well as subsequent to the formulation of hypotheses: hypotheses can be built with the help of operational definitions and they can be operationally verified. The concept 'operation' means in this argument, the putting into practice of theoretical projections of the past to the future. It is by operational means, then, that anticipatory behaviour is manifested as purposive activity conducing to the assurance of better conditions for the existence of the biological entity. The scientific knowledge of mankind is a highly perfected and theoretically deepened form of the projective knowledge of all biological entities down to, and including, the simplest amoeba. While it is an evident exaggeration to claim that the amoeba engages in a species of scientific activity, it is not an exaggeration to say that the behaviour whereby the amoeba assures its future requirements by a present reaction to stimulus has fundamentally the same ontic function for it as applied science (among other things) has for man.

But I do not wish to imply that 'projective existence' is in any sense *sui generis*, and radically different from basic existence. In an internally consistent monistic process-metaphysics there are no categorical differences between types and levels of being, only differences in degree. Basic and projective existences do not represent discontinuous levels of existence, but signify particular points on the curve of the evolutionary continuum. In a scheme such as this, one cannot legitimately postulate categorical differences between the simplest of beings (such as the material of the original background stuff of the universe) and the most complex systems of organic structures – whether men, or galaxies. Projective existence is manifested in all entities by the very token of their historical nature. The difference between what has here been termed 'basic' and 'projective' existence is one of degrees. The simple physical organism manifests a function which is largely concentrated on that specious lapse of time which is known, for lack of a better term, as 'the present'. In this context it means, in fact, a relatively short duration. Projective existence is manifested in a more complex entity, capable of explicating the universal ontic function to a degree where the lapse of time which it functionally encompasses is greatly increased. The increase is proportionate, however, to the progression-time of the entity as measured by its private clock. Thus projective existence is concordant with the nature of biological entities, since their nature is a resultant of their complex requirements and their complex requirements result from their advanced temporal standpoint. The duration involved in the self-determination of an atom is neither shorter nor longer than the duration involved in the self-determination of the human organism when their progression-time resulting in their structural complexity is taken duly into account. Every entity, by token of its historical nature, is concerned with duration and duration means the continuity of interaction between itself and the world. Thus every entity, by being what it is, namely a functional existent within the cosmic process, is concerned with all other existents as factors of its own determination during its existence. Hence its own future is not *entirely* contingent as regards its functional nature. Merely the length of time to which its functional control extends, changes. That change is proportionate to the progression-time of the entity: the more temporally advanced an entity is, the more it penetrates into the future on the basis of its more extensively known past.

Knowledge in Reflective Existence

Projective existence is implicit in basic existence; what I shall here term 'reflective existence' is implicit in projective existence. However, due to the assertion of 'basic existence' as the fundamental, although still unspecified manifestation of the universal ontic function, each further specified form of that function (hence also 'reflective existence') is implicit in it as potential. Therefore, not only is the type of knowledge ascribed to biological entities a potential for physical entities, but the type of knowledge attributed to psychological entities is a potential for physical entities as well as for biological entities.

The notions 'functional nature', 'private space-time', 'evolution' and 'progression-time' are not *sui generis* with respect to any one category of entities, but are shared by all. The differences between levels of existence are reduced to differences in realising potentials shared by all entities from the simplest to the most complex. Hence the 'psychic' features of man, as 'psychological entity', signify merely the manifestation of the ontic function at the particularly advanced level of temporal progression due to the particular set of spatial coordinations in which man found himself throughout his past history, and which he functionally improved as its favourable features permitted him to evolve his ontic function to higher levels of efficacy. The history of the particular as the factor of time, and its environment as the factor of space, have made man what he is: namely, "man". The predicate 'man' is misleading when taken as a factor of categorical differentiation between the organisms which it predicates and other organisms; 'man' is merely a species of organism determined by the set of space-time loci which constitute its historical route. Substitute any other 'particle' or 'stuff' in place of the original mould of man and 'man' will emerge. Not the particularity of the substance, but its position within the cosmic process, is the determinant feature. Thus, in the entity we term 'man', not the particularity of its components, but their structural organisation, is determinant. Man is an organism in the sense that an atom is an organism: by virtue of the further organisation of particular elements already manifesting some degree of differentiation. While such differentiation is relatively modest in the simpler atoms (consisting of the difference between positively and negatively charged units), it is highly varied and complex in man. The stuff of man includes more, and more differentiated items, than does the stuff of an atom or a molecule or even a cell, since 'man' is the functional organic compund of all these units.

Complexity in the structure of an entity presupposes the complexity of the function promoting its endurance. By this rule the function of the human mind may be considered a complex expression of the universal ontic function, corresponding in complexity and refinement to the actual existential requirements of the 'human being'. In our experience, humanity represents that species of entities of which it can be said that its ontic function is 'conscious'. In view of this fact, and by reason of schematization, man may be termed a 'psychological entity'. Here 'psychological' means a level of ontic function exclusive to this species. Contrarily to anticipatory behaviour, which is typical of man as well as of biological entities in general, the feature of man's ontic function which I shall term 'reflection', is not typical of any entity other than man. Although 'reflection' is realized only by man, it is latent as pure potential in all other species of entities. Reflection is exclusive to man, but it does not imply a new category of attributes; as I shall try to show, it can be logically derived from the concept of ontic function when man's highly complex projective existence is taken into account.

Basic and projective existence predicated of physical and biological entities have been classificatory concepts introduced to account for a continuous evolutionary process in terms of relative differences emerging in its course. 'Reflective existence' predicated of 'psychological entities' will be a similar classificatory concept which will be equally misleading if taken to indicate a categorical difference. It will be situated beyond projective existence, while including it, as projective existence has been situated beyond basic existence, though including it. In a sense, reflection must be a function of projection, both of which are qualified functions of basic existence. The question to be considered is how reflection follows as a necessary and logically consistent inference from the present scheme.

Consider then, that existence is an interaction which, when analyzed from the viewpoint of a subject, gives us the concept of its 'nature'. By such an act of abstraction the functional 'natures' of particulars emerge: the nature of the abstracted entity is such that it functions toward its space-time endurance, and the nature of the 'rest' of the world is such that it is a conditionary force, an environment relevant to this function. An entity specified to the modest degree to where it functions only as a basic existent is relatively ignorant of the 'rest of the world' as composed of entities possessing functional natures themselves. To such an entity, the world is one vast field of force, converging upon its space-time locus, and variously conditioning its endurance. The 'physical entity' is introverted (if one may borrow a term from psychology), being concerned with its own existence as its possibilities are disclosed by external influences.

In projective existence, however, 'biological entities' are already extroverted to some extent; for them the forces determining their existence are elements in a historical process having implications from past to present and from present to future. The knowledge of biological entities is of their environment as a relevant and historical setting for their existence. 'Psychological entities' (of which the only example in our experience is our own species) are even further extroverted. They regard the forces acting upon them not only as significant of a relevant historical environment, but as one which is purposively *modifiable*. The existence of psychological entities is based on the knowledge of the world as a modifiable set of entities, capable of providing an increasingly favourable setting for their own existence.

Knowledge of the environment in terms of entities of modifiable natures implies knowledge of the force or forces which can effect the modification. In such knowledge the environment is seen as composed of one vast subject, or of a set of interconnected subjects which are 'subjects' in the sense that they are subject to a purposively directed force acting upon them and provoking their modification. In turn, this implies not only knowledge of the existents in the environment in terms of subjects, but also knowledge of the forces acting upon these subjects as 'objects'.

This conclusion leads to the consideration that, when the entities of the environment are considered as subjects upon which objects act, and when this action is purposively regulated by exercising a measure of control over them, then that entity which represents the sole controllable force affecting the 'subjects' must be viewed as an 'object'. Evidently, that entity can be none other than the actual subject. Hence the subject 'reflects' upon himself and sees himself as an object in a world wherein he projects his own subjectness in the effort to modify it concordantly with the requisites of its own endurance. This process results in the objectivation of the subject[1], and conversely, in

---

[1] A basically similar idea has been expressed by Sartre in existentialist terms when he spoke of the objectivation of the 'I' by the 'others' in encounter, wherein the subject is robbed of his intrinsic freedom, and becomes an object for 'others' (*autrui*). But the concept of alienation is one conclusion to be derived from this process; the concept of reflection is another.

the subjectivation of objects. It involves the consideration of the subject himself, as an *external* force, acting upon his environment. It is a cognizance of the entity's own function-potential from the viewpoint of an affective force. It is the realization that the specification of external forces by internal nature is itself more than a blind reaction upon the forces themselves, but can be a planned instrument in the service of existence. It is an instrument operative across space and time, reacting in the form of a modified environment for the entity at a not yet reached space-time locus. If successful, the instrument provides for an operatively improved environment and thus becomes an effective form of ontic functioning.

Let us consider now what acts of knowledge the use of such an instrument presupposes. First, it means the knowledge of the environment as composed of modifiable entities. Second, it means the assessment of the operational variability of these entities. Third, it means the evaluation of the entity's own functional nature as a vector. Last, but by no means least, it means relating the functional nature of the entity as vector, to the operational variability-potential of the environmental entities. These together imply the knowledge of the environment as composed of variable entities, and knowledge of the self as controllable operative vector.

This knowledge refers either to the self as counterposed to the world, or to the self within the world. The environment can be constituted into one vast subject as the totality of objects which it contains, and of which it is the sum. Such a transcendental-idealist world is possible through an act of methodical intellectual synthesis. It becomes a world which remains counterposed to the self, but one where subject and object have changed places. It is a world which is acted upon by the entity, rather than a world which acts upon the entity. If, for a physical entity, the world is one vast pattern of influence acting upon it, for the reflecting psychological entity the world may be one vast subject, acted upon by the entity as a vector of a unitary pattern of objective force. Then, the abstraction of the entity in reflection takes the world as malleable subject, and the self as controlled dynamic object. But, in reflection the subject may also envisage himself as a being *in* the world. The pattern of influences external to the entity may be thought to originate in various, individual sources, represented by particular entities. Each of these entities may be subjectivated; the actual subject takes on the aspect of an object seen from its perspective. In that event, the actual subject objectifies himself as an object immanent to the realm of objects-functioning-as-subjects.

Subjectivating the world as a unified realm counterposed to the self is characteristic of some schools of transcendental idealism, while the assumption of immanence is implicit in practical common-sense and in pragmatism. But the choice itself does not affect the conclusion to which such assumptions give rise. In either event, the entity reflects upon himself by transferring his own subject-qualities to his environment and the object-qualities of his environment to himself. This transference is a further specified manifestation of the universal ontic function; it lends an increased assurance of optimal, long-range existence to the reflecting entity by affording knowledge of the modification-potential of the environment through cognizing it as a collection of ontic particulars. Reflection makes the highly explicated form of anticipatory behaviour typical of human beings possible: it permits the development of science, art and technology, by knowing the world as a series of 'objects' and 'living beings' possessing a given degree of relevance to the existence of the knowing subject. Hence the mutual relevance of entities in the universe results in reflection in function of existence, when the sufficiently high level of organisation represented by the complex compund individual known as 'man', has been reached.

Reflection presupposes the world, and not the world, reflection. Without the assumption of the prior existence of the physical world, the notion of 'reflection' is empty and meaningless. But when the physical world *is* presupposed, the mental phenomena connoted by 'reflection' follow from this prototype scheme of consistent, uncompromising realism.

PRINCIPLES OF REALISTIC KNOWLEDGE

The kind of knowledge deducible from a thoroughly explicated realist scheme is necessarily public; it concerns the knowledge of one entity in the act of experiencing another. It presupposes that 'the other' exists and seeks to determine *how* it exists according to the postulated principles of existence. Thus, 'knowledge' is deduced from the realist first principles rather than being founded upon an analysis of the items of direct experience. Presuppositionless empiricism is incompatible with the axiomatics of realist principles.

No claim of presuppositionless empiricism is made for the above scheme. The categories of knowledge I postulated above follow from the principles entailed by consistent realism; not immediate experience, but these principles function as verifier of the propositions advanced. Inasmuch, however, as adequacy cannot be at the cost of an irrelevance to empirical matters of fact, but must rather refer to the mode of explanation of the latter, the scheme must adequately explain what we experience (or think we experience) of the 'real' world, and conserve this reference to physical empiricism throughout.

The 'knowledge' attributed to all entities whatsoever is knowledge of 'others', if not *qua* other *entities*, then at least as a field of force converging upon the given entity and conditioning its existence. In fact, physical entities know nothing of 'others' as entities, but know their experience only as such a field of force, balanced by their internal distribution of forces. When the internal forces balance the external ones, the physical entity exists; when the balance is upset, the entity can no longer be said to exist as an individual constituted by the relational totality of its parts, but dissolves into the elements which have up to then constituted it.

Biological entities still know their experience as a field of force, but for them that field has become historical: it has a past extending to the future through the present. Thus actions undertaken in the present on the basis of knowledge gained in past experience can modify the field of force to represent a more suitable environment for the future of the entity. Anticipatory behaviour, constituting knowledge in projective existence, refers to such a historical field of force.

In the experience of psychological entities, the field of force is specified into substantive individual entities, known as such by the reflecting entity. This process results from the transference of the subject-nature of the entity to the environment and from the estimation of itself as an object exerting a given amount and type of influence. Hence the environment becomes a series of subjects (or one inclusive subject) for the reflecting psychological entity, and as a result he sees himself as an object in a world on which he purposively acts. Each higher level of knowledge includes each lower level, so that reflection includes, and indeed presupposes, projection, and projection includes and presupposes basic existence.

Toward the higher forms of knowledge, the field of force is specified into various sensory data by virtue of the development of sense organs. While the lower species of biological entities attribute these data to the world as a general field of force (i.e. as a vague source of influence affecting their existence); the higher species, and most particularly man, know them (realistically) as identifiable objects, functioning as physical causes of the felt influences.

The fact that anticipatory reasoning involves physical persons and objects for man and for some of the higher species of biological entities, and only a more or less unspecified field of force for the lower species of biological entities and for physical entities, is due to the exercise of projective functions by the higher biological species in the context of advance traces of reflection, and in man in the context of explicit and highly evolved reflections. When an entity engaging in reflection also engages in projection, he does so by evaluating the historical field of force as consisting of more or less specified and identified entities co-existing with him in the world. Functionally, projection does not presuppose reflection, while reflection presupposes projection. But the *explicit* forms of projection presuppose reflection, for it is through reflection that the affective field of force is specified into the ontic particulars which are involved in the explicit forms of anticipatory behaviour. The scientific as well as the artistic object can be an 'object' only through reflection, and the common operational object is similarly dependent upon reflective cognition. But there is no contradiction in affirming that primitive projection does not presuppose reflection, for anticipatory behaviour does not categorically necessitate the envisagement of the environment as a series of ontic particulars. Such an implicit and as yet non-reflective form of projection is already present in the simpler biological entities (i.e. in those equipped with elementary nervous systems) in that they react to the forces present in their environment in a manner conducive not only to their present existence but to their future well-being as well. For this type of 'instinctive' anticipatory behaviour it is not required that the environment be evaluated as consisting of distinct particulars; it is enough that the felt environmental forces be known to manifest an invariant order of succession, so that if a given force is present and is reacted to in a given way, it should be known (or instinctively felt) which other determinate kind of force will take its place.

Reflection, however, permits the cognition of substantive ontic particulars and, through them, the better knowledge of the environment. In turn, such better knowledge affords a greater temporal range of anticipatory forecasts and coordinated projective behaviour. Consequently, reflection permits the explication of the anticipatory functions of biological entities by man and renders him a projecting *and* reflecting, i.e. a more-than-biological, a *psychological*, entity.

There are no categorical differences between entities of any kind, only greater and lesser measures of functional efficiency corresponding to the various exigencies of existence in process. More complex entities have more delicate constitutions and require more refined varieties of function to exist. Mentation is at that end of the evolutionary scale which is the most advanced in our experience; but the diverse mental processes of man are significative of his advanced progression-time, and not of his possession of a quality *sui generis*.

The scale of evolution, from the haze of hydrogen atoms in interstellar gases to the complex patterns of thought and behaviour of civilized man, may be integrated into a vast encompassing scheme based on the axiom that the world exists regardless of whether it is perceived or not. Once this assumption is made, the empirical line of inquiry integrates experience into the world, and an analysis of experience is an analysis of the interaction of subject and environment. If the scope is enlarged, the proper topic of inquiry becomes the subject as 'one' among the 'many' of the natural universe. Experience is assumed to be of objective being, and since experience is a flux, flux is attributed to objective being. Hence 'the world', wherein we find subject and object as entities in interaction, becomes a realm of ebb and flow, of qualitative and quantitative change. This fluidity of experience is described by the term 'process'. But we must not forget that experience, assessed in the context of the realist's basic assumptions, also refers to concrete personal and individual unities and thus that it warrants the notion that all things that are, are substantial, ontically concrete individuals. This substantive principle is logically prior to the principle of change, determining the subject of which change is predicated. The ontological concreteness of individual beings, analysed through the heuristic principle 'process' represents one – not the only one, but a possible one – set of concepts and principles entailed by the basic assumption of realism.

The realist basic assumption is irreducible and unanalyzable, and hence it is neither provable nor disprovable. It is neither more nor less valid than the sceptical basic assumption of 'world-in-experience'. And, if on the one hand arguments based on the realist basic assumption are lacking in the experiential verifiability of arguments based on the basic assumption of scepticism, on the other they penetrate those regions of possible reality which are closed to the latter. Experience may be coherently analysed under the assumption that it is given 'in' the world, and the results of such an analysis are valid in the light of the assumed premisses. As long as neither the sceptic attacks the position of the realist, nor the realist criticizes the position of the sceptic, internal consistency in the system of each connotes the validity of the respective conclusions. The fact that a theory of satisfactory coherence and scope can be built on either set of basic assumptions means that the sceptic as well as the realist is qualified to explore one of the alternative avenues leading to knowledge of the world. The above, rather ambitious, scheme has been proposed in order to show that it is neither logically impossible nor empirically unwarranted to evolve a coherent and satisfactory theory on the premiss of realism, neither accepting support nor acknowledging criticism from arguments based on the premiss of scepticism.

PART IV

VERIFICATION

PRINCIPLE OF VERIFICATION

I have taken evident pains to show that reductionism in all forms is fallacious; that, in fact, no statement concerning 'being' entails any statement concerning 'consciousness' (except as 'mind' integrated in the domain of being) and hence no proposition of physical fact can be reduced to a proposition describing epistemic fact. If the universe of meaning following consistently from the assumption of 'consciousness', and the one following from the axiom 'being', are disjunctive, no reduction of one to the other is possible. In what, then, can *verification* consist?

Verification, I have suggested, concerns the demonstration of the isomorphic structure of the sceptical and realist arguments. The sense and significance of the demonstration of isomorphism is that it shows that meanings are assigned to terms in direct reference to the adopted root-axiom, and that these are directly determined by the chosen basic assumptions. These, on the other hand, are not determined by any argument, but are entirely axiomatic with respect to the systems. Hence the difference rendering the sceptic's and the realist's arguments disjunctive, reduces, in the final analysis, to axiomatic assertions of basic assumptions which could be analysed only to subconscious preferences in assessing the evidence. When immediate experience is taken as evidence of all things that may be, the universe of meaning of the sceptic is the result and there are no avenues open for penetrating into the universe of meaning attained by an affirmation of at least the objective origin of the evidence. Conversely, once the existence of things is taken as proven by the facticity of experience, the concepts and categories of the sceptic are left behind and are incapable of being consistently assimilated to the argument. But there is no contradiction in claiming that the meanings of such arguments are disjunctive while the function of terms determining the meanings is analogous.

There is no contradiction either, in claiming the value of verification for the demonstration of this analogy, since if analogy is demonstrated, it does not make sense to argue that the propositions refer to the realist's natural universe or to the sceptic's consciousness, since, if we assume that words are not labels, but functions within each set of propositions, their meaning, as determined by their use within each set of propositions, will be identical. Hence the basic assumptions of the sceptic and of the realist no longer lead to contradictory results, for, while it is still possible to doubt all evidence as well as to affirm its objective origin, neither doubt nor affirmation leads to significantly different conclusions. The objections of the sceptic are met on his own ground and that is perhaps the only way they can be countered. By this token some realistic propositions can be verified and those that can be so treated determine the scope of meaningful metaphysics.

Now I have proposed two internally consistent, but mutually disjunctive, arguments. I have argued from consciousness in one, and from being in the other. In arguing from consciousness, all I could affirm of "consciousness" without presuppositions was, that it exists. In order to derive 'knowledge' from such a merely existent consciousness, its experiences had to be rendered coherent by introducing a principle of organization which bridges the gap between what we ordinarily think we perceive and what we actually receive as data of our various perceptive organs. The act of consciousness required to fill this gap has been *intentionality*: in reference to it the unorganized series of sensory events could be explained as the sense-objects which we seem to perceive, and upon which rests our knowledge of the external world. But adding intentionality to existing consciousness has not entailed any proposition concerning other minds. There is no proof for the existence of anything *outside* consciousness in the analysis of experience, for all things other than the locus and fact of experience are data of experience, and that there is any 'physical left-over' behind or beyond them is purely a speculative conjecture. Hence the sceptical concept of experience is private, and whatever knowledge it offers is also private. This does not mean that it is incommunicable *per se*, but only that the idea of communication, presupposing as it does more than one entity, is meaningless in its context.

In the realist hypothesis I argued from the axiomatically assumed notion of 'being', i.e. I assumed that things, whatever they may be, exist independently of being perceived by any particular subject. The notions of space and time have been introduced as transcending the locus of perception and the *percipiens*, *qua* ontically existent entity, has been integrated into this encompassing space-time realm. The concept of experience deduced from the systematic ordering of experiential events as physical actualities in the natural universe has assigned a particular role to the experience which has been its tacit ground of inference: it made it into the experience of 'one' among the 'many'. Thus whatever events are given to the subject, his experience is public, for it contains reference to things and events which are existent and hence are also available to the experience of 'others'.

While it has been often thought that private experience is radically different from public experience, this is not necessarily the case, for both conceptions of experience are based on hypothetical, heuristically functioning notions which explicate the given experiential events as coherent actualities. The sceptic's heuristic principle should be something like my 'intentionality'; the realist's may well be my notion of 'ontic functionality'. Both principles refer to the same events, given to us in experience, but use different frameworks of explanation. Since neither framework of explanation can rely entirely on its root-axiom (for the sceptic's consciousness guarantees only that *it* exists, and the realist's beings, only that *they* exist) the introduction of heuristic principles to organize the events of experience into a coherent scheme need not mean a different principle of organization in the sceptical view than it does in the optic of realism: there may well be an area of coincidence in the conclusions. If that area covers all facts where coincidence is possible, it becomes meaningless to speak of the validity of the one as opposed to that of the other, for one cannot be valid unless the other is invalid, and there is no ground to deny the validity of either. Both are valid, even though they are contradictory. But if both can be valid and contradictory, then either the principle of contradiction, or the principles which contradict, are invalid. To make the former assumption is to remove the logical basis of the arguments and to eliminate the criterion of consistency based on the principle of non-contradiction. It remains to make the second assumption: the principles which contradict are invalid insofar as they are contradictory. To make this assumption we need to consider the terms contained in the respective propositions in function of their use within the language of the thinker making the proposition. We must further allow that the sceptic has a language (or 'language-game') which is as valid as that of the realist and that neither language is determined by its relation to ordinary language. Thus the two assumptions, (i) sceptical and realist languages are equally meaningful, and (ii) meaning is determined by use within the language of each, jointly result in the conclusion that if the proposition of the sceptic and of the realist are isomorphic, then notwithstanding the different meaning of their terms as labels, they determine the same principles. Consequently if and when a coincidence between the events referred to by the sceptic and the realist occurs, and further if and when not only the area of coincidence is given, but within that area the structure of the propositions determining the relevant principles is isomorphic, then we can disregard differences in wording, and consider the meanings identical and the propositions verified.

In brief, these are the principles of verification. We must consider next what are the chances for putting them into practice.

THE CORRELATION OF THE CATEGORIES OF
SCEPTICAL AND REALIST KNOWLEDGE

In order to clarify the possibilities of verification, the correlation of the categories of the 'argument from consciousness' and the 'argument from being' must be established. The correlation involves the categories common to both arguments: these are the categories of knowledge. In order to present a lucid picture of this correlation, I shall start by listing the categories of knowledge in each argument.

The categories of sceptical knowledge

Passive Intentions/Contemplative Knowledge
Active Intentions/Operational Knowledge
Theoretical Intentions/Inferential Knowledge

The categories of realistic knowledge

Knowledge in Basic Existence (Physical, Biological, Psychological Entities)
Knowledge in Projective Existence (Biological, Psychological Entities)
Knowledge in Reflective Existence (Psychological Entities)
Conversely, Physical Entities: Basic Knowledge
Biological Entities: Basic and Projective Knowledge
Psychological Entities: Basic, Projective and Reflective Knowledge

It follows that all categories of knowledge concern human knowledge on the sceptical side ('consciousness' can only be 'my' consciousness, hence it is necessarily human), while it is the knowledge of psychological entities which is the relevant one to human knowledge among the realist categories. Psychological entities, however, dispose of all the forms of knowledge we have distinguished, including reflective, projective and basic knowledge. Their knowledge is a synthesis of the three realist categories: basic knowledge is specified as purposive mentation through the presence of projective knowledge, and pro-jective knowledge is specified as knowledge of ontic particulars (physi-cal persons and objects) through the presence of reflective knowledge. Thus, the knowledge had by the psychological entity is not a mere aggregate, but the functional fusion of the kinds of knowledge it embraces: each particular type of knowledge is conditioned by every other and is moulded into the over-all pattern of functional mentation which represents, in the light of the realist scheme, the ontic function of man.

Since the knowledge of the sceptic is necessarily human and 'human knowledge' is by a psychological entity for the realist, and since the knowledge of the psychological entity fuses all forms of knowledge in functional harmony, therefore the correlation of the sceptical and realist categories involves all categories on the side of scepticism, and only the category of 'human' knowledge on the side of realism.

But this correlation is imperfect. When we analyse the elements of knowledge therein involved, we shall find that there is one category of realism which has no counterpart in the scheme of the sceptic. This category of knowledge is 'reflection': there is nothing corresponding to it in the sceptical view. Hence (assuming for the moment the validity of both schemes) the correlation is more correctly stated as follows.

Scepticism	*Realism*
Passive/Contemplative	(Human) Basic Knowledge
Active/Operational	(Human) Projective Knowledge (primitive form)
Theoretical/Inferential	(Human) Projective Knowledge (explicit form)

The area of non-correlation is then:

Scepticism	*Realism*
none	Basic Knowledge (of physical entities)
none	Projective Knowledge (of biological entities)
none	Reflective Knowledge (of psychological entities)

ANALYSIS OF THE CORRELATION

I. The Area of Correlation

The Area of Correlation involves all categories for the sceptic, and the basic and projective knowledge of psychological entities for the realist. Inasmust, however, as the predicate 'human' implies the presence of reflection, and reflection has no sceptical correlate, the realist categories are imperfectly correlated. My purpose here is to examine, first, to what extent the three pairs of correlates may be upheld as such, despite the implication of reflection in all the realist categories; and second, to consider whether or not the existence of the Area of Non-Correlation disproves the *verifiendum*.

The first pair of correlates includes 'Passive Intentions' giving rise to *Contemplative Knowledge* and *Knowledge in (Human) Basic Existence*. Can this correlation be upheld as the true coincidence of the principles involved? Now, I have defined 'passive intentions' as "those acts of cognition which involve the actually presented sense-data and do not penetrate beyond the realm of actuality into that of potentiality by means of practical operations or theoretical inferences". And I concluded that "knowledge limited to actually presented data has a character which may be denoted 'contemplative'." [1] On the other hand, knowledge obtained in basic existence has been defined by deduction from the notion of 'basic existence', as "the product of the past of the entity conjointly with the past of all other entities, but limited to the present of the given entity, and, as far as that entity is concerned, to the present of all other entities as well." [2] "Consequently the 'knowledge' of a physical entity (and the basic aspect of the knowledge of all existent entities) extends to those relationally communicated events which enter into the constitution of the given entity and determine its existence. The knowledge of the physical entity takes no account of the sources of the influence, only of their presence. It extends fully to the entity in question, and to the rest of the process-existents merely by virtue of the experience whereby their natures become objectified in the constitution of that entity." [3] Provided the principles determining the acquisition of knowledge in the two arguments do not contradict, it appears that the kind of knowledge obtained through 'passive intentions' coincides with that obtaining in basic existence: both refer to given actualities, and involve no cognition of the presented data other than that obtainable through their actual presence, *as* given. There are no inferences made as to the nature of the data, only their presented qualities are registered. Regardless of whether the data originate in a universal organic nexus

[1] *cf.* p. 113.
[2] *cf.* p. 176.
[3] *cf.* p. 177.

of space-time entities, or are merely elements in the content of an intentional consciousness, the knowledge to which they give rise in 'basic existence' coincides with the notion of 'contemplative knowledge' obtained by having passive intentions directed at the stream of experience.

The coincident types of knowledge, transposed to the human level, refer here to events given in perception. This knowledge is devoid of any cognitive act involving judgments about the perceived data; it signifies merely their awareness in the perceived form. Furthermore, there is no implication of any purposive reaction to the presented data. While there is a kind of response, it is not in the form of a planned reaction to whatever significance the data may have, but a mere accommodation of the data within the percipient system. This 'intro-verted' response corresponds not only to physical and chemical reactions, to the reaction to stimuli of higher organisms, but also to bare, non-evaluative sensory apprehension in human experience. There is no contradiction in ascribing such basic knowledge to psycho-logical entities, in addition to biological and physical ones. The qualitative divergences between physical and chemical reactions on the one hand, and reactions to stimuli and bare apprehensional perception on the other, are fused within the framework of passive-basic knowledge, restricted to apprehending those items of experience which actually enter into the determination of the human being.

The next pair of correlates are the categories 'Active Intentions' determining *Operational Knowledge,* and *Knowledge in Projective Existence* (primitive forms).

With respect to 'Active Intentions', I wrote "Whenever such [contemplatively known] objects are presented and are known through the 'passive' intentions, 'active' intentions can be introduced in order to positively modify the negatively (or less-than-fully-positively) relevant object." [1] And I concluded, "'operational knowledge' acquired through 'active intentions' penetrates further into the nature of actu-ality than does contemplative knowledge through passive intentions. Operational knowledge embraces not only actualities, but also potentialities . . ." [2]

Concerning knowledge obtained in 'projective existence' I shall repeat that "a biological entity does not behave purely in a manner which is conducive to its momentary existence, but tends to undertake

[1] *cf.* pp. 115-116.
[2] *cf.* p. 116.

acts which have their justification in meeting a requirement arising in the future." [1] "But not merely has the scope of knowledge of biological entities been changed and widened – also their type of knowledge is different from physical entities. The facts known by the biological entity are known not only as actualities, but also as historical processes. They are known as events which have their grounds in the past and their consequences in the future." [2]

The principles defining the acquisition of knowledge have again to be axiomatically assumed (I shall discuss them presently) and the question limited to whether the kind of knowledge ascribed to 'active intentions' coincides with the kind obtained in 'projective existence'? Consider that the operational knowledge acquired in active intentions is based on contemplative knowledge through passive cognitions, but is more penetrating than the latter: operational knowledge extends to potentialities, while contemplative knowledge involves only actuality. Similarly, knowledge in projective existence extends past the range of knowledge in basic existence: the latter takes the universe only as an influence objectified in the constitution of the given entity, while the former knows it as a *historical* field of force, having its ground in the past and its consequence in the future. Now the 'potentiality' inherent in a contemplatively known object relates to the actuality of that object as the future of a given pattern of influence relates to its past. The already known element is actuality, the element discovered about that actuality is potentiality. In the argument from consciousness, potentiality is referred to the presented conformation of sense-data in the stream of experience. In the argument from being on the other hand, potentiality is referred to the spatio-temporal nexus of entities affecting, by virtue of the solidarity of the universe, the analytically abstracted subject. From the standpoint of that subject the universe consists of a pattern of actual nexus determined by the entity's own past conjointly with the past of all reality and having its consequences in the future; from the viewpoint of intentional consciousness experience consists of presented sense-data conformations of a given level of relevance to intentionality disclosing, however, further degrees of relevance as potentiality. Similarly, the processing of external influence through purposive operations by an ontic entity entails the discovery of the operational potentialities in experienced actuality. Thus there is no contradiction in affirming that the categories of active

[1] cf. p. 179.
[2] cf. p. 180.

processes and projective existence are correlates and that the principles of knowledge they afford, coincide.

On the human level, the type of coincident knowledge may be said to represent 'operational cognition', i.e. a pragmatic type of comprehension of apprehended items holding practice to be the criterion of veridical knowledge. While in bare apprehension each perceived datum was such as perceived and no judgments as to its properties and attributes were made, here those judgments are advanced which follow from purposive (respectively 'intentional' and 'functional') experimentation with the given objects. Such "purpose" is concordant with the act of consciousness (intentionality), and with the act of being (ontic functionality), and results in the discovery of the modifiability of the presented datum. When the modification-potential of actuality is discovered, it acquires a new dimension: that of inherent potentialities from the viewpoint of intentional consciousness, and that of a historical field of force from the viewpoint of the ontic entity. As regards the realist scheme, this process is also ascribed to biological entities, but not to physical ones. It transcends the range of physical and chemical reaction, but is present in a primitive form in the simplest responses to stimuli wherein the response accords not merely with the immediate stimulus, but with the set of stimuli of which the given stimulus is a component. In man, this anticipatory process is greatly extended as regards temporal scope, since man behaves in accordance not only with events which he expects to follow immediately upon those he actually experiences, but also makes long-range forecasts. (The latter involve explicit inferences; these, however, belong under the heading of the next pair of correlates.) Projective knowledge as correlate of behavioural knowledge implies inferences in an implicit form. Thus, the implicit anticipatory behaviour which man has in common with lesser biological species coincides directly with the sceptical category of 'operational knowledge'.

The third and final categories in the Area of Correlation are 'Theoretical Intentions' yielding *Inferential Knowledge*, and the explicit forms of *Knowledge in Projective Existence*.

"Inferential knowledge," I said in the relevant chapter, "includes things which are not given to consciousness in the form of sense-data and constituted sense-objects, but which reside in the given data and objects as pure, even if theoretical, possibilities." Consequently, "Inferences refer to the *possible values of actual objects* inferred from knowledge of their actual values and of the relation of their actual values to their operational values." [1] Concerning the explicit forms of 'knowledge in projective existence' I shall recall the following propositions. "Man treats his environment in terms of sources of influences which are not merely momentary and unforeseeable, but as a series of grounds having future consequences and as a series of consequences having past grounds." "Reasoning from an actual event as ground of its anticipated consequence involves projection of past experience into the future; reasoning from an actual event as consequence of a past ground means explaining the present in terms of a past by which it is determined." [2] And I concluded, "The scientific knowledge of mankind is a highly perfected and theoretically deepened form of the projective knowledge of all biological entities down to, and including, the simplest amoeba." [3]

When we collate these statements within the context of the arguments wherein they have been advanced, we shall find, first, that the scope of the inferential knowledge postulated in the 'argument from consciousness' has been widened to include all possible values of actuality which are potentially knowable through the formulation of hypotheses and their testing through 'effector sensations'. The latter are used as a means of testing the validity of the possible values of actual experience, thus helping to transcend the range of the operational and actual values. Inference is to pure, theoretical possibility, as revealed in the relation of actuality and operational potentiality.

Second, the scope of knowledge has been similarly widened in the explicit forms of knowledge in projective existence. The explicit projective knowledge of psychological entities extends beyond the range of the operationally knowable facts of the world, to those which may only be known through hypotheses verifiable by means of finding the key 'epistemic correlates' of the postulated aspect of reality. When hypotheses are verified, the result is the theoretical postulation of objects which are either held to exist at a spatio-temporal locus sufficiently removed from that of the observer to prevent their direct inspection, or to be of such size that their direct observation is rendered impossible. Hence explicit forms of projective knowledge correspond to theoretical-inferential knowledge, in that both include knowledge of objects theoretically inferred from direct apprehensions. Explicit 'projective knowledge' differs, however, from 'theoretical-inferential knowledge' in that the postulated objects are held to be real even

---

[1] cf. p. 117.
[2] cf. p. 181.
[3] cf. p. 182.

though not inspectable within the realist framework of the former, while they are considered as pure possibilities inherent in inspected actuality within the sceptical framework of the latter. But the difference is due to the respective frameworks, and represents an interpretation, rather than a qualification of these forms of knowledge.

The knowledge here discussed represents theoretical inferences from experience. It is a fact, however, that such inferences deal with objects, while the cognition of the environment in terms of physical objects (ontic particulars) has been ascribed to 'reflection' in the realist scheme. Hence the validity of this correlation is open to question, there being no correlate to 'reflection' in the sceptical scheme. However, *if* we should find that the phenomenon of reflection has a corresponding phenomenon for the sceptic, the presence of 'objects' in the projective knowledge of man would not constitute a disproof of the correlation, for reflection itself could be verified by reference to scepticism. This is a question to which I shall return and attempt to decide upon, in the next section.

II. *The Area of Non-Correlation*

I have dealt above with the categories of the sceptical and the realist schemes which are capable of correlation. I have shown, I believe, that if 'reflection' can be verified by the sceptic, there is no reason to disbelieve that the function of terms in each of the three pairs of correlates could be analogous. I shall now have to consider the area wherein the sceptical and the realist categories *cannot* be correlated. This area includes three realist categories of knowledge: the basic knowledge of physical entities, the projective knowledge of biological entities and the reflective knowledge of psychological entities. There are no sceptical categories directly indicated for any of these realist categories. The question is, does this entail the unverifiability, i.e. the 'meaninglessness' of the realist scheme as a whole?

Now, while it has been maintained that unverifiability by empirical, 'basic' or 'protocol' statements entails the meaninglessness of the given propositions (and thus metaphysical statements failing to meet such criteria have been held 'expressive' rather than 'cognitive' or 'factual'), it is seldom demanded that each particular proposition should be directly verifiable by the immediate facts of experience. If this claim were made, not many propositions of a realist nature could be validated as being 'meaningful'. Rather, those propositions should be considered meaningful which are verifiable in virtue of being a component in a system of which the key notions are verifiable. In other words, verifiability is to be taken as a property primarily applicable to the body of internally consistent propositions and derivatively applicable to any proposition within that system by virtue of the proposition's being a part in the system. In view of the fact that in the context of the realist basic assumptions some statements transcend direct sensory experience and are only verifiable by these if experience is evaluated as referring to the physical world denoted by the given system of assumptions as a whole, no such 'surplus' propositions are verifiable by propositions derived from an analysis of experience in the context of scepticism except in virtue of its being a part of a realist system.

It is evident that such a principle of verifiability leans heavily on the coherence theory of truth, but it nevertheless represents the sole workable means of testing the validity of propositions referring to other-than-experiential events. The premiss "being" entails such propositions, but the premiss "consciousness" does not. If, but only if, the non-correlated categories come into the heading of 'necessary unverifiability', entailed by the adoption of the realist premiss, and only if the propositions contained in these categories follow without contradiction from verifiable propositions, can the latter be said to be meaningful, though verifiable only by virtue of being a part of a partially verifiable system.

As regards the first two categories, it may be safely maintained that this, in fact, is the case. Whatever knowledge we ascribe to 'physical entities' and to 'biological entities' necessarily transcends any kind of knowledge we find in an analysis of experience in the context of the sceptical basic assumption. The 'knowledge of a physical (biological) entity' is merely an aspect of *my* experience, and 'my' experience is communicated to 'my' consciousness. It is perhaps redundant to claim that 'my' consciousness is human, but it is clear that if I cannot equate my consciousness and knowledge with the experience and knowledge of another entity, knowledge of other-than-human entities is not directly verifiable by any consistent 'argument from consciousness'.

However, unverifiability does not render these concepts and principles meaningless, for it is not excluded that they should consistently follow from verifiable propositions. Now, the verifiable propositions of the realist scheme are those concerning the knowledge of the 'psychological entity', i.e. of man. While it cannot be shown that the knowledge of physical and biological entities is *deduced* from the knowledge attributed to man, it can be shown that all these kinds of knowledge follow from the same basic principles of the scheme, in that they represent particular forms of the 'universal ontic function'. Thus, if human knowledge follows from the scheme and is verifiable, then the knowledge of physical and biological entities is indirectly verifiable, since it follows from the same scheme as human knowledge does. If the 'argument from being' is internally consistent, propositions concerning other-than-human entities are indirectly verifiable and potentially meaningful. There is no contradiction in holding such propositions verified, if and when propositions concerning human knowledge are held to be verified. Consequently, the lack of sceptical correlates to these two realist categories of knowledge does not automatically entail the meaninglessness of these propositions.

The case is somewhat different when we consider 'reflective knowledge'. Such knowledge is human, and the sceptic is competent in the sphere of human knowledge. Hence, if the realist notion of reflection is meaningful, there should be direct evidence of 'reflection' in the sceptical analysis of experience. But there is no category in the above prototype 'argument from consciousness' which would correspond to the meaning of 'reflection'. This may be simply due to a deficiency in my argument. But, I believe that this objection does not apply here. To appreciate my point, consider that there *cannot* be a meaning to 'reflection' under the assumption that the world is given in experience, for the very fact of such an inquiry presupposes reflection: experience is entirely 'introverted' and its analysis is through introspection. 'Introspection' in this use is synonymous with 'reflection': to know the world, means to introspect, i.e. to reflect upon one's experiences. Therefore, if any knowledge of the world is had, it is had through reflection. The realistic distinction between 'reality' and 'judgment of reality' and between 'world' and 'self' becomes meaningless. For the consistent sceptic the only reasonable distinction is between the *content* and the *act* of consciousness. The act is immanent in the content and cannot be said to exist without it in space and in time. When 'the world' is a judgment of immanent contents, it is a set of concepts or representations in consciousness, explained by reference to a posited act of cognition. The known is ontologically indistinguishable from the knower; the distinction lies purely in the epistemological differentiation between the 'content' and the 'act' of consciousness.

To affirm that reflection is a specific category of cognitive act would be equal to assuming an external world prior to the analysis. In my 'argument from consciousness' I could not prove the existence of the world outside, and independent of, consciousness; all I could assert was that consciousness exists, and that its existence presupposes an act whereby its contents are organized into the 'world-phenomenon' with which we are continually confronted. There is no space and no time external to consciousness (or, more exactly, no acceptable knowledge of such space-time, in the light of the sceptic's criteria); whatever is given, is given not only *to* consciousness, but also *in* consciousness. Whatever is presented to consciousness is part of its contents, and the constitution of the world is at the same time the constitution of the ego. It follows that any reflection on data presented to consciousness is reflection on the world as well as on the ego. It is, in other words, reflection on the 'ego-world'. Hence, 'reflection' is explicitly presupposed in every discussion of the data of consciousness and is implicitly presupposed in any discussion of any thing or event having the remotest of connections with experiential data. All empirical discussion, on whatever topic, presupposes reflection: in order to speak of something we must know it, and we can know it (in the sense of being acquainted with it) only by knowing the elements of the thing in question in experience; denial of this proposition implies the affirmation of innate ideas and apriorism. When we know a thing in experience *and* we talk about it, then we reflect upon our knowledge; denial of *this* proposition implies that we can talk about things without thinking of them in any way. Hence reflection is presupposed whenever we say anything about anything and it can be denied only by recourse to innate ideas or to the notion of speaking without thinking. I doubt that either one of these alternatives needs to be seriously considered. If so, then considered discourse on any topic involves reflection, and reflection, in the sceptic's argument, can only be reflection on the ego-world. The reflection is also a datum in the ego-world and is available for further reflection, which in turn is similarly available. Thus, there is an infinite regress, but it involves the ego-world and not the ego counterposed to (since reflecting on) the world. The point is that *every* reflection involves an infinite regress, for I cannot conceive of any act of reflection upon which I could not reflect anew (though I must necessarily stop at some level in practice). The sceptic's reflection concerns all that there is to experience and since experience is all that there is to his world, reflection concerns the ego-world. *When* there is reflection, *then* it is reflection upon experience; and *if* there are propositions advanced concerning experience, *then* there is reflection. Hence when we speak of our experience in any context, we are reflecting; as a result, the *class* of sceptical categories (consisting of propositions concerning experience) coincides with the realist category of 'reflective knowledge'.

Although no correlate to 'reflective knowledge' can be found in a consistent sceptical argument, the class of all propositions of such an argument implies reflection. Consequently, reflective knowledge as evaluated in the realist argument coincides not with any one category of the sceptical scheme, but with all its categories. There is no structural analogy of propositions demonstrable in this coincidence, but there is a strict implication in meaning: propositions concerning experience can be advanced, if, and only if, reflective knowledge is a fact. Thus, the apperceptive elements of human knowledge are not inconsistent with the categories of the sceptic: on the contrary, they are presupposed by the very fact that sceptical categories can be formulated. 'Reflection' is equivalent to methodical scepticism, even though it has neither been derived from, nor does it entail, the adoption of the sceptical basic assumptions.

THE FUNDAMENTAL ANALOGIES

The above considerations were based on the prior acceptance of the principles determining the acquisition of knowledge, and these principles thus functioned entirely axiomatically in these explorations of the correlations of the various forms of knowledge. But only if the function of 'intentionality' is analogous to that of 'ontic function' in the respective arguments, can the above correlations be considered decisive for verification. I shall, therefore, be concerned to give a general outline of the analogies between 'intentionality' and 'ontic function'.

Consider, then, that both 'intentionality' and 'ontic function' signify *acts:* one an act of consciousness, the other an act of being. The essential and basic feature of intentionality, as the principle of the act of knowledge, is that it defines knowledge by reference to an intention directed *at* something. And the essential and fundamental feature of ontic function as the principle of the act of being specified to the level of the human mind, is that it functions *for* something. Both are aimed at some particular state; in both cases the state concerns ultimately the entity which is aiming. In the sceptical view there are no other entities and in the realist view there are many. But this makes no difference to the statement that intentionality, as well as functionality, are recursive acts: the end for both is something specific concerning the entity itself. In the case of intentional consciousness, the recursive function of intentionality is to obtain what I have termed 'the intended state of consciousness'. This state is defined as being such that it is constantly (though not necessarily directly) intended. The recursiveness of ontic functionality, on the other hand, is part of the nature of the psychological entity and is aimed at assuring his own 'stability'. If the 'state of consciousness' and the 'stability of the entity' have identical functions in their respective arguments, then the function of terms in the Area of Coincidence are likely to be analogous.

What then, we must ask, is the decisive factor concerning each of these principles? I believe that with respect to the 'intended state of consciousness' it is 'preferentiality': an entirely subjective quality intended and describable as 'pleasant'; it is an ideal toward which intentionality is directed. On the other hand, the decisive factor concerning ontic function is that it aims at improving the 'stability of the entity', and this is an objective factor: stability represents that state of organization of the given entity whereby its existence is rendered eminently compatible with its evironment. By this I mean that it is so organized that in view of the conditions prevailing in its actual space-time locus it is apt to extend its space-time existence to its furthermost potential. It entertains a set of nexūs which favours the space-time continuity of the entity to the greatest degree permitted by the degree of organization to which the entity has attained during the course of its history. The 'nature' of the subject promotes such a state of organization and thus we may say that there exists a drive toward stability.

But how does the subjective quality of preferentiality relate to the objective state of stability? Taken on the respective levels of scepticism and realism, there is no possible relation; these concepts are mutually exclusive. But the question here is whether they could have the very same function in both arguments? That, I believe, is the case. Preferentiality is a quality of experient consciousness, and stability is a property of the organic subject. To say that stability is communicated to consciousness in the form of preferentiality with the result that a strict implication occurs between these terms (organic stability then, and only then, when sensation of preferentiality) is to utter a perhaps profound, but hopelessly non-demonstrable proposition. It is non-demonstrable for it disregards the disjunction between epistemic and physical facts, between statements referring to subjective experience and those dealing with objective existence. The best we can do is to show that preferentiality has, in the context of the sceptical argument, the same function as stability has in realistic theory. Then, if the meaning of these terms is their use in the theories, we do not have *two terms* with strict implication, but *one function*. Inasmuch as the terms derive their meaning from their function in the argument, their meaning will be the same, notwithstanding their semantic differences. "Preferentiality" relates to "intentionality" as "stability" relates to "nature of the entity" and the meaning of these terms is determined by this relation. Preferentiality is the hallmark of the subjective state which is the object of intentionality; stability is the feature of the objective state which is the object of ontic functionality. When we bracket 'subjective' and 'objective', we obtain two states toward which purposive activity is directed. The relation arising between the object of the activity and the possibilities of attaining it, involve a greater or lesser number of other entities (it is immaterial here whether we call them 'epistemic' or 'ontic') and may involve all entities entering into the experience of the given percipient. The attainment of the state results in the organization of the experienced entities into identifiable, coherent things and events. The mode of organization is always by reference to an *act* of knowledge or to an *act* of being ('intentionality' or 'ontic function') and to a *state* of the experient. The resulting organization represents knowledge of the entities.

The area of this fundamental analogy between the two sets of propositions is restricted to the sphere of experience admitted by the sceptic, with the sphere admitted by the realist (but not by the sceptic) constituting the area of the indirectly verifiable 'realist surplus'. The vital point is that the area of coincidence does manifest a fundamental analogy: the various modes of knowledge occur in both arguments in reference to an *act* and to a *state*, and produce identical processes of knowledge. The analogous function of the 'acts' (intentionality and ontic functionality) with respect to the 'states' (*of* consciousness and *of* ontic entity) determines the fundamental isomorphism of basic propositions in the two arguments. This becomes evident if we admit into our argument *both* intentionality, conducing to the intended state of consciousness *and* ontic functionality, conducing to the state of stability of the given entity. Knowledge is had through the intentional striving toward preferentiality as well as through the functional activity aiming at stability, with the result that *within* the Area of Correlation (i.e. that area which concerns immediately verifiable human knowledge) the sceptic would have no reason to disagree with the realist on any point other than the use of words. For, whether I call the events of my experience 'sense-objects constituted from the private sense-data available to my consciousness' or 'physical objects known through the public sense-data stimulating my sense-organs', and whether I think of myself as a 'pure consciousness' or as 'one ego-object amid objects' makes no difference to *what* I know, only to how I *denote* the objects of my knowledge. That, however, is determined by the adoption of the basic assumptions of scepticism and realism, and no argument based on these assumptions can either prove or disprove them. But if I know the same things regardless of whether I am a sceptic or a realist and only refer the objects of my knowledge to different conceptual frameworks, I can reduce the resulting propositional differences to insignificance by considering the function of the words determinant of their meaning. Fundamental analogies between sceptical and realist arguments entail the recognition that their meanings are non-contradictory, if within the coinciding area of inquiry the structure of the propositions is isomorphic.

VERIFICATION OF THE
ANALOGOUS PROPOSITIONS

With respect to the principles of knowledge, the Area of Correlation can be upheld as an area of analogous propositions. Where there is such analogy, the structure of the arguments should be isomorphic. Thus even if meanings-as-labels are mutually exclusive, meanings-as-use should coincide. This hypothesis must be determinable by using a common language for both sets of propositions. To demonstrate this point we must eliminate the 'label' meaning of the terms and retain only their function. This can be done by introducing signs as propositional variables. The signs represent the singular function of all terms in their respective contexts. If both a sceptical and a realist argument can be expressed by one proposition using signs as variables, the given proposition is considered verified: it applies to epistemic as well as to physical facts, regardless of the differences of meaning inherent in the words taken as labels. It follows that propositions so verified would satisfy the criteria of proof I advanced: the proposition understood in the sceptical value of the variables would satisfy the premiss-criterion 'experientiality' and the theory-criteria 'consistency' and 'economy'; the proposition understood in the realist value of the variables would meet the premiss-criterion 'adequacy' jointly with the theory-criteria 'consistency' and 'economy'.

(i) *The sceptical values of the propositional variables.*

X Private sense-datum or 'epistemic fact'   (the class of X is the content of consciousness)

Z intentionality (act of consciousness)

S intended state of consciousness (the intended conformation of sense-data)

P preferentiality (relevance of particular data to the intended state)

F volitionally controlled effector sensations
E class of sense-objects
E_1 actual value of sense-object
E_2 operational value of sense-object
E_3 possible value of sense-object

(ii) *The realist values of the propositional variables*

X public sense-datum   (the class of X is the universal field of
         or 'physical fact'   force as convergent upon the space-time
                                   locus of a given entity)
Z ontic functionality specified according to the space-time stand-
         point of a given particular, i.e. its 'nature' (act of being)
S state of optimum stability of a particular
P relevance of a sense-datum for the existence of the particular
F behaviour of the particular (active response to sense-data in
         accordance with the nature of the entity)
E class of physical objects (i.e. ontic entities)
E_1 inspected physical object
E_2 operationally defined physical object
E_3 theoretically postulated physical object

(iii) *Verification by means of the propositional variables*

I. PERCEPTUAL KNOWLEDGE

Each X is an element in E_1 known through Z in function of S and
identified by its actual P-factor

II. PRACTICAL KNOWLEDGE

Each X is an element in E_1 (as above) and also in E_2, the latter known
through F as a means at the disposal of Z in function of S and identified (also) by its operational (i.e. actively realizable) P-factor.

III. THEORETICAL KNOWLEDGE

Each X is an element in E_1 (as in I) and in E_2 (as in II) and also in
E_3, the latter known by the inference $E_1 \supset E_2. \supset . E_3$, and identified
(also) by its possible (inferred) P-factor.

    The above propositions apply to knowledge derived from the scep-
tical 'argument from consciousness' as well as to that deduced from the

metaphysical scheme entailed by the realist 'argument from being'. If the verification is correct, the following synonyms result:

private sense-datum (epistemic fact)	public sense-datum (physical fact)	(X)
intentionality	ontic function specified to the human level	(Z)
intended state of consciousness	maximal organic stability (i.e. optimum conditions for long-term human existence)	(S)
preferentiality	relevance of the environment for human existence	(P)
effector sensations	purposive behaviour	(F)
class of sense-objects	class of physical objects	(E)
actual value of a sense-object	inspected physical object	(E_1)
operational value of a sense-object	operationally defined physical object	(E_2)
possible value of a sense-object	theoretically postulated physical object	(E_3)

The above terms are synonymous if we allow equal validity to the anguage of the sceptic and of the realist, and determine their meanings according to the function of their terms within propositions. The *premiss-synonyms* thus emerging are 'epistemic facts' as the matrix of consciousness, and 'physical facts' as the experience of 'others' by the ontic entity; the *heuristic synonyms* are 'intentionality', directed toward preferentiality, and 'ontic function', striving toward stability, as well as 'effector sensations' and 'purposive behaviour'; the *deductive-synonyms* are 'sense-objects' and 'physical objects'. The latter synonyms are divisible to 'sense-object of actual value – inspected physical object', 'sense-object of operational value – operationally defined physical object' and 'sense-object of possible value – theoretically postulated physical object'. Terminological differences are due to the denial of external space-time by the sceptic and its affirmation by the realist, with the result that the 'here-and-now' of the realist becomes the equivalent of the 'immanent space-time' of the sceptic. Hence inferences concern potentialities and possibilities inherent in actuality for the sceptic, and objective events at spatio-temporal loci beyond the range of direct inspection for the realist. But in view of the analogous function of the key terms in the two arguments, the basic assumptions of experientially immanent and experientially transcendent time are invalidated, together with the mutually contradictory meanings attaching to the sceptical assumption that the world is given in experience and the realist assumption that experience is given in the world.

PART V

REFLECTIONS ON FURTHER IMPLICATIONS
AND SUMMARY

OTHER MINDS, SOCIAL REALITY AND MEMORY

In these final reflections I shall consider how some of the major areas of inquiry I have not considered explicitly in the foregoing investigations relate to my treatment of the problem of scepticism and realism. Thus, in a sense, I shall briefly explore what I have not done but perhaps should have done, and draw conclusions as to the consequences of having done what I did do.

I shall be the first to admit that there are weighty implications of scepticism and realism to fields of inquiry which I have not considered. On the one hand the scope of the investigation has been already so extenuated that further studies would have very likely blunted the edge of the argument; on the other I do not consider myself competent to deal with complex problems belonging to the fields of research of specialized sciences. But a few words concerning the relation of some of the more outstanding problems to my theory on scepticism and realism are in order.

Of primary importance among the problems I have not dealt with, but which are particularly relevant to scepticism and realism, are the problems of our knowledge of other minds, of social reality and of memory. These form parts of more complex problems pertaining to the scope and varieties of human knowledge, but an exhaustive treatment of such problems would require several volumes and exceed both the intentions and the capacities of this writer. Yet, taken in themselves, these problems manifest a relevance to the single basic problem with which I have presumed to deal, justifying my saying a few words about them.

Often considered basic to the diverse problems coming under the collective heading of 'knowledge of other minds', is the question of *intersubjectivity*. Although the problem of 'other minds' is real, it seems to me that there is a sense in which it could be said that the problem of

'intersubjectivity' is not. My reason for suspecting this is the combination of the word 'inter' with the word 'subjectivity'. If the arguments
by which I exemplified the consequences of taking the sceptical and
the realist basic premises seriously are, on the whole, correct, 'inter'
belongs to realist discourse, and 'subjectivity' to the sceptical one.
But this is not a matter of mere terminology. The type of meaning
attaching to 'inter' presupposes several entities, and hence realism to
some extent and in some form. On the other hand 'subjectivity', if
taken at its full value, means that as far as any given subject is
concerned, there are only objective contents of experience, and not
necessarily 'others' such as himself. Thus 'inter' presupposes the many,
and 'subjectivity' connotes the one. This will surely be considered an
exaggerated view of the issues, but I wish to maintain that it nevertheless is the consistent one.

It would be intrinsically fallacious to attempt to derive knowledge
of 'other minds' from an analysis of experience, for 'other minds' are
either given or they are not, but their existence cannot be proven by
an analysis of experience under the assumption that they are given 'in'
it. Contrary to the impossibility of proving the partners presupposed
by 'inter' in 'intersubjectivity' when 'subjectivity' is taken at full
value, 'inter' becomes self-evident and unproblematic if 'other minds'
(in this sense we should mean 'other real individuals') are axiomatically asserted to exist, and if experience is analysed in the context
of the assumption that it refers to the apprehension of these 'others'.
We can well justify 'inter' then, but not 'subjectivity', since certainly
the subject whose viewpoint we adopt is not taken as a 'pure'
subject, but rather as one real individual among others. But if we
already know (or think we know) that there are 'others' we have no
reason to consider that this knowledge has to be derived from the experience of one. Even if the knowledge of others needs to be verified
and justified by an analysis of experience, if the analysis is made in the
realist context, such verification is surely unproblematic: once we
assume that our apprehensions are *of* other people, there is plenty of
evidence in our daily experience of their existence.

To my mind the problem of 'intersubjectivity' is illegitimate: it is
either insoluble, or spurious. In neither event is it a 'problem', unless
we acknowledge as such questions to which we know either that there
is no answer, or that we already have the answer. Thus, even if I have
not considered it explicitly, a clear negation of the *problem* of intersubjectivity may be derived from the implications of my treatment of

scepticism and realism. It is not the consistent sceptic and the consistent realist who make a problem of intersubjectivity, but those who would like to draw on the rigorously experiential method of the one as well as on the adequate conceptual equipment of the other. But instead of answering the question concerning our knowledge of other minds, the arbitrary synthesizers of the sceptical method with realist notions have only succeeded in making a problem out of it.

The problem of intersubjectivity has further implications, however, since it represents one of at least two major approaches to the problem of social reality. One of these may be termed the 'subjective' or 'phenomenological' approach, and the other the 'objective' or 'naturalistic' one.[1] If my assessment of the problem of scepticism and realism is valid as regards the problem of intersubjectivity, it is also valid with respect to the problem of social reality. Thus it would seem that a purely consistent subjective approach cannot legitimately refer to 'social reality', for it cannot conjoin its conception of 'reality' with the term 'society', since 'reality 'should be restricted to the being of the subject, and 'society' connotes the being of 'others' in addition to the subject. On the other hand the objectivitistic-naturalistic approach, operating from the premiss of realism, can legitimately undertake a systematic study of the problems raised by the assumption that experience refers, among other things, to intercourse among people in a social community. Let us consider these propositions.

When we speak of 'society' we mean a set of nexūs existing between various individuals forming a structural whole. The term has meaning only if we allow that more than one individual is given, for any given individual by himself is not a 'society' but only part of a society. (Individuals can be analysed to being a 'society of components' if we take them as 'subjects' and not as 'superjects'. But, it is precisely as 'superjects' that individuals could imply human society.) To speak of society, we must presuppose the transcendence of the individual and his coordination within a larger network of relations. Thus the given individual has to be inductively generalized. However, the difficulty with this is that in the eyes of the consistent sceptic there is no ground for such an induction. The sceptic can always assert that 'my' consciousness exists, and 'others' do not, for only the existence of consciousness is apodictic. As Ayer points out, even a telepathic experience (if we

[1] For a collection of essays illustrating the methods and concepts of both these approaches as well as an excellent bibliography, see *Philosophy of the Social Sciences*, edited by Maurice Natanson, New York, 1963.

wish to admit its possibility) is private to oneself, and there would be no contradiction in allowing that it exists even though the other person's experience did not.[1] Hence by posing the criteria of the sceptic, we can reduce all other minds and all other men to data of experience, given to 'my' consciousness. Under this assumption it is impossible to maintain that society exists and that the problem of social reality is not spurious, for society without 'others' is self-contradictory. But, it may be objected, evidence of 'others' and hence of society, is present also in 'my' (and presumably in every) consciousness, in the form of a drive, or psychic motivation toward social intercourse, consisting of diverse feelings of obligation and moral responsibility.

Such a 'drive' or tendency may well be maintained. Köhler, for example, points out that in some respects it is essentially similar to quite evident physiological drives.[2] But where does this assumption get us? If we argue consistently from consciousness, we have no reason to postulate an external space-time to which experienced events refer. A drive present in consciousness is more consistently and economically referred to a form of intentionality directed toward some 'preferential' data. These preferential data are those which in a realistic view are signified by the presence of 'others' in the diverse forms of social intercourse. For the sceptic these data remain data, and do not, merely by their presence, confirm knowledge of 'others'. Society is meaningless for the consistent sceptic; its knowledge rests upon the knowledge of 'others', and that knowledge is based on the presence of certain sense-data which do not, in themselves, carry the signification of 'others' apodictically. Hence any motivation or drive toward social intercourse can be accounted for by the notion of intentionality adhering to preferential data; this solution is far more economical and self-consistent than assuming the existence of 'society'.[3]

[1] Ayer, op. cit., 'The Privacy of Experience'.

[2] Köhler uses the term 'vector' to indicate the various directed attitudes of the self "which depend upon the self and upon given objects, or more precisely, upon the relation which obtains at the time between the characteristics of the former and those of the latter." (Gestalt Psychology, Ch. IX) He finds a 'vector' of social intercourse in that after prolonged solitude most persons experience a drive toward social contact which is quite similar to vectors (such as the need for food, drink, or a mate), which are determinable by knowledge of the interior side of their 'bipolar' organisation.

[3] I do not contest the fruitfulness of sociological inquiry on the subjectivist pattern, only its purely philosophical (logical and empirical) validity. On fields such as sociology, subjectivist inquiry, even if not free from unacknowledged presuppositions, may produce valuable results. Covert inconsistencies are not sufficient reasons to disvalidate the insights into societal processes obtained by such thinkers as Max Weber and Alfred Schutz; they are sufficient reasons, however, to criticize the logical consistency of their procedures.

"Society" is repudiated in the 'argument from consciousness', but it follows from the 'argument from being'. There, it represents an ontic entity constituted by the organic interfunctioning of its members, i.e. of human beings. Such an entity has its own temporal level of evolution ('progression-time') and its private space-time. It is an entity like all others, but, from the viewpoint of our species, it is a compound-individual of which we, as lesser compound-individuals, are parts. We can regard society as an ontic compound-individual and we can attribute to it the pattern of experience which is its due within the process of existence in the universe. We can find all the features of basic and projective existence in society, just as we can find them in psychological and biological entities. Every society interrelates with other societies, and their relevant environments are constituted by the conditions for social existence of their members. The endurance of a society is conditioned by its own history conjointly with the history of other societies, and with that of all factors which constitute the relevant social environment. Its history is expressed in the specifics of its 'nature' which can be analysed to the national characteristics which it incorporates. The total pattern of social relations determined by the national civilisation expresses its nature in the form of the ontic function which determines its existence as a space-time entity. As such, it has a basic, a projective, and even a reflective existence. Its basic existence concerns the bare survival of its members as an interdetermined group of people. (The existence of a primitive tribe comes close to exemplifying this contention.) Its projective existence lies in the organisation of the body politic with a view toward meeting situations that are likely to arise in the future, by anticipating the consequences which are assumed to follow from actual conditions. Its reflective existence is manifest in the debates on the correctness of its economic and political course in the light of its international relations, signifying an act of reflection upon the power represented by the given society from the viewpoint of other societies. Our 'own' society can thus be seen 'from the outside' as a vector acting upon its social environment. The greater temporal range of social planning, when contrasted with that of individuals, reflects the higher progression-time of the social entity. Its richer historical route, and wider relevant environment gives society dimensions which throw their shadow over a wide extent of space and time. For the purposes of an exploration of social reality, we could postulate 'social entities' and attribute to them all the forms of knowledge which we could assign to psychological entities; we would be merely pressing the inquiry further along the lines indicated by the categories of the 'argument from being'. Such procedure is permissible in the context of realist schemes, since any inquiry into the nature of reality can also inquire into the nature of social reality. And the investigation of social reality presupposes the conceptual equipment for considering society *real*. Consequently, the determination of the essence of society presupposes an ontology.[1]

To illustrate this contention, consider a statement of extreme historicism, such as, "the human essence is no abstraction inherent in each single individual. In its reality it is the ensemble of the social relations".[2] Shortened, this statement reads, 'in its reality the human essence is the ensemble of social relations'. Now, this is a dogmatic proposition taken by itself; we must refer it to some evidence by which it could be verified. If the evidence is gathered on the objectivist pattern, the statement represents a deduction from an ontology. As such, its truth is dependent upon the truth-value of the ontology. But such a statement may also be referred to the subjectivist (i.e. sceptical) framework, in which event it would appear that an analysis of human essence provides the premiss for the conclusion that, it is, in reality, the ensemble of social relations. But then, the proposition becomes incurably analytic. For, inference is from human essence, and human essence for the subjectivist is first of all his own. Thus the basic premiss is the essence of Marx. To be in a position to assert then, 'Marx's essence is the ensemble of social relations' we require proof *in* an analysis of his essence of the existence of social relations. In addition, we require means of checking that Marx's essence is in fact equivalent and identifiable with the ensemble of social relations. Unless such proof is found (and I have argued that it cannot be found) the statement 'the human essence is the ensemble of social relations' becomes the tautology, 'the essence of Marx is the essence of Marx'. The term 'social relations' functions as the term 'essence of Marx' since no meaningful difference between them has been established. Thus, if individual 'nature' or 'essence' is taken as the empirical ground for determining social nature or essence, the resulting conclusion is a tautology. The only alternative is to assume the existence of the world and with that the existence of 'others', for in that case "social" becomes a legitimate predicate. (It should be noted, however, that Marx referred this statement to objectivist evidence and thus, despite any criticism that

[1] *cf.* my *Essential Society*, Part I.
[2] Karl Marx, *The Sixth Thesis on Feuerbach*.

may be advanced of his inverted Hegelianism, it must be allowed that his statement, even if it is not necessarily sound, can at least be valid.)

The last area of inquiry I shall consider here is that of *memory*. The problem of recall and its associated questions have always impressed me as being unsatisfactorily solved by the various philosophical and psychological theories. The variety of theories dealing with memory is impressive, ranging from behaviourism to the mnemic and trace-theory; they cover propositions concerning recall made within the framework of many philosophical and psychological schemes. I shall not take positions, but will restrict myself to explicating somewhat further what has already been implied by my previous arguments (which were not meant to deal with memory, but were obliged to assume it), showing that the major problems encountered in a study of memory can be seen in the light of both of the knowledge processes I described, with the result that there would be no contradiction in maintaining the analogy of the major aspects of these processes in both schemes in view of specialized analyses of memory-phenomena.

We have two points of reference in the knowledge-process: the 'act' (intentionality/functionality) and a 'state' (*of* consciousness/*of* stability) to which the act refers. One of these is fixed in relation to the other. We may, for example, consider that the act is a fixed point of reference in relation to which the states 'move', in the sense that one state succeeds the other. The structure of the succession is relevant to the act because the act involves the modification of that structure in the attempt to obtain the desired state. Hence the act is continuously involved in (i.e. is 'directed at') the succession of states. These states are the events of experience, signifying either preferentiality' or 'stability' and function as points of reference for the act. Inasmuch as whatever the act may be, if it is to be effective, it must last through the series of states, the effective presence of memory is implied.

It is immaterial to this argument whether the events are held to move and the act to remain fixed, or *vice versa*, as long as relative movement between these two termini is given. I may say that my experiences succeed each other and I remain fixed; I may also say that the events of my experience are fixed facts and I 'pass through' them. The first statement corresponds to the argument of the sceptic, whose experiences change but who has no grounds to affirm that *he* changes since the ego remains the pure locus of the experiences; the second statement coincides with that of the realist who asserts that not the temporal change in the relationship of events constitutes the passage of time, but a shifting of his own point of reference. The essential fact is that the knower and the known shift relatively to each other. This permits the inference that several states coincide with one act, with the result that each state in the series is retained in reference to the structure of change. Now the structure of change in the series is both qualitative and quantitative. There are qualities which undergo modification, as well as quantities; and while immediate experience is qualitative, its changes can be quantified. If we allow for both qualitative and quantitative elements in the structure of change, then the act which refers to the change can retain its qualitative as well as its quantitative elements. The qualitative elements, when retained, can result in sense memory (i.e. memory in the form of sense-impressions and series of images) and the retained quantitative elements may afford factual memory in the form of a recall of the structure of past events. Habit memory is indicated if we consider that the structure of change includes, as an essential element, an associated form of reaction, so that our own behaviour in given types of recall is part of the events recalled. Thus, in 'remembering what we did' we acquire the kind of habit-memory which enables civilized men to fulfill the complex functions of their daily existence.

This is surely a rather vague and most general statement of the issue. But what I wish to point out here is merely that a relative shift of knower and known is entailed by the argument from consciousness as well as by the argument from being, with the result that recall of the changing events of experience, although 'intentional' in one and 'functional' in the other, is equally indicated in both. Neither the sceptic nor the realist can do without memory, and neither has a monopoly on its explanation. As long as we affirm the knower-act-known relation, memory is a property of the act referring to the known and functioning for the knower. In this respect it is immaterial whether we call the *knower* a 'pure consciousness' or 'one being among many', the *act* 'intentionality' or 'ontic function' and the *known* a 'sense' or a 'physical' object. The relation of these terms determines knowledge, and if the act is represented by an adequate heuristic principle, the relation of the terms should be sufficient to account for the diverse phenomena of recall.

These brief remarks concerning the complex problems of 'other minds', social reality and memory, were designed to show that these and related problems can be fruitfully considered in the light of explicit and consistent scepticism and realism: they do not contradict either, although the emphasis shifts considerably according to the chosen context. But the shift of emphasis poses the problem of scepticism and realism; it does nothing to solve it. The roots of this problem lie already with the formulation of the questions we ask concerning reality. The point I wished to make here is merely that we can, and do, ask coherent questions and expect, and receive, rational answers in the context of scepticism as well as in that of realism.

BASIC CONCEPTS AND CONDITIONS
OF MEANINGFUL METAPHYSICS

The arguments I have advanced for scepticism and for realism had the task of exemplifying these positions and not of affirming them. I do not wish to maintain that either solipsistic scepticism or constructivistic realism represents the true method of philosophical construction. I do wish to maintain, however, that being clear about the consequences of adopting scepticism or realism as a basic assumption can help us to have a better grasp of the problems and possibilities offered to us in view of our capacity for rationally systematizing our apprehensions of the world and of reflecting upon our unique position in it. Both are empirical procedures and both are justified in the light of their basic and seldom explicated assumptions. My purpose was to throw some light on the elementary phases of philosophical thinking which are usually taken for granted, but which are nevertheless decisive to the problem of meaning in metaphysics. It is time now to summarize the final results.

The argument from consciousness and the argument from being are prototypes and, as such, their specific principles are of secondary importance. Of primary importance is that the principles of the former represent an explication of scepticism and result in solipsism and that the principles of the latter exemplify realism and provide the foundations of a metaphysic. When we abstract from the postulated solipsist and metaphysical schemes and consider only their significance, we are left with a final conclusion which is not dependent upon the specifics of the principles I advanced. This conclusion obtains upon the verification of the metaphysical scheme as a total system of assumption by the solipsist scheme and states that in view of their function within the system, the principles of the former are equivalent to the principles of the latter.

Equivalence of function can be translated as identity of meaning under the theory that the function of terms within propositions and the function of propositions within the systems determine their meaning. Hence, meanings were shown to be identical in systems of solipsist scepticism and metaphysical realism.

The signification of the identity of meaning is represented by an equation. It consists of equating the system describing and explaining the intimate workings of one's own consciousness with the extensive workings of the universe. Scepticism results in a total concern with the act and the content of knowledge within consciousness; realism knows no checks to prevent it from being involved in a metaphysic dealing with the facts and the acts of being. If the two systems use equivalent principles having identical meanings, the content and the act of knowledge in consciousness have all properties which the fact and the act of being have in the universe. This is not a dogmatic statement, but a conclusion justified by the fact that terms and propositions of analogous functions *can* be used to refer to the events of our immediate experiences and the events of the natural universe. The prototype arguments had the function of demonstrating that this *can* be the case, and not that it necessarily *is*. But if the demonstration possessed sufficient power of conviction to make this possibility a path worth exploring, my purpose in formulating these arguments will have been fulfilled. Before closing, I would like to consider briefly with what propositions we would be left if we accepted the identity of the *content* and the *act* of knowledge with the *fact* and the *act* of being.

The propositions concerning consciousness tell us *how* we know that which we know. The propositions concerning being tell us *what* the things are which we know. Their equation means that the act of knowledge and the act of being are one and the same act (i.e. they are describable by the same principles). If the act of knowledge is the act of being, then we know in function of being and exist in function of knowing. The former satisfies realism, the latter scepticism. But, since this is an equation, it can be read either way, with the consequence that *both* realism and scepticism can be satisfied without involving contradictions. The proposition 'the act of knowledge is the act of the knower' can also be read 'the act of knowledge is the act of being'. Therefore, we have bridged the gulf between scepticism and realism by approaching it from the side of scepticism. But there is also the proposition, 'the act of being is the act of *a* being', which can now be read, 'the act of being is the act of knowledge' (i.e. it is the act whereby the 'being' in question *is* known and is *there* to be known). Therefore, the gulf between scepticism and realism has also been bridged from the side of realism.

Knowledge is a process and being is a process. If the two are identical, we know what we know in function of *our* being, and the things we know are there to be known in function of *their* being. But the 'we' refers here not merely to human beings, but to all things there are, i.e. all that 'have being'. Each existent thing 'knows' every other, and we know other things *because* we are ourselves existent. The 'little universe' inside our heads is part of the 'big universe' outside, and it affords a view of the latter. When we look out at the 'big universe' we speak of an act of knowledge; when we realize that we exist among others we look at ourselves and at the other things and see the 'little universes' which together make up the big one.

It would be difficult to pigeonhole such a notion in any of the existing and convenient categories of philosophical positions. It is not idealism or panpsychism, for the act of knowledge is not attributed as such to beings, but is equated with an ontological act of being. It is not materialism or physicalism, for the act of being is taken as an act of knowledge and it applies as such to the events of experience. To describe this thesis it is sufficient, I think, to say that it transcends the problem of scepticism and realism, showing that both are valid in the light of their basic assumptions, but that the basic assumptions of each present only one side of a coin that has two sides of equal validity and importance. 'World-in-experience' and 'experience-in-world' entail, respectively, the 'little' and the 'big' universe as conclusion, – but the two are identical. Hence when we look at one, we also see the other. And since if we look at either one we engage in an analysis of our consciousness as well as in an analysis of the natural universe, we engage in a metaphysic which cannot be reproached with meaninglessness.

If scepticism and realism are valid as distinct systems of assumptions, they are mutually contradictory. Metaphysics presupposes realism and meaning presupposes scepticism; therefore, meaningful metaphysics is a contradiction in terms. But if scepticism and realism are valid as distinct systems of assumptions and if they contradict because of the adopted framework of reference, but the framework exhibits the same propositional structure, the contradiction is spurious. Hence, scepticism and realism contradict as distinct systems, but are consistent as isomorphic structures, and when function determines meaning, scepticism and realism have identical meanings albeit expressed in different terms. Therefore, since metaphysics presupposes realism and meaning presupposes scepticism, and scepticism and realism are non-contradictory, meaningful metaphysics is possible.

INDEX